Interpreting the axe trade documents the changing character and context of stone axe production and exchange in the British Neolithic. Drawing on a variety of studies, the authors explore some of the problems and potentials that attend archaeological discussions of exchange at both a theoretical and a methodological level. Out of this critique arises an argument for an integrated approach to the production, circulation and consumption of past material – an approach which acknowledges the subtle and complex roles that 'things' may play in the reproduction of social life. These arguments provide the basis for a case study which explores the links between the social contexts within which Neolithic stone axes circulated in Britain, and the social and material conditions under which those objects were originally produced. Field survey, excavation and detailed technological studies at the largest stone axe source in Britain are set alongside analyses of the changing character and social context of axe circulation and deposition across the country as a whole. These different analytical threads are then woven together in the final section of the book, where the authors suggest that the patterns explored in the course of their work reflect major changes in the nature of social life during the Neolithic.

NEW STUDIES IN ARCHAEOLOGY

Series editors

Colin Renfrew, *University of Cambridge*
Jeremy Sabloff, *University of Pittsburgh*

Interpreting the axe trade

Frontispiece   Aerial view of the Langdale Pikes looking west. Photograph: Bob Bewley. Crown copyright reserved.

RICHARD BRADLEY and MARK EDMONDS

Interpreting the axe trade

Production and exchange in Neolithic Britain

CAMBRIDGE
UNIVERSITY PRESS

Published by the Press Syndicate of the University of Cambridge
The Pitt Building, Trumpington Street, Cambridge CB2 1RP
40 West 20th Street, New York, NY 10011–4211, USA
10 Stamford Road, Oakleigh, Victoria 3166, Australia

First published 1993

Printed in Great Britain at the University Press, Cambridge

A catalogue record for this book is available from the British Library

Library of Congress cataloguing in publication data

Bradley, Richard, 1946–
Interpreting the axe trade: production and exchange in Neolithic
Britain / Richard Bradley and Mark Edmonds.
     p.   cm. – (New studies in archaeology)
Includes bibliographical references and index.
ISBN 0 521 43446 7
1. Axes, Prehistoric – Great Britain. 2. Neolithic period – Great
Britain. 3. Commerce, Prehistoric – Great Britain. 4. Great
Britain – Antiquities. 1. Edmonds, M. R. (Mark R.) 11. Title.
111. Series.
GN776.22.G7B73 1993
936.1–dc20   92–21642 CIP

ISBN 0 521 43446 7 hardback

For Clare Fell

CONTENTS

ILLUSTRATIONS

TABLES

ACKNOWLEDGEMENTS

Archaeologists rarely do their fieldwork on their own. When they are working in a mountainous area an effective team is essential, and this we had at Langdale. We are extremely grateful to all who worked on the sites, often under very difficult conditions, and in particular to those who undertook special responsibilities in the project: Mark Bowden, Martin Cook, Roy Entwistle, Steve Ford, Annette Hazell, Pete Hinge, Frances Raymond and Julian Thomas. Other important contributions were made by Chris Gaffney, Jamie Quartermaine, David Sanderson and Ian Sanderson. We are also grateful to our fellow workers in the specialist studies that followed the completion of our fieldwork, in particular Phil Meredith, Mark Robinson, Jim Smith and Roger Suthren. Pollen analysis was carried out by Paddy Boyd, Adam Hadley, Melanie Hall, Pete Hinge and Malcolm Reid, working under the supervision of Michael Keith-Lucas. We must thank Rupert Housley, Jim Innes and Mark Robinson for discussing the environmental evidence with us, and the British Museum Radiocarbon Laboratory and the Oxford Radiocarbon Accelerator Project for dating samples from our work. We are also indebted to Bob Bewley for his superb air photographs and to Colin Renfrew for his support and good advice.

Our fieldwork could only have been carried out with the support of the National Trust and their Archaeological Advisors, David Thackray and Philip Claris. We have also received considerable encouragement from Tom Clare of Cumbria County Council and from the staff of the Cumbria and Lancashire Archaeological Unit. Two of the people already mentioned, Jamie Quartermaine and Philip Claris, had already mounted an impressive field survey when our work began, and we are most grateful to them for access to their results before publication and for much valuable discussion. We received a similar measure of help and encouragement from the staff of the local museums, especially Colin Richardson at Carlisle Museum where our finds and site records are available for consultation.

The project was funded by grants from the British Academy, the Prehistoric Society, Reading University and the Society of Antiquaries. The thin-sectioning of hammerstones from Pike o' Stickle was funded by an additional grant from the British Academy. The Science Based Archaeology Committee of the Science and Engineering Research Council provided a grant which has allowed us to extend our investigation of the mechanical properties of the raw materials used for making axes.

Clare Fell's contribution really speaks for itself, for she brought the Great Langdale complex into the archaeological literature over forty years ago and has continued to inspire investigation of these sites ever since. She has been unfailingly generous with her advice, hospitable and wonderfully encouraging. We dedicate this book to her.

I

NEOLITHIC BRITAIN AND THE STUDY OF EXCHANGE SYSTEMS

I

Making the connections

Introduction

The best way to introduce this book is by telling a story.

The basic elements are familiar, for the story is Italo Calvino's version of *The Count of Monte Cristo* (Calvino 1969).The scene is Château d'If, and the protagonists are the prisoners, Edmond Dantès and the Abbé Faria. Both of them wish to escape, but their approaches are subtly different from one another. Faria digs his way out of their cell, but all his plans go wrong and his tunnels lead him further into the fortress. On the basis of Faria's mistakes, his fellow prisoner constructs a map of the castle. If Faria is so energetic that he comes near to the perfect escape, Dantès spends his time imagining the perfect prison – it is a prison from which escape is entirely impossible.

His reasons are very simple. If he can conceive the perfect prison, it will either be the same as the real one – in which case there is no point in trying to leave it – or it will be one from which it is even harder to escape than the Château d'If. In that case all is not lost: 'We have only to identify the point where the imagined fortress does not coincide with the real one, then find it' (p. 152).

Thus the prisoners have two methods at their disposal. Faria digs blindly in the hope that he will escape, and Dantès draws together the results of the Abbé's tunnelling in order to create a model of the fortress as a whole. Those basic approaches epitomise the methods used in prehistoric archaeology on either side of the Atlantic.

No doubt the contrast is overdrawn, but since the 1960s research in the United States has been led by an explicit body of theory: questions of explanation have had pride of place, and the archaeological 'record' has been approached through a series of hypotheses, some of them derived from research in other fields (e.g. Binford 1987). In Europe, on the other hand, a tradition of detailed description has been difficult to shed, and here some of the more sophisticated interpretations of the past have developed out of a process of pattern recognition. Nowhere is this clearer than in the study of exchange, where work in the two continents has drawn on quite different traditions of research.

The material studied in this book is no exception. It demonstrates quite clearly how tenacious an empirical approach can be. The non-flint axes made during the Neolithic period in Britain have been examined by petrologists using essentially the same techniques for half a century: a programme of research which must be unmatched for sheer persistence (Keiller, Piggott and Wallis 1941; Clough and Cummins 1988). Yet their results were hardly used in studies of prehistoric exchange systems until about ten years ago (Cummins 1979; Hodder and Lane 1982). In effect, the first forty years of research were devoted to detailed *description*. Neolithic specialists accepted that axes had travelled over considerable distances, but it seemed enough to map the extent of their distribution and to observe any changes in that evidence over time. For the most part, interpretation of these patterns was regarded as self-evident. To all appearances, it was also a secondary consideration.

This approach to the material record is deeply entrenched in Europe. It is the archaeology of the Abbé Faria, tunnelling energetically and getting nowhere. We can compare the exhaustive characterisation of stone axes with the lists of metal analyses compiled by the Stuttgart laboratory (e.g. Junghans *et al.* 1960), or with the great catalogues of metalwork published in the series Prähistorische Bronzefunde. Each is a testimony to the energy and devotion of its authors, yet there are few signs that these studies have had much impact on our understanding of broader patterns of production and exchange. Either these compilations are viewed as worthwhile ends in themselves, or their sheer bulk is so inhibiting that they remain on the library shelf: lists of artefacts sundered from their material and historical contexts. Despite their thorough documentation, they rarely attract the attention of archaeological theorists.

To some extent the situation has changed over the last few years, and many prehistorians working in Europe have acknowledged the impact of processual archaeology. Its attitudes have more in common with the position of Edmond Dantès, yet there is a danger of taking the comparison too far. Where European prehistorians had placed the major emphasis on cataloguing and characterisation, the new generation of scholars turned to quantitative modelling. Exchange systems were studied by formal methods, some of them derived from geography or economics, and most of the developments to establish themselves securely concerned methods rather than theory. There were important changes in the ways in which data were collected and analysed, yet there is a sense in which the impact of the New Archaeology has been surprisingly limited.

Its ideas were adopted as part of a wider reaction against the excessive empiricism of the post-war years, and to some extent its reception was coloured by thinking in social anthropology. Anthropologists working in the United States had more in common with archaeologists and even taught in the same university departments. Certain ideas were shared between the disciplines; there was the same emphasis on cultural adaptation, on social types and progressive evolution, and in some cases the new interest in exchange was informed by ideas from formalist economics. This contrasts with European anthropology, where the dominant influence was probably that of Lévi-Strauss. Research workers took more interest in understanding societies *from the inside* and had turned their attention to the symbolic dimensions of human behaviour. The differences are epitomised by the title of Marshall Sahlins' famous polemic (Sahlins 1976). European research placed more emphasis on *culture*, whilst the New Archaeologists of the 1960s and 1970s were interested in *practical reason*. Exchange systems are a case in point. Processual archaeology emphasised the importance of precise *measurement*, whilst European social anthropologists showed a greater concern with *meaning*. In this situation, the techniques pioneered by American archaeologists took on a life of their own. There was little common ground with

European social theory, and no sooner had the precepts of the New Archaeology been absorbed by prehistorians than Edmund Leach denounced it as the offshoot of an obsolete anthropology (Leach 1973).

In effect, the methods of the New Archaeology were introduced into an intellectual climate in Europe in which a number of its assumptions were no longer so acceptable. Although archaeology and anthropology could be taught together in European universities, there were areas in which the subjects had diverged to an alarming extent. Among these was the study of exchange. As we shall see, the New Archaeology ensured that data were interrogated and ordered with a growing sophistication, so that now a whole battery of analytical techniques were available. But at the same time, these methods had become increasingly divorced from anthropological studies. To adapt a famous saying of Oscar Wilde, archaeology and anthropology had become two subjects divided by a common interest.

Many writers have sensed a new rapprochement between these disciplines (e.g. Rowlands 1982; Hodder 1982a). In this chapter we argue that after twenty years of productive research, formal methods for the analysis of exchange systems are starting to reveal their limitations. It is to social anthropology, and particularly the tradition associated with Marcel Mauss, that we must look for further progress. The first part of this chapter traces the development of exchange studies in processual archaeology and the difficulties that gradually became apparent in that work. The second section shows how some of the same issues have been approached by social anthropologists and advocates a new synthesis of these two fields of research. In the remaining chapters we try to practise what we preach. We turn to one of the largest bodies of data in prehistoric archaeology and offer a new study of the 'axe trade' in Neolithic Britain. In Calvino's story Edmond Dantès' escape from the Château d'If depends on his ability to put Faria's observations to good use. With fifty years of petrological analysis at our disposal, we shall try to do the same.

Exchange systems in prehistoric archaeology

The petrographic analysis of stone artefacts is so well established that it is difficult for two British authors to appreciate the impact of characterisation studies on prehistoric archaeology. By linking specific products with identifiable sources these studies provided one method of evaluating the diffusionist interpretation of European prehistory. They reduced the importance of purely stylistic comparisons (Dixon, Cann and Renfrew 1968) and, used together with radiocarbon dating, they prepared the way for a reading of the evidence that emphasised *local* processes rather than the migration of people (Renfrew 1969). At the same time, characterisation studies were a prerequisite for the development of more subtle regional analyses, providing one method of charting the character and scale of resource use. Such work has taken two general forms: analyses which use the overall distribution of a particular raw material to define an analytical region, and those where the distribution of different raw materials helps to identify 'interaction zones' (Pires-Ferreira 1976; Renfrew and Dixon 1976; Plog 1977).

For the most part studies of stone axes in Britain have operated at the broader geographical scale and have been concerned with describing their distribution across the country as a whole (Clough and Cummins 1979). Only recently has much interest been shown in exploring the relationship between the products of *different sources* (Chappell 1987). This change of attitude is due to the work of Colin Renfrew and his colleagues who studied the distribution of obsidian in the Aegean and the Near East (Renfrew, Cann and Dixon 1968; Renfrew 1969), although similar work was carried out over the same period in the New World (Flannery 1972; Beale 1973). Renfrew's initial objective was to reassess the geographical connections that formed the basis of the diffusionist model, but in doing this it became important to identify the kinds of process that were responsible for the spatial patterning seen in the archaeological record. It was no longer enough to describe the distribution of particular artefacts or raw materials; it was important to identify the processes behind different dispersal patterns.

Such studies were important because they raised the possibility that detailed analysis of the movement of objects from one area to another – or, more precisely, studies of the frequency with which they were used and discarded – would shed light on the institutions involved in promoting and maintaining contacts. Many of the early analyses took a similar form and focussed on the changing number of objects in relation to their distance from the source, a method with an established pedigree in geography and economic anthropology. They highlighted a recurrent pattern in the movement of goods outward from their area of origin. Almost without exception, their numbers decreased with distance from the source, a pattern of use and discard which Renfrew was to formulate in his 'Law of Monotonic Decrement':

> In circumstances of uniform loss or deposition and in the absence of highly organised directional (i.e. preferential nonhomogeneous) exchange, the curve of frequency or abundance of occurrence of an exchanged commodity against effective distance from a localised source will be a monotonic, decreasing one. (Renfrew 1977, 72)

This was an analytical device which was designed to isolate anomalies and also to distinguish between what Renfrew called *contact* and *supply zones*. One aspect of this work was to prove particularly influential, for he suggested that an exponential fall-off curve could be explained by a model of 'down-the-line exchange' or balanced reciprocity. This was a pioneering attempt to forge a quantitative link between a specific anthropological model of exchange and its material residue. Moreover, it followed from that argument that significant departures from the basic fall-off curve might reflect the intervention of different agencies in the movement of goods between their source and their ultimate destination (Renfrew 1975). In other words, formalist analytical techniques could be used to identify 'types' of exchange that substantivist anthropologists placed along an evolutionary continuum (Dalton 1977). These ranged from 'reciprocal' and 'prestige-chain exchange' to 'freelance trade', 'directional trade' and even *laissez-faire* capitalism. Each was held to have specific implications for the organisation and complexity of the societies in which they operated. Thus in Sahlins' typology reciprocity could be linked to segmentary societies, whilst redistribution would be correlated with chiefdoms or states (Sahlins 1972). In a similar vein, Ian Hodder showed how regression analysis of different fall-off patterns could distinguish between the movement of low-value, often bulky goods which had travelled a short distance, and the movement of higher-value goods, whose distributions extended much further (Hodder 1974; Hodder and Orton 1976, 124).

These were exciting developments of the original model since they held out the prospect of extrapolating from distribution patterns to social organisation through a fuller understanding of how the exchange of goods had been organised. Inevitably, as more applications of these methods became available, empirical and theoretical problems began to be identified. Many of these surfaced in two volumes dealing explicitly with approaches to prehistoric exchange, both of which drew heavily on the conceptual framework mapped out in earlier studies (Earle and Ericson 1977; Ericson and Earle 1982). At an empirical level it seemed as if the predictive power of Renfrew's two-dimensional model could be enhanced through the incorporation of additional factors that might have influenced the regional distribution of material (Wright and Zeder 1977). These included the nature of transportation and access to and from the area of origin, the character and chronology of the sites used in the analysis, the density of population in different regions, and the availability of alternative resources (Wright 1969; Ericson 1977; Singer and Ericson 1977; Ammerman, Matessi and Cavalli-Sforza 1978; Finbow and Bolognese 1980). The last factor was to be explored in a study of Neolithic axes in Britain, which employed a 'gravity model' based on the 'attractiveness' of artefacts from different sources (Chappell 1986; cf. Hallam, Warren and Renfrew 1976; Hodder 1978). As Torrence points out, however, such an approach only offers a basis 'for describing and comparing distributions which are already reasonably well documented' (1986, 27). Valuable as this may be, it does not provide sufficient grounds for inferring the character of the processes that lay behind those patterns.

Stone artefacts are especially well suited to such studies, and this may be why the early analyses of obsidian distribution have proved of such lasting value. We must also consider the relationship between consumption and exchange in relation to the physical properties of different raw materials. The problem is partly one of archaeological visibility. In propounding the Law of Monotonic Decrement Renfrew had referred to 'circumstances of uniform loss or deposition', but not all the artefacts that were exchanged would have entered the archaeological record. Metals were frequently recycled and the products of different ore sources might be mixed together – a problem which confronted the Stuttgart analyses mentioned earlier. Ceramics could also be recycled, as broken pots were used to temper new ones, but stone is virtually indestructible. In the case of lithic artefacts complete recycling is not an option; although objects may be extensively reworked, a raw material like obsidian will retain its essential characteristics. Moreover, the production, re-use and maintenance of lithic artefacts leaves a direct trace in the form of debitage, and this often provides a basis for inferences concerning source, technology and chronology. Indeed, Ammerman and Andrefsky (1982) argued that any study of the regional distribution of lithic materials should incorporate an assessment of the reduction sequences employed at different locations. On this basis it would be possible to establish how far the level of consumption on any site reflected its involvement in artefact production.

There are further problems in using the evidence of consumption to infer the character of exchange. There has been some progress in measuring the proportion of imported materials 'dropping out' of the system, but as evidence of how they had circulated this is tantalisingly indirect. Most studies have been concerned with objects or materials that were 'routinely discarded' when their use-life was over, yet, as we shall see, this approach makes questionable assumptions about the nature of material culture and the roles that it plays in social life. The problem becomes more obvious where particular objects might have been associated with personal identity or prestige, or where they had been deployed in specialised transactions (e.g. Moholy-Nagy 1976). In such cases they may have entered the archaeological record as formal deposits, for example grave goods or votive offerings. Their distributions could differ markedly from those of objects that were discarded with less formality. For example, Sidrys demonstrated that different amounts of obsidian were entering Classic Maya sites according to their status in the settlement pattern (Sidrys 1976, 1977). Two separate regression lines could be calculated to summarise the movement of this material away from its source; the density of obsidian in the excavated deposits on major centres was about six times that encountered at minor sites. This might have happened because the movement of obsidian was articulated through these locations, but it seems more likely that it reflects two different patterns of consumption.

A more serious problem emerged in Renfrew's later work, for it became apparent that a number of quite different agencies might have been responsible for the same types of patterning in the archaeological record (Renfrew 1977). The two types of regression identified by Hodder still retained some validity, but simulation studies and ethnographic research were starting to show that essentially similar fall-off curves could be created by a range of quite distinct processes (Ericson and Earle 1982). Still more discouraging, fall-off curves very much like those believed to identify particular kinds of exchange could all be created by the random movement of goods outwards from their source (Elliott, Ellman and Hodder 1978). By extension, even where distinctive spatial patterning could be recognised, it was by no means certain that this reflected one kind of socioeconomic relationship. For example, centrally administered redistribution might result in the same spatial patterning as the operation of a market economy.

Faced with such problems, several authors concluded that formal models would be most useful where they could be assessed in relation to additional sources of information. Nevertheless their discussions continued to work from the assumption that there might be a direct relationship between different levels of social complexity and different forms of exchange. Many of these arguments feature in Ericson and Earle's edited volume *Contexts for Prehistoric Exchange* (1982), although the significance attached to the word 'context' varies considerably between different authors. Earle, for example, talks of a 'more detailed contextual analysis that considers the broader economic, social, political and ideological forms in which exchange is embedded' (Earle 1982, 7–8; cf. Spence 1982). This statement echoes a strong substantivist vein among the contributors. Other papers place more emphasis on methodology, and here 'context' is used as a synonym for provenance. Despite the range of different viewpoints, many of the authors acknowledged problems created by the massive scale at which earlier studies had been undertaken, and looked for more detailed patterning at the local level. Finbow and Bolognese (1982) suggested that the solution to some of these problems might be provided by trend surface analysis, whilst other contributors showed that patterning at a local level could even contradict the trends detected on a broader scale of analysis (Bettinger 1982; Earle and D'Altroy 1982). In other words, Renfrew's model might work well at a regional level but did not account for variations which stemmed from more local factors, such as site specialisation or the presence of sociopolitical boundaries (Bettinger 1982). The argument was underlined by McBryde's ethnohistoric studies of Aboriginal exchange, which were published at about the same time (McBryde 1979; McBryde and Harrison 1981).

Another approach has been to investigate production sites. We find the same attempts to identify consistent relationships between different forms of social organisation and the character and organisation of production (Singer and Ericson 1977; Sheets 1978; Ericson and Purdy 1984; Torrence 1986). This kind of reasoning characterises Ericson's discussion of obsidian exchange in California (Ericson 1982), but it is most clearly articulated in Torrence's analysis of the obsidian quarries of Melos in the Aegean (Torrence 1986). Her work focusses on the lithic reduction sequences practised at the stone source, with special attention to questions of standardisation and specialisation, as measured by technological features such as error rates. Torrence draws on ethnographic and historical accounts of stoneworking in different socioeconomic settings in order to define a continuum of productive efficiency. This she describes as 'a framework for measuring exchange'. Different points along this continuum have different social correlates and reflect the existence of quite different forms of exchange. On that basis she rejects the hypothesis that Melian obsidian had been extracted and worked by specialists. Research by Muller (1987) on Mississippian exchange systems has something in common with this study, for here again close scrutiny of the evidence for shell artefact production led to a reinterpretation of distribution patterns thought to identify specialist activity.

Muller's study is more wide ranging than Torrence's, and makes two observations that serve to highlight the true complexity of the issues. First, he comments on how the discovery of fine or exotic artefacts can lead to circular interpretations. Their presence in graves tempts archaeologists to infer that the deceased had enjoyed a special position in life. They then go on to suggest that high status depended on the ability to secure those objects; the character and role of exchange are inferred from exactly the same material. Secondly, Muller shows how the distinctiveness of the artefacts found in his study area has been exaggerated. This contrasts with the way in which *the same objects* were treated at Spiro, nearly 1000 km away. Here these artefacts are concentrated in a small region, where they are best represented in a restricted set of burial mounds. Both observations point to the difficulty of drawing inferences about the value of certain artefacts from the circumstances attending their production. In this case the value accorded to shell artefacts may have changed as they circulated in contexts some distance from their area of origin. In much the same way, Ammerman and Andrefsky's discussion (1982) of obsidian exchange in Calabria shows how the significance ascribed to particular objects may change according to their context.

Problems in the study of exchange

Many of these studies have been stimulating, but they do have their limitations. So many problems have arisen that we must question the assumption that the refinement of formal methods of analysis can ever provide a satisfactory 'framework for measuring exchange'. There is the critical problem of equifinality. There seems little virtue in pursuing quantitative analyses of artefact distributions if we lack any grounds for inferring the nature of the processes responsible for their creation. All that we shall achieve by that work are more precise and all-encompassing *descriptions*. These remain important for comparing different exchange systems with one another, and for tracing their changing configurations over time, but at a still more detailed level their role will be quite limited. The problem is no longer one of scale, for the most serious difficulties result from the assumptions that lie behind such formal analyses. As Hodder notes, most studies have been predicated on the idea that progress can be made by *assuming* that people in the past considered costs and benefits along formal economic lines (Hodder 1982b). Torrence's study is a case in point, for it is only by making this assumption that she is able to apply the same scale of measurement to people as different from one another as hunter-gatherers procuring workable stone for their own use, and the makers of gunflints for sale in the modern world market (Torrence 1986). We do not deny the value of heuristic models in thinking about the archaeological record. The problems arise because we equate predictions made on this basis with explanation or broader understanding:

> To say that Y amount of pottery is found at a site because it is X distance from the source and because the relationship between X and Y fits a regression formula is hardly an adequate explanation of the exchange process. In the same vein, concepts from modern economic theory may be adequate for describing and 'predicting' the past, but since we cannot be sure that scarcity, maximisation and surplus are relevant concepts for past societies, attempts at explaining why a particular formal pattern is found are liable to be of limited value.
> (Hodder 1982b, 202)

There are other problems with the idea that particular dispersal patterns should reflect the character of past societies. It would be easy to focus on the extremes encompassed by different case studies and to extrapolate between them in order to locate those societies that fall outside their remit. We could arrange the various systems of production and consumption according to their scale and complexity as if this mirrored a real sequence of development. Dalton came close to doing so in his contribution to *Exchange Systems in Prehistory*, whilst Earle and D'Altroy hint at an evolutionary sequence in their discussion of 'staple' and 'wealth finance' systems (Dalton 1977; Earle and D'Altroy 1982). Marxist scholars are no less vulnerable on this account, and they too have looked for links between specific modes of production and particular types of social formation, although in non-capitalist societies these are based on a different conception of exchange (e.g. Friedman and Rowlands 1977).

Such approaches do have their attractions, but we hesitate to follow that course since it brushes aside the problems raised by particular analyses in favour of a general model so far removed from the data that it loses any analytical power. It would make it difficult, and possibly unnecessary, to explore the conditions under which particular networks developed or the purposes that they served. At the same time, social typologies have had an unhappy history. Feinman and Neinzel, for example, have shown that schemes of this kind establish no more than a one-dimensional index. Once we extend the scope of our analysis, the sharp outlines disappear. Those cross-cultural correspondences that appear to hold do so at such a level of generality that they tell us nothing about the conditions in which particular practices were employed (Feinman and Neinzel 1984). Such approaches leave little room for competition or conflicts of interest.

If it is difficult to extrapolate from spatial patterns, it is still harder to infer social institutions from the evidence of production sites. Yet in a number of cases this is exactly what has been done. Thus for Torrence, and for Singer and Ericson, production sites or quarries provide a unique context in which to study 'a complete exchange system' (Torrence 1986, 91; Singer and Ericson 1977). Similar ideas have been propounded by Earle (1982). We agree that the archaeological potential of production sites has very rarely been realised, but take issue with the idea that they can be studied in isolation. There is no intrinsic reason why the relationships between production, distribution and consumption should be either predictable or direct. It is the nature of their articulation under specific historical conditions that needs to be explored, and this cannot be assumed a priori. Otherwise studies of artefact production merely substitute one partial analysis for another.

In effect, the last two decades have seen the development of a battery of sophisticated techniques for studying prehistoric exchange. Most of these have been concerned with examining broad patterns of artefact dispersal. This work has been supplemented by a more limited number of studies of production sites, but these share the same disadvantage, that the character of the entire system is being researched through just one of its component parts. Moreover, with a few notable exceptions, research in this field has emphasised the frequency or *scale* of consumption, rather than the *character* and *context* of artefact use and deposition. The life history of different artefacts seems predestined, from the moment they are made until they enter the archaeological record. As a result we sustain an extraordinary loss of detail. The summary character of these models does little justice to the richness of the material that they address. If we are to catch something of what is lost, we must go beyond the methods of processual archaeology and explore the potential of other sources.

Alternative perspectives

A useful starting point for this discussion is a review article by Ian Hodder (1982b). He argues that if archaeologists are to study exchange in its social context, 'as part of a system of production' (p. 207), they should not limit themselves to the character of the artefacts involved. What is needed is a wider understanding of their contexts, including any patterns of association and avoidance. This is consistent with his more recent suggestions concerning the development of a contextual archaeology (Hodder 1989 and 1991). At the same time, the artefacts employed in a particular exchange network are not selected at random. We must also investigate their symbolism. He sums up the possibilities as follows:

> Exchange involves the transfer of items that have symbolic and categorical associations. Within any strategy of legitimation, the symbolism of objects is manipulated in the construction of relations of dominance. The exchange of appropriate items forms social obligations, status and power, but it also legitimates as it forms. A fully contextual approach to exchange must incorporate the symbolism of the objects exchanged.
> (1982b, 209)

That statement encapsulates a number of ideas which have been influential in more recent work. They differ from the approaches described so far because their origins lie in another tradition of social anthropology. Its tenets are rarely considered by those promoting formal models of exchange. We referred earlier to the influential collections edited by Earle and Ericson; it is extremely revealing that Marcel Mauss' *The Gift*, surely the starting point for studies of this kind, is cited only once (Earle and Ericson 1977; Ericson and Earle 1982; Mauss 1954). Marshall Sahlins' book *Stone Age Economics*, published as recently as 1972, is referred to in only a quarter of the papers, and the same fate seems to have overtaken a volume on *Social Exchange and Interaction* edited by Wilmsen in the same year (Wilmsen 1972). Its contents were more in the tradition of Marcel Mauss but this book never had the influence that it deserved.

As both Mauss and Sahlins recognised, exchange in non-Western societies is really a form of diplomacy, and for this reason it cannot be understood in purely 'economic' terms. Rather, it is concerned with the creation, protection and manipulation of *social* relationships. It plays a central role in mediating marriage ties, kinship bonds and alliances, and is crucially important in competition for status. In this sense it is deeply implicated in the classification and circulation of *people* (Lévi-Strauss 1969; Gregory 1982, 30). At the same time, a number of writers consider that exchange also has a strategic role, for giving can be a way of 'inflicting debt' (Earle 1989). Every gift presupposes another in return, and lasting differences of social position may result when debtors are unable to discharge their obligations. Such obligations may include the transfer of portable artefacts, the provision of hospitality or the contribution of labour.

These ideas are useful but there are more subtle ways in which exchange can sustain or subvert political relations. Weiner (1985) suggests that in non-market societies exchange is quite different from commodity sale and can involve a process of 'keeping while giving'. Recent studies show how inalienable wealth can play a central role in creating and reproducing inequality (Damon 1984; Strathern 1984 and 1988;

Lederman 1986; LiPuma 1987; N. Thomas 1991). There are even cases in which the terms used to denote particular exchange networks are the same as those referring to specific power relations (e.g. Leach and Leach 1983).

A number of authors have explored the important conceptual distinction between the circulation of *gifts*, where a lasting relationship is formed between the participants, and the movement of alienated *commodities* (Godelier 1977; Gregory 1982). The two transactions can be conducted within very different temporal frameworks (Ingold 1986, chapter 6). Thus the immediate reciprocity which characterises the transfer of commodities 'cancels out the obligation of exchange at that moment, and the commodity is alienable. The gift requires future reciprocation, and thus symbolises a lasting obligation over time' (Barrett 1989, 308). In addition, Barrett distinguishes between different forms of gift exchange according to the way in which they reproduce social relations. He contrasts *cyclical exchanges*, where the symbolic importance of the gift is transformed at various points, with *tributary gift giving* where authority is established primarily through the hereditary claims of a chief. Rowlands takes a rather similar view, arguing that gift exchanges are inextricably involved with power relations. Here the inalienable character of a gift:

> implies not only that it or an equivalent must be returned, but that being able to enforce this is, in itself, a means of domination . . . For wealth to be inalienable implies both the power to keep while giving, and the power to exclude others from the right of temporary possession. In other words, the term suggests property relations, certainly different from capitalist notions of ownership, but none the less a *definition of persons and social relations in terms of the possession of things*.
> (1987, 6–7; our emphasis)

We must be wary of hardening the distinction between commodities and gifts until they 'stand for' capitalist and non-capitalist relations respectively. That would be to overlook the active roles that commodities play in contemporary social life (Miller 1985). All exchanges create a relationship between the participants, even though this can be masked or mystified (Bourdieu 1977). Nor should we overlook the 'calculative, impersonal and self-aggrandising features of non-capitalist societies' (Appadurai 1986, 11). These are important criticisms, and they serve to show how different forms of production and consumption may coexist in the same historical context. Even so, in non-capitalist societies objects can remain attached to people, and for this reason the exchange of material symbols must be one of the media through which social strategies are conducted.

It may be useful to think of exchange in terms of the establishment of *genealogies*, for the object of exchange 'acquires a past through its engagement in social relations, in the same way as does the natural world' (Ingold 1986, 269). The history of the contexts through which an object has passed is effectively the history of the social relationships that this passage created or maintained. Moreover, since it objectifies that history (Mauss 1954, 167), the exchanged item takes on a symbolic character, acting as both metaphor and mnemonic. The problem is that while objects may change their meanings as they are exchanged, the recovery of those meanings will be very difficult to achieve (Barrett 1987).

The significance of material culture is not restricted to specialised transactions. Its engagement in the routines of everyday life may play a part in inculcating specific ideas about the cultural and natural worlds (Bourdieu 1977, 1990; Barrett 1988). This body of unconsidered ideas and associations may be drawn upon when particular items are treated as overt symbols. The notions associated with material items may slip in and out of focus according to their engagement in social discourse, and for this reason there is little merit in perpetuating the rigid distinction between *function* and *symbol*. Hodder (1982b) is right to suggest that the choice of items for exchange is far from arbitrary, but if we take this argument further, we must acknowledge that the significance accorded to an object – or even to the act of exchange – may be different from one context to another. This can be overlooked if we concentrate on the symbolic properties of artefacts to the exclusion of their other attributes. The ideas invested in material items are neither inherent nor immutable; they are ascribed through practice and are determined according to context. This point has been emphasised by Appadurai (1986), who uses the term 'regime of value' to emphasise the importance of the context within which particular objects circulate. In such cases its 'value' is really a matter of political judgement.

The same basic ideas have wider implications. They extend beyond the process of cyclical exchange, mentioned earlier, and can also be applied at a broader scale of analysis. For example, Godelier (1977) contrasts the inalienable exchange of salt among the Baruya with its first introduction from outside the local system. Like Gregory (1982), he argues that the objects or materials obtained through commodity transactions may subsequently be used in gift exchange. To some extent the same notion is present in Sahlins' work. He argues that the very nature of exchange will vary according to the social or moral distance separating the participants: close kin may be bound by generalised reciprocity, whilst negative reciprocity characterises dealings with strangers (Sahlins 1972). The links between these categories should not be drawn too sharply, for this would result in a conception of social groups as tightly bounded entities. This would not be appropriate for pre-modern societies (Rowlands 1987, 4).

The idea that artefacts may be imbued with a different significance as they circulate in different spheres plays a fundamental part in discussion of 'prestige goods economies' (Frankenstein and Rowlands 1978; MacCormack 1981). The operation of such a system presupposes the juxtaposition of two social formations with very different characteristics. In most cases research has concentrated on core/periphery relations between states and tribal systems, where items derived from the more complex society play a central role in the creation and protection of authority in the other group (e.g. Ekholm 1977; Rowlands 1987). Such relationships are inherently unstable, and the precarious balance of power achieved by these means is easily upset. This can happen through the subversion of exchange networks, the emulation of prestige items or even their deployment in inappropriate contexts (Meillassoux 1968; Strathern 1971; Miller 1985).

Relationships of this kind may not have been common in prehistoric Europe, but comparable arguments extend to societies that shared a similar structure. This is the basic premise of 'peer polity interaction', which depends on the idea that communication between elites in different sociocultural settings may provide a medium by which they sustain their authority (Renfrew and Cherry 1986). Changes within a given polity may be affected by changes in the nature or frequency of external contacts. As Mary Helms has argued, objects or ideas derived from geographically distant areas may serve as important resources in arguments over the distribution of power (Helms 1988). On the other hand, such arguments also arise from internal tensions and conflicts of interest, and these must be given due weight. External stimuli are important, but they can only be perceived in terms of 'the internal characteristics and logical properties of local cultural traditions' (Sørensen 1989, 199).

Again the most important point is that the significance of exchanged items may be altered as they move between one polity and another. This is true even though they are acquired through networks of alliance and obligation that extend beyond the local system. At the same time, such networks can act as a stimulus for major conflicts of interest. These might relate to the negotiation of age or gender distinctions, as well as competition between broader groups. Indeed, as Larick has shown, *the same artefacts may even be drawn upon in the reproduction of a number of different discourses* (Larick 1985, 1986). Where divisions are sustained by the passage of material items, existing relationships can be subverted in several ways. Subordinate groups in the social hierarchy may emulate the status items of their superiors; new exchange networks may be established that threaten existing alliances; and artefacts may be procured and deployed under new conditions (Davis 1985; Miller 1985; Appadurai 1986). In other words, the ideas objectified in particular categories of material culture are vulnerable and can be manipulated.

There are three levels at which it might be possible to exercise control over these processes. Following Kristiansen (1984), we could argue that the character and context of *deposition* act in just this manner, by controlling the volume of material in circulation. This idea has been applied to a number of archaeological contexts (Bradley 1990a). On the other hand, we should recognise that the deposition of elaborate artefacts may be related more directly to the creation and protection of hierarchy. In this case the idea that deposition was employed as a measure against 'inflation' would have little relevance (Gregory 1980). We should also note that the cycles of exchange and deposition discussed by Kristiansen span several generations and extend over enormous geographical areas.

Alternatively, control can be exercised over the *production* of particular items, an argument championed by Earle, who discusses the relationship between craft specialisation and chiefdoms (Earle 1977; Brumfiel and Earle 1987). Restrictions certainly can be placed on the contexts in which it is appropriate for particular items to be made. On the other hand, ethnographic research has shown that the presence of such restrictions is not necessarily linked to the emergence of a clear political hierarchy. Rather, they may be founded on kinship or age and gender divisions (e.g. Burton 1984a; 1984b; McBryde 1979). By extension, the web of social relations might be maintained as effectively through control over *access* to the items that pass along particular networks. In other words, restrictions might be placed upon the contexts in which the significance of those items was transformed (McBryde and Harrison 1981; Traube 1986). For example, proscriptions might surround the choice of exchange partners or the locations at which it was appropriate for transactions to take place. In each case this would have the effect of maintaining the integrity of the spheres in which particular artefacts could circulate.

All these processes may have been effected through the evocation of ideas sanctioned by tradition, but it should still be possible to infer their operation from archaeological data. Even if we reject any link between deposition and 'inflation', spatial and temporal disjunctures in the conditions under which artefacts were taken out of circulation may provide clues to the role that those objects played in the reproduction of social life. It is this point which is overlooked when we talk of the routine 'discard' of items. Whilst it may be useful to distinguish between the unconsidered disposal of materials and formal or votive deposition, any changes in a society's tacit attitudes towards the disposal of material culture may reflect wider transformations in its principles of classification and order (Douglas 1966). Much the same argument applies to the evidence for the production and circulation of artefacts. Archaeologically detectable changes in the character and context of their use may provide a starting point for a broader investigation of how their circulation affected the categories of the contemporary world.

Summing up

These observations have serious implications for our studies. They highlight some of the problems to be faced in analysing exchange, and they emphasise, if emphasis is needed, the naïvety of supposing that the exhaustive characterisation of artefacts could lead to immediate understanding. The fifty years spent provenancing stone axes in Britain are no substitute for a grounding in archaeological theory.

Several observations are crucial to our case. We have suggested that it is unwise to extrapolate the character and social context of an entire exchange network from just one kind of data. Nor can we assume that one-to-one correlations exist between specific forms of production, circulation or consumption and broader social 'types'. From this perspective the importance of many of the studies undertaken by processual archaeologists has little to do with their predictive power. Rather, their strength lies in the opportunities that they provide for detailed description and for drawing wider comparisons.

At the same time, our arguments have been tempered by observations made within social anthropology regarding the ways in which material production contributes to the broader process of social reproduction. As a result, the focus of this study moves from the definition of social types to the roles played by the production, circulation and consumption of a particular range of artefacts in sustaining political relations. In offering a new study of the 'stone axe trade' in the British Isles we shall be concerned with the part played by long-distance exchange in a number of small-scale regional systems, and the ways in which they were transformed.

This shift of emphasis has important methodological implications. In particular, it forces us to think about the manner in which we employ many of the analytical techniques described in this chapter. We have seen the dangers of treating exchange systems as homogeneous entities and extrapolating from one part to the whole. For that reason we must be more aware of the relations *between* different classes of archaeological data, moving back and forth through different scales of analysis. We need to contrast a number of separate aspects of the empirical record if we wish to understand the purposes that stone axes served within particular regimes of value and how relations between different regimes were articulated.

To attempt this experiment at all, we need to compare and contrast three basic areas of the archaeological record which have often been dealt with in isolation from one another. These are: the character, context and chronology of stone axe production; the character and organisation of their distribution through time; and the changing conditions under which they were deposited. To these we must add a fourth element, a well-documented culture sequence, for unless this is available, it will be impossible to set our findings in their broader context.

We began by describing the extraordinary development of stone axe studies in the British Isles and commented, perhaps unkindly, that forty years had been devoted to characterisation studies before these objects played any part in broader discussions of the nature of exchange. That material still waits to be investigated in detail. The research which forms the core of this book is a first step towards that goal.

2

Neolithic Britain – background to the case study

Introduction

Stone axes probably circulated throughout the Neolithic period in Britain. Yet it is clear that during that time there were important changes in the nature of society and its political geography. There has been a tendency to relate them to the exigencies of a 'farming' economy, but recent research has shown how they may actually reflect major transformations in a variety of *different* fields of social life: changes that cannot be explained simply by shifts in the character and intensity of subsistence. This chapter sketches the Neolithic sequence in the British Isles, highlighting the main chronological and regional divisions that have emerged in that research. Having done this, we shall be better placed to review the state of stone axe studies, for only then can we move beyond a view of these artefacts as reflections of an economic regime, to consider the wider roles that they might once have played.

European prehistorians often feel constrained by the Three Age Model, which divides up the prehistoric past on purely technological grounds. Whilst few attempts have been made to reject this scheme altogether, it is usual to modify it from within. Thus it did not take long to recognise that the 'Stone Age' was in special need of subdivision, and earlier this century the period was broken into three. There remains a tendency to study these three phases as homogeneous entities. This involves the assumption that the boundaries between them mark the thresholds across which all aspects of social life were transformed simultaneously. Moreover, the work of the last few decades has replaced the material distinctions that formed the basis for the original scheme by a series of economic archetypes, with the implication that changes in the nature of subsistence provide the basis for changes in other spheres. Thus the middle phase of the Stone Age, the Mesolithic, has come to characterise the activities of hunter-gatherers, and the Neolithic those of the earliest farmers. At the same time, the Neolithic has also been defined in terms of its material culture, for it saw the first widespread use of polished stone tools and pottery (Figs. 2.1 and 2.2).

These issues are important because the British Neolithic falls somewhere in between these two working definitions. It is not clear whether the adoption of domesticated resources happened rapidly in Britain, and it seems unlikely that farming was introduced by large-scale settlement from the Continent (Kinnes 1988; Whittle 1990). Although there is evidence for the use of domestic livestock, particularly cattle, from the early fourth millennium BC, there is little to suggest the widespread cultivation of cereals. Even at this simple level, there remain some grounds for uncertainty. The domestic animal bones are nearly always discovered in formal

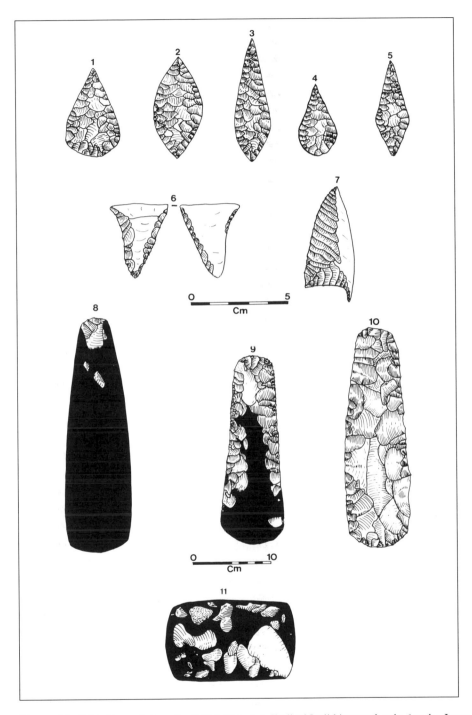

Fig. 2.1 Neolithic flintwork from the British Isles. 1–5, Earlier Neolithic arrowheads; 6 and 7, Later Neolithic arrowheads; 8–10, flint axeheads; 11, polished knife.

deposits, some of them at settlements, but many more are found in association with a series of ritual monuments, where there is little evidence of habitation (Grigson 1981). In addition, increasingly sophisticated methods for the recovery of carbonised remains show that wild plants could have been more important than domesticated species throughout this period (Moffet *et al.* 1989). In the light of such uncertainty, the other definition of the term 'Neolithic' raises a series of new questions. Polished axes, distinctive 'leaf-shaped' arrowheads and ceramics are frequent finds in this period (Figs. 2.1 and 2.2), although some of the axes may have precedents among Mesolithic groups in Ireland and Wales (Woodman 1978, 108–14; David 1989, 248–9). These distinctive artefacts are also among the principal elements shared with communities on the Continent. In effect, the appearance of novel artefacts, and the elaboration of existing forms, happens without a dramatic shift in the economic basis of society. We must begin by questioning the assumption that they can be 'explained' as responses to new subsistence practices, or as the consequences of a process of 'settling down'.

Such uncertainties extend to the level of everyday activity. The fixed settlements that had once been associated with farming populations on the European mainland elude archaeologists in Britain, and house plans of any kind are only rarely discovered (Megaw and Simpson 1979, chapter 3; Darvill 1987, chapter 3). Even the contemporary tool kit has features in common with that used by 'Mesolithic' hunter-gatherers, and it may have been designed to be both flexible and portable (Bradley 1987; Edmonds 1987). Similarly, the Earlier Neolithic flint scatters are small and rarely prolific, again suggesting a largely mobile pattern of activity. None of this evidence indicates a sudden 'economic' change, especially since there is reason to believe that subsistence patterns had been undergoing a gradual modification for some time (Mellars 1976). In the Later Mesolithic period there are already indications of more intensive land use (Simmons and Innes 1987). This evidence suggests a major focus of settlement on the shoreline, which would have been sufficiently productive for year-round occupation (Bonsall *et al.* 1989). There are also signs of increasingly frequent firing of the woodland, which was apparently intended to improve the resources available to browsing animals.

These arguments would hardly justify treating Neolithic Britain as a self-contained field of study. The changes of material culture were undoubtedly significant, but what really distinguishes the archaeological record is that for the first time the British landscape contains a range of monuments, some of them of great size and elaboration (Renfrew 1973). These have close counterparts on the Continent. It is all too easy to fall into the trap of inferring an agricultural system in Britain in order to explain how monument building was 'financed'. Such arguments do not carry conviction. They encourage a view of monuments as largely secondary phenomena – as 'luxuries' constructed following the establishment of a new, more productive economic regime (see Case 1969). As a result, they provide little basis for exploring the roles that these sites might have played in different aspects of social life. On a more pragmatic level, this interpretation also conflicts with the economic and environmental evidence that is currently available.

Other problems arise from the ways in which research has been structured. As Julian

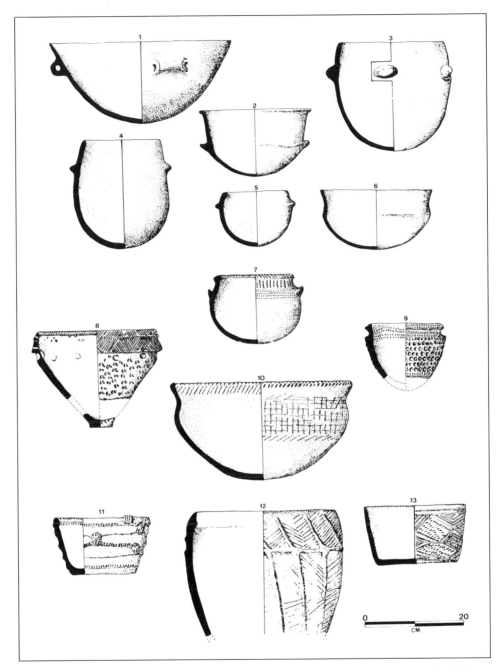

Fig. 2.2 Neolithic pottery from the British Isles. 1–7, Earlier Neolithic pottery; 8–10, Later Neolithic Peterborough Ware; 11–13, Later Neolithic Grooved Ware.

Thomas (1988) has argued, the transition between the Mesolithic and the Neolithic marks a threshold across which different concepts and techniques come into play. Mesolithic specialists tend to concern themselves with the subsistence economy and can be curiously blind to social factors, whilst Neolithic scholars are often more interested in social processes but can combine this with an uncritical acceptance of assumptions about the nature of the economy. Thus the Mesolithic–Neolithic transition is also the meeting point between two different methodologies. No doubt some of these differences arise from the material records of the two periods and the way in which they encourage analysis at different levels of material and chronological resolution, but this is no justification for the major conceptual shifts that can be seen in so much of the literature. In the case of the Neolithic, the character of subsistence practices may not have changed completely, but when we consider that it shares both monuments and material culture with widely scattered communities on the Continent, purely economic arguments are robbed of much of their power. The period has been cogently summarised in these terms:

> The process of becoming Neolithic consisted of a transformation of the *social relations of production*. This could be achieved by the end of the fourth millennium bc because it was now possible to transfer the Neolithic lifestyle, as an entity, from one community to another. What it consisted in was not pigs, sheep, grain but *knowledge*, including arcane and magical knowledge.
> (Thomas 1988, 63)

In terms of subsistence and settlement, the Neolithic sequence can best be divided into two broad phases (Megaw and Simpson 1979, chapters 3 and 4; Bradley 1984a, chapters 2 and 3; Darvill 1987, chapters 3 and 4). As we have seen, in the earlier of these, lithic scatters are small and suggest a pattern of fairly short-lived activity. Flint technology also implies a rather mobile pattern of settlement, not unlike that of the preceding period. In the later phase, both these features change, although in nearly every area domestic structures remain as elusive as ever. The tool kit no longer seems to be designed for portability. Flintworking is more wasteful and is characterised by a broader range of expedient tools, as well as a much wider variety of finished forms, some of considerable size (Bradley 1987). It is also possible to detect changes in the selection of raw materials. Lithic scatters are both extensive and prolific, although this need not be interpreted as evidence of sedentism. At the same time, larger areas of the landscape seem to have been used (Gardiner 1984; Edmonds 1987).

We can compare this sequence with the far more prominent evidence for monuments and exchange. From the outset, we need to make a simple division between two rather different regional developments in Britain (Fig. 2.3). The better known sequence is epitomised by the evidence from Wessex (Richards 1990; Barrett *et al.* 1991), whilst its northern counterpart is best documented on the Yorkshire Wolds (Manby 1988). In studying their development and interaction, we shall highlight two parallel sequences of change, the first running from about 3800 BC to 3300 BC, and the second extending down to the first appearance of metal around 2300 BC. Our understanding of the second period is complicated by the development of a more

Fig. 2.3 The regions of the British Isles described in the text.

extensive interaction sphere with its point of origin much further to the north in Orkney.

The key sequences are found in areas with very similar characteristics. Both the Wessex downland and the Yorkshire Wolds provide fairly well-watered chalk plateaux, rising to a height of 200 m or more. They were probably mantled by loess, an extremely fertile silt of Pleistocene origin, and each is flanked by unusually productive areas of lower ground. In some respects the Yorkshire Wolds stand out, and in a recent paper Higham (1987) has shown how they enjoy a more favourable range of natural resources than other parts of northern England. This has always made them a major focus for human settlement. It is less clear why Wessex should have been so favoured, as there are other parts of southern England which share the same characteristics. On the other hand, it is important not to exaggerate the significance of these two areas, for in each case the archaeological record has been preserved fortuitously through their use as sheep pasture during later periods. Not only does this introduce a bias into our appreciation of the archaeology: it has also meant that these regions have an unusually long history of investigation. We should remember that lowland areas can produce very similar archaeological evidence, but the fact that this is less well preserved sets limits on its interpretation. In this sense the evidence from Wessex and Yorkshire has to stand for more extensive regional systems in southern and eastern Britain respectively. Those smaller regions with concentrations of monuments and complex artefacts have been described as the 'core areas' of Neolithic Britain.

There may also be certain historical differences between these two key sequences, although it is too soon to say how far these have been coloured by the ways in which research has developed. It is not clear to what extent the chalk uplands had been used during the Later Mesolithic period, and, taken overall, datable material is sparse. In Wessex the situation is being redressed by systematic field survey, and in one region it is now established that the density of Mesolithic occupation sites on the clay with flints mantling the chalk is at least as high as anywhere else in the country (Arnold *et al.* 1988). On the Yorkshire Wolds, there is greater room for uncertainty, as systematic field survey has hardly been carried out. On the other hand, a recent study has provided evidence that the chalkland vegetation may have experienced drastic modification at this time (Bush 1988).

The Earlier Neolithic sequence (Fig. 2.4)

Although an interval may have elapsed between the first adoption of domesticates and the initial appearance of monuments, it is only with the latter development that the sequence really begins, and at present it seems that the construction of earthworks may have started first in Yorkshire; dates of a similar order of magnitude also come from less intensively researched landscapes elsewhere in northern and eastern Britain. These monuments were associated with the dead and can be traced back to about 3800 BC (Manby 1988). In the south rather similar monuments were established, but a somewhat smaller proportion of the sites belong to quite such an early stage. In the latter area, the clusters of funerary monuments could be flanked by distinctive

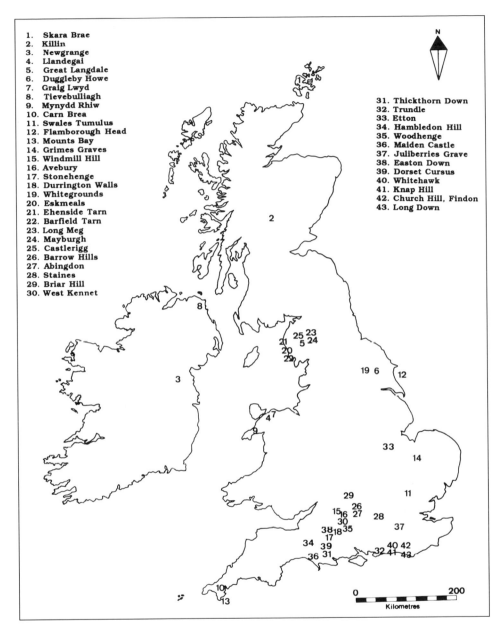

1. Skara Brae
2. Killin
3. Newgrange
4. Llandegai
5. Great Langdale
6. Duggleby Howe
7. Graig Lwyd
8. Tievebulliagh
9. Mynydd Rhiw
10. Carn Brea
11. Swales Tumulus
12. Flamborough Head
13. Mounts Bay
14. Grimes Graves
15. Windmill Hill
16. Avebury
17. Stonehenge
18. Durrington Walls
19. Whitegrounds
20. Eskmeals
21. Ehenside Tarn
22. Barfield Tarn
23. Long Meg
24. Mayburgh
25. Castlerigg
26. Barrow Hills
27. Abingdon
28. Staines
29. Briar Hill
30. West Kennet
31. Thickthorn Down
32. Trundle
33. Etton
34. Hambledon Hill
35. Woodhenge
36. Maiden Castle
37. Juliberries Grave
38. Easton Down
39. Dorset Cursus
40. Whitehawk
41. Knap Hill
42. Church Hill, Findon
43. Long Down

Fig. 2.4 Neolithic sites mentioned in the text.

enclosures, characterised by interrupted ditches (*causewayed enclosures*) (Megaw and Simpson 1979, chapter 3; Bradley 1984a, chapter 2; Darvill 1989, chapter 3). These probably originated after the funerary monuments were established in the south. Developments in the north took place at, or possibly beyond, the limits of their main distribution.

The funerary monuments of these areas show both similarities and differences (Fig. 2.5), and the same is true of the practices that took place there. The traditional characterisation of this period is that it sees the construction of *long barrows*: rectangular, trapezoidal or oval mounds which cover the disarticulated remains of a large number of individuals. Their bones might have been housed in a turf or timber ossuary, which performs the same function as the better-known megalithic chambers in regions with suitable materials for their construction. In this ideal scheme, the bones of men, women and children might be mixed together after they had lost their flesh. Grave goods would be excluded from these deposits (Bradley 1984a, 19–25; Darvill 1987, 68–70).

This portrayal is not actually wrong, but it is so generalised that it conceals more detailed evidence for regional and chronological developments. There seems little reason to doubt that human remains could undergo a period or periods of treatment before they were brought into these chambers; indeed, it seems almost certain that some of the bones were taken away again. It is a moot point whether they were unfleshed through exposure, primary burial or by some other means, but in most instances it is clear that the bones were rearranged in an ideal order beneath the monument. They might be classified by age, sex or body parts, and in rare instances skeletons could be reconstituted using bones that actually belonged to different individuals (Bradley 1984a, 19–20). In no region are there sufficient deposits of this kind to account for more than a small part of the population, and in any case other remains may be found as loose bones or as inhumation burials with settlements and causewayed enclosures (Kinnes 1979, 120–7). Flat graves may also have existed in isolation, and there are signs that there had been a cemetery of this type outside one of the causewayed enclosures in the Thames valley (Claire Halpin pers. comm.).

In short, it seems as if the deposits in elaborate funerary monuments may have served a variety of purposes. Although only a small proportion of the population appears to have been interred in these contexts, the transformation of individual identity would have allowed the mortuary deposits to stand for the corporate group as a whole. At the same time, it seems that the order of these deposits may also have played a part in the reproduction of distinctions within society, drawn on the basis of age and gender (Shanks and Tilley 1982; Thomas and Whittle 1986).

At a more detailed level there are important differences between the traditions epitomised by the evidence from Wessex and Yorkshire. In the latter area there are certainly signs that human bones were circulating among the living just as they were in Wessex, but in this case when the bones were deposited in long barrows they could be purposefully destroyed by setting the whole structure on fire (Thorpe and Richards 1984; Manby 1988). This did not take place at every site, but where it did happen it would have prevented the bones from circulating as relics. This may have been

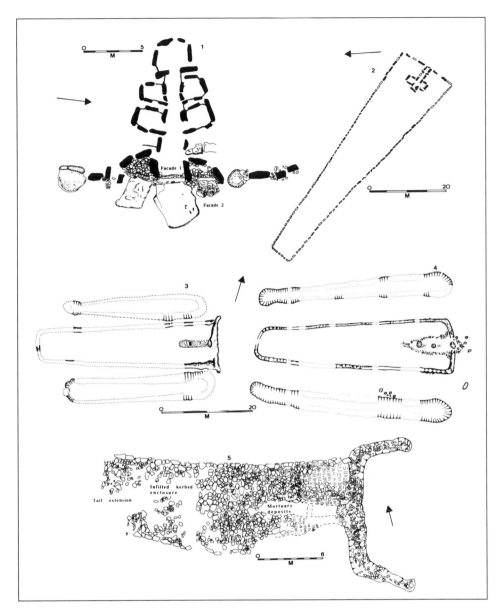

Fig. 2.5 Earlier Neolithic mortuary sites in England. 1, detail of the façade and burial chambers at West Kennet; 2, Waylands Smithy; 3, Willerby Wold; 4, Fussell's Lodge; 5, Street House.

intentional, for similar practices are documented on only one site in Wessex (Morgan 1959), where an emphasis may have been placed on more lasting relationships between the living and the dead. At the same time, from about 3800 BC onwards there are signs that a different set of mortuary practices were developing in northern England. It broke with tradition entirely, for in this case bodies were buried fully articulated. They are usually associated with a different type of monument – a round barrow rather than a long barrow – and the dead might be provided with grave goods. Such burials are often those of men, and can be accompanied by unusually finely made arrowheads or other elaborate artefacts (Kinnes 1979; Manby 1988). This tradition of round barrow burial was to extend over a long period in northern and eastern England, and with the addition of later deposits, some of the covering mounds grew to an enormous size (Kinnes *et al.* 1983).

This explicit emphasis on the burial of individuals, often accompanied by grave goods, contrasts with the normal sequence in southern England, where long barrows are much the commonest form of funerary monument until about 3300 BC. Even so, the evidence does change its form. The important difference is that in this area changes seem to have happened by manipulating the cultural rules established at the start of this sequence (Thorpe 1984; Barrett *et al.* 1991, 51–3). There is also a striking connection between the use of long barrows and that of causewayed enclosures. Both undergo subtle changes of character during the Earlier Neolithic period. These may very well have run in parallel with one another (Thorpe 1984; Edmonds in press).

Because the evidence from Wessex is better known, it can easily be treated as a model for the period as a whole. That is very misleading. So long as the discussion was conducted in terms of *types* of monument rather than their sequence, it gave enigmatic results. Long barrows were built with increasing frequency in the years after 3800 BC and clusters of these monuments were accompanied by causewayed enclosures from about 3600 BC onwards (Fig. 2.6). The latter were conceived on a large scale, so that it was only natural to suppose that there would have been a relationship between the increasing amounts of labour invested in their construction and a broader process of political centralisation. The causewayed enclosures might be viewed as the centres of separate territories, each marked by a concentration of between twenty and thirty-five long barrows (Renfrew 1973). Similarly, it seemed as though there should be a direct relationship between economic growth in the region and the ability of different communities to conceive monuments on an increasing scale (Case 1969). That argument was important because it also supplied a clue to the ending of this sequence, for around 3300 BC long barrows stopped being built and causewayed enclosures also went out of use. Perhaps this had happened because the environment was no longer able to sustain such efforts and the social system broke down (Whittle 1978). In any event there followed a phase of relative inertia before a new process of social development occurred.

This scheme no longer looks quite so attractive. It is now possible to trace more gradual changes in the character of both kinds of monument. For example, long barrows may not have changed their outward form to any extent, but radiocarbon dating reveals subtle changes among the deposits found on these sites. There is a

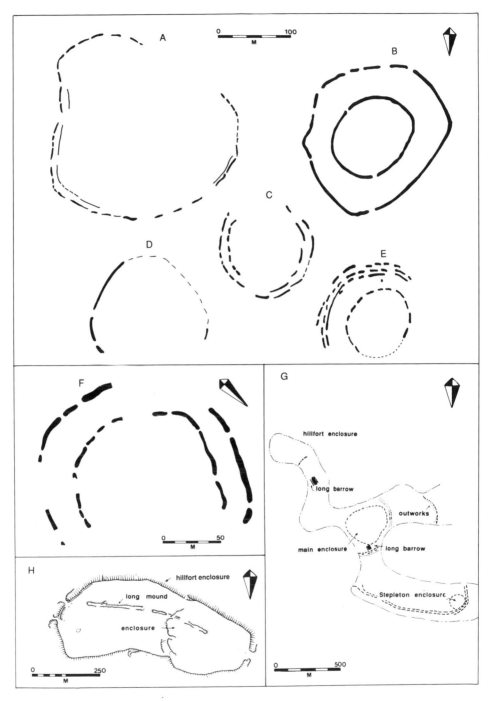

Fig. 2.6 Outline plans of selected causewayed enclosures. A, Haddenham; B, Robin Hood's Ball; C, Great Wilbraham; D, Etton; E. Orsett; F, Staines; G, the Hambledon Hill complex; H, the Maiden Castle complex.

progressive shift away from collective deposits and towards the burial of articulated skeletons. The number of individuals represented on these sites might also be reduced, and there was a parallel change from the representation of men and women in approximately equal proportions towards the burial of adult males. In a few instances they were now accompanied by grave goods (Thorpe 1984; Barrett *et al.* 1991, 51–3; Bradley 1992a).

There are also links with the changing character of the causewayed enclosures. These may have played many roles, but environmental evidence from the chalkland suggests that they occupied relatively marginal positions, often in woodland, in contrast to the long barrows which seem to have been located nearer to the settled area (Thomas 1982; Gardiner 1984). Such enclosures appear to have served as aggregation sites for a wider population; indeed, they are almost the only locations to contain extensive flint industries during this period (Healey and Robertson-Mackay 1983). Many of the enclosures provide evidence of feasting (Pl. 2.1), and some may have been involved directly in rites of passage, for they contain fragments of human bone and sometimes entire skeletons (Edmonds in press). More important, the largest of all these enclosures, the great complex at Hambledon Hill, appears to have been one of the locations where bodies were initially exposed (Mercer 1980). Two particular features of this site strengthen the link with long barrow rituals. The human remains found here, especially a series of skulls deposited in the ditch, were mainly those of young people, who are underrepresented in long barrows. At the same time excavation identified a series of pits inside the principal enclosure where bodies appear to have been exposed until they had lost their flesh. These features were associated with items of personal equipment and non-local artefacts, recalling the grave goods found in other areas.

A further characteristic of the enclosures will play a part in later chapters, but it needs to be introduced now. The artefacts found on these sites have certain unusual features. They may have been imported from other areas, and some of these enclosures produce an unexpectedly high proportion of axes and decorated pottery, as well as other exotica (Smith 1971; Bradley 1982). Where adequate evidence is available, they are particularly associated with the *later* phases in the life of these monuments. This is especially interesting because there are indications that the status and significance of these sites may have changed through time. They could have played a wide variety of roles in different areas, but there seems little reason to doubt that initially many served as ceremonial sites, located in peripheral positions. Sometimes they were placed towards the boundaries between social territories, as suggested by local styles of pottery and monuments (Holgate 1988). Because Earlier Neolithic settlements have been so difficult to identify, it has been an obvious temptation to suggest that causewayed enclosures may have served this role. The case could be supported by a range of excavated evidence, but this was confined to a very small selection of sites. They did produce evidence of structures, but it was striking that several of these enclosures also showed evidence of remodelling at a late stage in their development. This involved the recutting of the surrounding ditches in order to remove most of the causeways, and the construction of considerable ramparts, not unlike those of Iron Age hill forts. It seems likely that this sequence reflects a major transformation late in the history of these monuments. Sites that had originally provided a context in which different groups might come together played a rather different role as specialised or high-status settlements (Bradley 1984a, 34–5; Darvill 1987, 73–4). It may also be no accident that several causewayed enclosures are paired with late long barrows, and that in three cases their mounds covered *individual* burials (Bradley 1992a). Perhaps the changing character of these enclosures reflects the same process of social differentiation as the evidence from contemporary graves. If so, it is some indication of competition that the demise of long barrows in Wessex occurs at a time when some of these fortifications were attacked.

The Later Neolithic sequence (Fig. 2.4)

Despite the major changes that took place in southern England during the later fourth millennium BC, there is a sense in which our regional sequences can still be distinguished along rather similar lines. Developments differed between individual core areas, but the sharpest divisions remained those between the north and south. In northern England relations of inequality could have been based mainly on personal

Plate 2.1 Animal bone deposit in the inner ditch of the Windmill Hill causewayed enclosure. Photograph: Alasdair Whittle.

prestige, whilst in the south they could still be mediated through relations with the supernatural and the proximity of the ancestors.

This contrast is strongest towards the end of this period, but there are signs that it goes further back. Both regions share one peculiarly British form of monument, the cursus, the two largest examples of which are found in southern Wessex and the Yorkshire Wolds respectively (Barrett *et al.* 1991, 36–58; Kinnes 1984, 37). Such earthworks are enormous parallel-sided enclosures, at once alignments and extended avenues. Little is known of their character or chronology, but it seems as if they originated whilst long barrows and causewayed enclosures were still in use and continued to be built after both those types had lapsed. Cursus monuments evidence a lasting interest in the dead. Some of these monuments are aligned on existing burial mounds, and occasionally their layout may also reflect the movements of the sun. The largest monuments are designed so that such effects would only have been visible from certain vantage points, access to which could be limited by the enclosing earthwork. At the same time, the way in which they link funerary monuments to the movement of the heavens could be one more indication of the interpenetration of sacred and secular authority (Barrett *et al.* 1991, 53–8).

The sequence in Wessex provides evidence for a lengthy history of intermittent activity around these monuments, and they may have retained their importance for a long time after they were built (Barrett *et al.* 1991, chapters 3 and 4; Richards 1990, chapter 10). In northern and eastern England the situation is unclear, but on the Yorkshire Wolds it is known that the tradition of long barrow burial ended, whilst round barrows went on in use (Thorpe and Richards 1984; Manby 1988). As we have seen, these are associated with individual burials and grave goods, and in this case the repertoire of burial offerings may have changed more rapidly than the form of the monuments themselves. Offshoots of this system are distributed widely and can be found in many of the major river valleys, extending south as far as the Thames and north into lowland Scotland (Kinnes 1979, 1985, 41–4). The North Sea coast was of especial significance, and these long-distance connections were emphasised by the movement of elaborate artefacts.

In southern England the sequence is harder to define, and certainly it appears that Wessex no longer played such a prominent role. Although activity continued around older monuments, involving a series of structured deposits in the secondary levels of long barrows, enclosures and cursuses, few new earthworks seem to have been constructed, and round barrows on the northern English model are present in only limited numbers (Kinnes 1979). It seems possible that a series of small circular enclosures, again with segmented ditches, belong to this transitional phase, but only two have been excavated, one of them the earliest monument at Stonehenge (Woodward 1988; Atkinson 1956); significantly, the latter was located within a few hundred metres of a cursus. More attention was paid to older monuments than was devoted to the creation of new ones. It may be no exaggeration to suggest that in northern England, where individual burial was already well established, the Neolithic sequence continued without a major break. On the southern chalkland, however, there are fewer signs of sustained development.

The latter sequence was to be influenced from an unexpected source. Whilst the tradition of round barrows had been developing in northern England, another, ultimately more ostentatious series of funerary monuments had come into existence along the Atlantic seaboard. This involved the use of the distinctive megalithic tombs known as passage graves, whose wider distribution extends from Scandinavia to Iberia. Our interest is in the developments that took place in Ireland and Orkney, where massive stone-built tombs are found together with the circular earthwork enclosures known as *henge monuments* (Eogan 1986; Renfrew 1979; Davidson and Henshall 1989; Hartwell 1991). Those in Ireland remain very poorly dated, but the Scottish examples originated quite early in this phase (Harding and Lee 1987). They seem to have played an essentially ceremonial role, and provide evidence for large-scale aggregations, accompanied by feasting and the deposition of complex and well-travelled artefacts. They occur in nearly all of the core areas of the Later Neolithic, where they are often found among clusters of other monuments, including those surviving from the earlier phase. The construction of these earthworks made enormous demands on human labour, and a number of the sites contained elaborate settings of timbers or upright stones (Harding and Lee 1987). In areas of highland Britain, where large earthworks were more difficult to build, their place was probably taken by massive stone circles (Burl 1976; Barnatt 1989). Sites in both of these groups include basic astronomical alignments. Like the causewayed enclosures described earlier, henges and stone circles may have played rather different roles from one region to another. Even so, these sites provide one of the key ingredients in a long-distance network which was ultimately to extend into southern England.

Another ingredient comes from a similar source. In common with passage tombs in Brittany and Iberia, the Irish examples were lavishly decorated (Shee Twohig 1981). The art of these Irish tombs is entirely abstract, which makes it particularly difficult to interpret (Eogan 1986, chapters 7 and 8). There is a suggestion that it depicts the entoptic phenomena which can be experienced under trance conditions (Bradley 1989), but for our purposes the association of these distinctive symbols with great monuments to the dead is indication enough of its special significance. The passage tombs of Ireland and Orkney have many features in common, but there is one important difference. Passage grave art is uncommon in Orkney (Shee Twohig 1981, chapter 4), but some of the same motifs appear on Neolithic pottery in that area. That characteristic style is known as *Grooved Ware* and is found in association with stone-built tombs and henges (Figs. 2.7 and 2.8; see Wainwright and Longworth 1971, chapter 6).

Elements of this tradition extended into other parts of Britain, although the process was a protracted one. As a result, the two major developments that happened during this period – the use of round barrows and the development of henges – show considerable chronological overlap and tend to be associated with different artefact assemblages (Thorpe and Richards 1984). Just as henge monuments are normally linked with Grooved Ware and its associations, the grave goods known from round barrows are generally found with a separate ceramic style (*Peterborough Ware*) which can be traced back to the decorated pottery of the Earlier Neolithic. Both may have

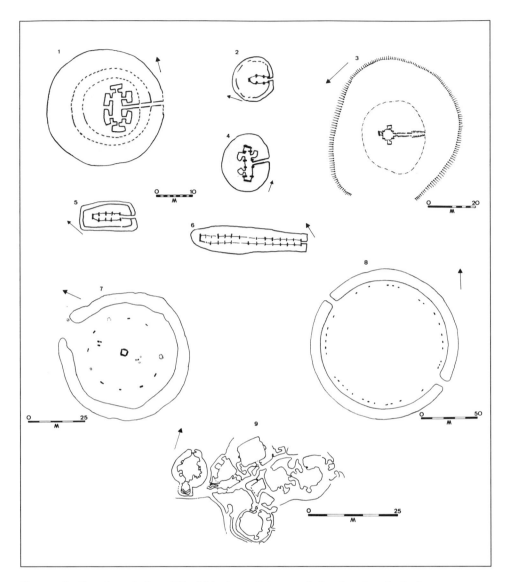

Fig. 2.7 Outline plans of selected Neolithic sites in Orkney. 1–6: chambered tombs (1, Quanterness; 2, Bigland round; 3, Maes Howe; 4, Isbister; 5, Knowe of Yarso; 6, Knowe of Ramsay); 7 and 8: henge monuments (7, Stones of Stenness; 8, Ring of Brodgar); 9, the settlement at Skara Brae.

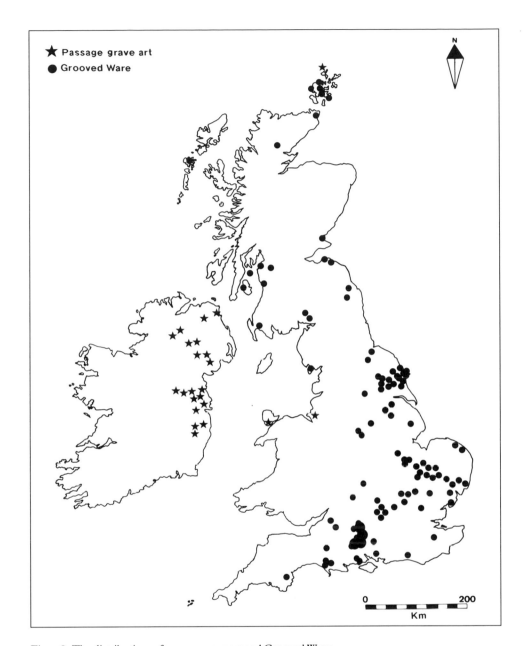

Fig. 2.8 The distributions of passage grave art and Grooved Ware.

played quite limited roles, and, as Julian Thomas points out, vessels in each group were deposited with such formality that their uses may have been limited to particular social transactions (J. Thomas 1991, chapter 5). Alternatively, they may have been employed by people of different social position, in which case the divisions between these two artefact assemblages could reflect the existence of ranked spheres of exchange – particular objects could pass only between those of equivalent status (Bradley 1984a, 46–57).

The processes by which these changes took place remain rather uncertain, but it is clear that over the period between 3000 and 2500 BC Grooved Ware and its associations were adopted increasingly widely, and that its diffusion accompanied the first appearance of large henges. As this happened, the Grooved Ware network seems to have assimilated some of the characteristic components of the Peterborough Ware tradition (pp. 57–61). It seems likely, however, that both assemblages still remained in use in different core areas. Although each is represented on what seem to be domestic sites, round barrows are less common in those regions with the new ceremonial centres.

The long-distance movement of artefacts, practices and ideas is evidenced most obviously in Wessex. This was one of the last areas to come within the Grooved Ware ambit, but it was the region that saw the building of the largest henge monuments of all (Wainwright 1989). Unlike their counterparts in areas further to the north, these earthworks provided evidence for an extraordinary level of consumption, including large-scale feasting, the use of imported artefacts and the formal deposition of pottery carrying motifs that still bore witness to links with distant areas (Richards and Thomas 1984). There is perhaps an echo of the ways in which causewayed enclosures had been used so many generations before, but now this region exhibits an archaeological record unparalleled in its complexity outside Orkney and the Boyne Valley.

The contrasts between different regional traditions in the Later Neolithic are important, but they must not be exaggerated. There are regions like East Anglia where the outlines are blurred (Cleal 1984), and in some of the other core areas little is known about the monuments or the pattern of settlement. In many respects Wessex presents an extreme case, albeit an interesting and well-documented one, and it need not represent the sequence of development followed in other parts of the country (Harding 1991). In particular, the emphasis on ritual and the supernatural that seems to be evidenced there was hardly compatible with the movement of personal prestige goods that was becoming such an important feature on the European mainland at this time. This was associated with Beaker pottery and the introduction of metals. For the first time for a thousand years, it is likely that alliances extended outwards into Europe. Thus it is that Beakers and their associations are best represented in those regions that already reveal an emphasis on the individual (Thorpe and Richards 1984). In Wessex, on the other hand, the earliest burials with similar material avoided the location of the large henge monuments and did not extend across the landscape until a later stage. That complicated transition brings the Neolithic period to its close.

Production and exchange in Neolithic Britain

To anticipate what will be said later, there is something of a mismatch between the extraordinary efforts that have gone into the analysis of non-local artefacts in Neolithic Britain and the extent to which this work informs the broader analysis of the period. As we shall see, there have been suggestions that certain of the major enclosures could have acted as foci through which such objects passed, but this has been used as a clue to the functions of these monuments and not to the character of society itself. Similarly, the presence of far-travelled artefacts in formal deposits, within these monuments or elsewhere, has added support to the notion that they must have served as valuables, but less interest has been shown in quite how they might have circulated. Until about ten years ago these objects were regarded with circumspection, as if they might entrap the Neolithic specialist into unwarranted flights of fancy.

That is not the situation any longer, although some might take the view that such reticence had been well judged. The emphasis on careful description did have one great merit, for we now possess sufficient chronological information to talk about changing configurations in the movement of these objects (Smith 1979), however reluctant we may have felt to clothe these in human terms.

At the outset we can consider the evidence of flint axes, the first variety to be investigated in detail. These originate in several areas. They could be made from surface material, where the stone had been insulated from frost damage by superficial deposits like clay with flints, or where it was exposed in the sides of cliffs or similar formations. Alternatively, it had to be won by the more laborious process of mining. In every case the material was limited to areas of chalk, with the result that potential sources tend to be found in a broad zone extending between south-west England and the Yorkshire Wolds, or close to the coastline of southern and eastern England (Fig. 2.9). There were further deposits in Ulster. All too little is known about the extraction of flint on or close to the surface, although one open-cast quarry has been excavated near Belfast (Collins 1978). Sites on the clay with flints had been used for raw material, and also as locations for settlement, from the Mesolithic period onwards, although most of the axe making to take place there dates from the later Mesolithic (Gardiner 1990).

Flint mines occur in three main regional groups: in Sussex, Wiltshire and Norfolk. All have seen some excavation, but only the mines at Grimes Graves have been examined on a large scale recently (Mercer 1981a). Although all these sites produced axes, they were not limited to these objects, and work at Grimes Graves suggests that other kinds of artefact may have become increasingly important through time (Saville 1981). The chronology of these mines is only partly understood. Those in Sussex seem to be limited to the Earlier Neolithic period and may even have begun life before 3800 BC. The assemblages at these sites are dominated by axes. There are also Later Neolithic and Earlier Bronze Age artefacts, but they come from the upper levels of the shafts, suggesting some reworking of discarded raw material (Gardiner 1990, 120–1). The age of the important Wessex group has still to be established, and the only radio-carbon date falls in the late fourth millennium BC. Again there is evidence of later activity around the mine shafts at Easton Down, but this is probably one of the rare settlement sites of this period (Stone 1931b). The major complex at Grimes Graves in

Norfolk provides a total contrast. This must be one of the best-dated sites in prehistoric Britain and has seen a sustained programme of excavation and radiocarbon dating. The results are remarkably consistent and suggest that the mines began operation during the Later Neolithic period, with a peak of activity around 2500 BC (Burleigh *et al.* 1979). Again the site was re-used as a settlement during the Bronze Age (Mercer 1981a, 36–8).

Despite the long chronology of these mines and the striking changes in their distribution, they do share certain consistent features. Apart from the technology of extracting the rock – by deep vertical shafts from which horizontal galleries strike out to follow seams of flint (Pl. 2.2) – there seem to be indications that only the preliminary shaping of the artefacts was carried out at the stone source, pre-forms or roughouts being removed to other locations for the more time-consuming process of grinding and polishing (Healy 1984, 23–5; Gardiner 1990, 121). This observation highlights a second characteristic shared by the mines in Sussex and Norfolk, for both seem to have been located in relatively marginal areas. Grimes Graves is some way from the intensively settled land of the river gravels or the Fen Edge (Healy 1984), whilst the largest group of flint mines in Sussex is located in between the two main concentrations of long barrows, causewayed enclosures and contemporary flint scatters (Gardiner 1990, 122). In this case the choice of location is likely to have been deliberate, as raw material of similar quality can be found elsewhere on the South Downs.

The characterisation of flint artefacts is still at an early stage, and work on flint axes has been restricted to a small sample, most of which come from causewayed enclosures. Whilst this does provide some chronological control, it means that the results are weighted towards the earlier part of this period (Craddock *et al.* 1983). Nonetheless it confirms the wide distribution of Sussex products during this phase and the apparent absence of major competing sources. The distribution of Sussex axes even extends into East Anglia, later to become the most prolific source of these artefacts. The sample is too small, however, to allow us to comment on the structure of this distribution.

The southern and eastern distribution of flint mines is balanced by the generally highland distribution of the other rocks used for axes (Fig. 2.9). Again there are some complications. Whilst most of the raw materials were obtained from their natural sources, an unknown proportion of the axes were made from glacial erratics of the same composition, and these can be found in different parts of the country (Briggs 1976 and 1989). Otherwise the development of stone axe studies has proceeded in the opposite direction to the investigation of flint mines. We have seen how such mines and their contents had been researched for many years before suitable methods were devised for tracing the distribution of the products. With very few exceptions, the highland axe sources were not located until the characterisation of their products was under way, at which stage it became possible to follow certain groups of axes back to their area of origin (Grimes 1979). Since a single raw material might have more than one possible source, these petrological groups were given numbers rather than topographical names. In some cases it seems likely that all or most of these sources have been located on the ground, and in these cases site names enjoy a general currency. Many of the stone sources have still to be identified by fieldwork, however, and even now very little is known about the production sites and the ways in which they operated. That is one omission that this book seeks to remedy.

The sources of these axes were much more widely dispersed than the flint mines (Fig. 2.9). Petrological analysis was soon to show that only some of them had been exploited on a large scale, although cover has been rather uneven, and not enough axes have been studied in Scotland and Ireland. The most important stone sources were at a location close to Mounts Bay in Cornwall (Group I), Graig Lwyd in North Wales (Group VII), Tievebulliagh in Ulster (Group IX) and the location of our own fieldwork in the Lake District of Cumbria (Group VI). Together they produced most of the axes that can be attributed to specific sources. The Cumbrian stone source was the most prolific of all and accounts for 21% of the axes of known origin (Clough 1988, 4–5). More minor rock sources were identified over a wide area, including south-west England, the Welsh Marches, south-west Wales, north-west Wales and the southern Highlands of Scotland. Together these account for another twenty-six petrological groups, although a number of these supplied perforated stone implements of somewhat later date (Smith 1979; Clough 1988).

Unlike the flint mines, very little is known about these stone sources, and the archaeological remains at most of them have not even been surveyed. Up to 1984 they had seen so little fieldwork that the largest investigation was probably that of

Plate 2.2 An early flint mine excavation in Sussex.

Hazeldine Warren at Graig Lwyd (Warren 1922). Smaller-scale excavations had taken place at Mynydd Rhiw in north-west Wales, the source of Group XXI axes (Houlder 1961), Great Langdale, the main source of Group VI, and Tievebulliagh and Rathlin Island, the two major sources of Group IX (Mallory 1990; Whelan 1934). During the preparation of this book, a source of Group VIII axes was investigated in south-west Wales (G. Williams pers. comm.) and one of the writers also undertook work on the source of Group XXIV axes at Killin in the Highlands of Scotland (Edmonds and Sheridan in press). Despite this activity, there were reliable radiocarbon dates from just two of these sites, Great Langdale and Killin. This meant that any chronology would have to be compiled by studying the associations of axes found in stratified deposits elsewhere in the country.

This brought to light several striking patterns. Quite a high proportion of the known stone sources were being used during the Earlier Neolithic period, but it was not until about 3400 BC that their products travelled far outside their respective source areas (Smith 1979; Cummins 1979). Like the products of the smaller sources, their distribution showed an even fall-off away from the production sites. After that time, however, axes from North Wales, the Lake District, and to some extent those from Ulster, had a much wider distribution, in each case extending into areas with a good flint supply. The same was true of the products of the main Cornish stone source (Group I), whose area of distribution did not extend far outside south-west England until the third millennium BC. A striking feature shown by the products of the workshops, particularly those in Cornwall and Cumbria, was that their products no longer exhibited an even fall-off with distance from the source area. Rather, they might be underrepresented in the local region and could occur in unexpectedly high proportions towards the outer limits of their distribution (Cummins 1979). Despite this curious pattern, different areas of the country were dominated by the products of just one of these sources, leading Cummins (1980) to postulate the existence of territorial divisions at this time.

Because the characterisation of flint axes is such a recent development, it has not been possible to compare these patterns with the distribution of flint mine products. Nor do we know the ratio of stone to flint axes in some parts of the country (see Darvill 1989). In other respects it is possible to compare the character of these two industries. It is clear that, like the flint mines, many of the highland stone sources were producing implements other than axes. The evidence has not been recorded systematically, but this is certainly true of Tievebulliagh and Graig Lwyd (Sheridan 1986, 23; Warren 1922), although it seems as if only the axes may have circulated far outside the local region. Again the production of flaked axes may have taken place in two stages, as it did at the flint mines, and there seems little doubt that only the preliminary stages of working took place at the stone source, leaving the grinding and polishing to be undertaken at a distance. This can be demonstrated for those rocks which fracture in the same way as flint, but not, of course, those axes made by pecking, since this process leaves next to no trace in the archaeological record. That could be why the source of the Group I axes has never been located on the ground (Coope 1979).

If flint mines could be located in marginal areas – outside the main settled landscape

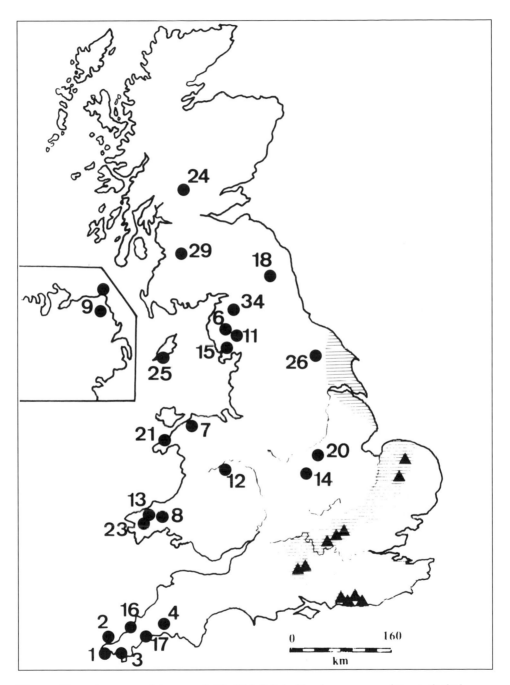

Fig. 2.9 The main sources of stone axes in Neolithic Britain. Numbers correspond to petrological groups. Those specifically mentioned in the text are Great Langdale (6), Graig Lwyd (7), Tievebulliagh (9), Mynydd Rhiw (21) and Killin (24). The chalk is shown by the shaded area, and the main groups of flint mines by triangles.

or on the boundaries between different social territories – the stone axe sources took the same tendency to extremes. Where they have been examined on the ground, they often occupy spectacular settings and remote places, and few of them could have been close to extensively settled areas. At least two of these locations – Graig Lwyd and Rathlin Island – would have been approached by sea. If further demonstration of this point is needed, the Cumbrian sources exist in a mountainous landscape, and some of the major concentrations of extraction sites are to be found within a short distance of the highest point in England. Raw material with the same physical properties could have been obtained with much less effort (Bradley *et al.* 1992). The overall pattern is so consistent that it cannot have come about by chance.

So far this account of the 'axe trade' has been quite uncontentious, but a price has had to be paid, for little or nothing has been said of the ways in which it might contribute to the broader pattern of development mapped out earlier in this chapter. That is because the crucial transition from description to explanation has proved to be so controversial. Yet it is only by taking that step that the gaps in our knowledge will be highlighted and the important issues laid bare. Those are the difficult questions that we shall consider in chapter 3.

3

Studying stone axes in Neolithic Britain

The language used to discuss the movement of axes could hardly be more revealing, for at once it betrays a tendency to interpret this phenomenon in terms of modern economics. The word 'exchange' is rarely used, and most accounts talk, however loosely, of an 'axe trade'. The production sites are described throughout the literature as 'axe factories', and those who are held responsible for this activity are considered as 'specialists', 'traders', 'entrepreneurs' or 'middlemen' (typical examples of this terminology can be found in Houlder 1961 and 1976 and Cummins 1979).

There are several reasons why these views have gained so much currency in Britain. In the early days of characterisation studies it was hard to credit the sheer scale of the operation, with very large numbers of axes proving to be of exotic origin. To a certain extent this impression was misleading, for much of the pioneering work was done before it became apparent that the Neolithic period had lasted much longer than had originally been supposed. In fact its length increased almost fivefold with the systematic application of radiocarbon dating (compare Piggott 1954, Fig. 64 with Smith 1974, Figs. 13, 17 and 18). At the same time, it was easy to be impressed by the quantity of stoneworking debris that still survived on the surface at some of the major sites. This was particularly true with the identification of those at Graig Lwyd, Tievebulliagh and Great Langdale, and only heightened the impression that these were the bases of a massive 'industry' (Bunch and Fell 1949). At this stage there was nothing to indicate the length of time over which they had been used. Moreover, in the absence of much attempt to understand the physical character of production, it was impossible to establish the relationship between the number of axes being made and the quantities of debitage that were left behind.

The same problems influenced perceptions of the flint mines, particularly since nearly all the work was carried out on the mine shafts themselves, rather than the flaking floors around them (Curwen et al. 1924; Curwen and Curwen 1926). This meant that the most striking feature of these sites was the investment of human labour that had gone into extracting the rock from deep in the chalk, but there was little to indicate how much of it had been used or what was being made there. More recent experiments have provided some of the answers, and now it appears that it is easy to overestimate both the amount of energy needed to extract the stone and the size of the workforce (Felder 1979; Mortimore 1979; Mercer 1981a, 28–36). Again, more sophisticated excavation methods, allied with the systematic use of a radiocarbon chronology, reveal that very few of the shafts on a large site like Grimes Graves need have been used simultaneously. Careful study of the Neolithic spoil heaps even suggests that work took place intermittently and perhaps seasonally (Mercer 1981a, 28–36). In the absence of such a chronological framework, our ability to draw useful inferences is limited.

Even when chronological variations in the distribution of stone axes came to be identified, there was little willingness to ask whether similar changes might have taken place at the production sites. Could the scale of axe production have changed over time? This would have serious implications for their description as 'factories', but in the literature no concessions are made to the possibility of internal variations on these sites. We have assumed that the nature and organisation of production remained stable, when both the scale and character of activity may have changed through time.

Taken together, these assumptions have left their mark: so much so that when Grahame Clark (1965) drew attention to the social dimension of the 'axe trade' in the ethnographic record, his comparisons with the British evidence were considered inappropriate because of the character of the distributions (Smith 1974, 286, note 78). Curiously enough, few archaeologists have postulated an industrial labour force engaged in earthwork building over the same period, even though such tasks would have involved a far greater investment of energy (for a partial exception see Green 1980, 190–1).

Such an uncritical attitude to the 'axe trade' has its roots in our conception of what it meant to be 'Neolithic'. Far from reflecting a drastic transformation in social relations, mediated through material culture, the period has been defined in economic terms. As we have seen, the evidence for this interpretation leaves much to be desired, but for the proponents of this view what could be more natural than the mass production of artefacts for clearing the native forest? In that case the increased movement of axes during the Later Neolithic would hint at a process of economic intensification sufficient to finance the building of large henge monuments. In fact such arguments miss the point entirely, as it is difficult to correlate the main periods of land clearance with those in which polished axes were distributed on a significant scale (compare Bradley 1978, 105–7 and Smith 1979). Moreover, it is feasible and also efficient to clear areas of woodland by burning, ring-barking or overgrazing (Rackham 1976, chapter 2). Axes would probably have been at least as important for woodworking, and there is plenty of evidence, from tool marks and even from discoveries of hafted implements, that they were used in this way (Coles *et al.* 1978).

Further problems arise because there has been no real attempt to establish the context of axe production; it is simply assumed that it must have been in the hands of full or part-time specialists. The only discussion that impinges on this question is where occasional agricultural tools, like the quernstone from Stoke Clump in Sussex (Wade 1924), are discovered in the filling of flint mines. Otherwise attention focusses on the spatial organisation of axe making. Roughouts tend to dominate the record on and around the stone sources, whilst fully polished artefacts are found on more fertile land some distance away (Gardiner 1990). So-called 'grinding slabs' have occasionally been identified in the latter area (Manby 1965). Only rarely have we asked whether this spatial distinction reflects a division between producers and consumers, or whether the same people might have been responsible for both kinds of evidence. Even less concern has been shown with the character of the production process. One of the few exceptions is Alan Saville's analysis (1981) of the debitage from a recently excavated mine shaft at Grimes Graves. This reveals a very low degree of standardisation in the form of the artefacts and the means by which they were made. There is little to suggest that those working on the site were concerned to reduce errors in production.

Reconstructions of how the axes were distributed owe more to recent experience than they do to familiarity with anthropological research. If there were skilled craftsmen working at the sources, then, the argument runs, there must have been knowledgeable middlemen ferrying the products to areas of high demand. It was generally accepted that an entrepreneurial class of traders moved large numbers of axes over considerable distances, in order to satisfy the everyday needs of farmers (Houlder 1976). The axe trade developed to offset a scarcity of local stone sources.

In some cases more specific institutions were postulated. We have already seen how the circulation of axes made in Cornwall and Cumbria extended over large areas of the country, and how their products are highly represented towards the outer limits of their distribution (Figs. 3.1 and 3.2). These observations have encouraged quite specific interpretations. First, the overrepresentation of Cornish axes close to the Thames estuary is explained by a pattern of seaborne trade bringing them in bulk from their source area in the south-west (Cummins 1979 and 1980). The use of coastal transport is not unlikely in itself, and at least two of the other stone sources (Graig Lwyd and Rathlin Island) are ideally located for this arrangement. In any event axes were certainly crossing the Irish Sea between Ulster, the Isle of Man and north-west

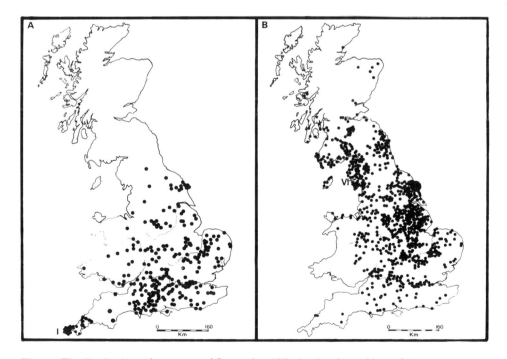

Fig. 3.1 The distributions of stone axes of Groups I and VI, showing the positions of the sources.

England (Sheridan 1986; Coope and Garrad 1988). For Cummins, bulk trade is only the first stage in the dissemination of Cornish axes, for he suggests that they passed through a secondary distribution centre in the Thames estuary before reaching their ultimate destinations. The same notion of secondary distribution foci is used to explain the distribution of Cumbrian axes in the east Midlands: 'all the axes had been dumped in north Lincolnshire and trickled down from there over the rest of the area' (Cummins and Moore 1973, 221). It is not clear how this final stage of that journey was accomplished, but again it seems as if we are dealing with a system in which the significance of stone axes remained the same despite their changes of context.

There may be another influence behind this conception of the axe trade, but on this occasion it originates within archaeology itself. In his later work Gordon Childe attempted to define the distinctive character of European society, and emphasised a number of features of the modern world that could be traced back into prehistory. One of these was the independent entrepreneur, operating outside the political framework of the time. In his studies of the European Bronze Age Childe emphasised the importance of the detribalised smith as an agent in spreading innovations and a source of local inventiveness (Childe 1958, 169). The smith's activities were to be traced partly through artefact distributions and partly through the contents of hoards, concealed for later use but never recovered (Pl. 3.1). This perspective colours discussions of the axe trade, and precisely the same interpretations are applied to the small collections of axes found in Neolithic hoards in Britain (Smith 1921).

In fact, there are serious problems with these models. Modern economic principles

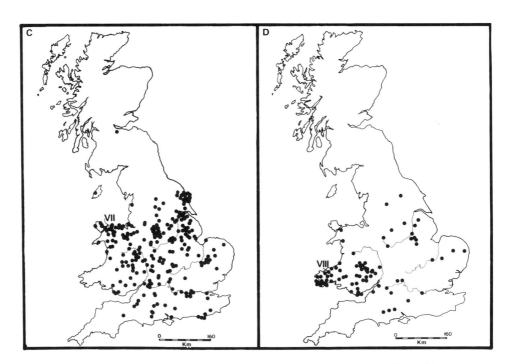

Fig. 3.2　The distributions of stone axes of Groups VII and VIII, showing the positions of the sources.

have been applied quite uncritically, and the distribution maps that underpin Cummins' interpretations are not entirely satisfactory. They are based on the *relative proportions* of different axes found in sample quadrats extending across the country. This means that the *absolute quantity* of stone axes is not considered in this analysis, with the result that some of the highest proportions of non-local objects come from areas with very few finds. This reliance on relative proportions also means that the pattern is artificially inflated by the rarity of axes from some sources rather than the frequency of those from others. In any case this analysis is limited to non-flint axes, where it would be more useful to observe the changing ratio of those made in both sets of raw material (see Darvill 1989). A more helpful portrayal of the data is provided in Sylvia Chappell's recent study (1986). She considers these distributions in relation to a gravity model, which seeks to predict the spread of the products of different stone sources in relation to their attractiveness in the eyes of the consumer, the latter being measured by the proportion of different types in the country as a whole. Although the concept of 'attractiveness' raises certain problems, this method of study is important because it places the recognition of anomalies on a more systematic basis. Although some of the concentrations of non-local axes shift their positions in this analysis, the products of the same stone sources prove to be overrepresented in distant areas.

A second problem is one which we considered in the opening chapter. There we saw how fall-off curves thought to typify separate kinds of exchange system could be reproduced by simulation. These experiments suggested that very similar patterns

Plate 3.1 Stone axe hoard from Malone, Ulster. Photograph: Ulster Museum.

might be created by random processes. A comparable approach has been taken to the distributions of some of the major groups of stone axes in the British Isles (Elliott, Ellman and Hodder 1978). This indicated that the closest approximations to their actual distributions occurred where they moved across the country in a series of short steps. This is entirely consistent with a model of hand-to-hand exchange, rather than a more complex distribution network. It provides no support at all for the idea of bulk transport over long distances and undermines any case for the existence of independent traders or middlemen.

Lastly, the complex interpretation put forward by Cummins and others takes no account of the changing condition of the axes themselves. It treats all the finds as equal and equivalent. In fact, some are intact and apparently unused, some show evidence of resharpening, and others have been reflaked to put them out of use or to provide the raw material for making different artefacts. Such variations concern both form and size (Hodder and Lane 1982; Chappell 1987). In most cases we can distinguish between those axes that have kept their original form and others which had been substantially altered. The main size threshold is much the same for those from quite different stone sources and occurs within a length range of about 13 to 15 cm. The reworked axes also show the greatest variety of forms. Again this seems to be consistent with the idea that such artefacts were used over a long period before they reached the outer limits of their distribution.

Archaeologists have studied variations in the form and size of axes because it is so difficult to interpret one-dimensional distribution patterns. Again research has been based on questionable assumptions. The most important of these is the distinction between function and symbol discussed in chapter 1. Several studies have followed this distinction in the belief that the morphological characteristics of axeheads will offer clues as to their social significance. There has been a tendency to arrive at an intuitive classification of these axes, based largely on their size. Comparison with ethnographic examples suggests that the largest axes (generally those with little or no signs of use) may have played a symbolic role. Annable, for instance, makes the simple assumption that the values of Cumbrian axes varied in proportion to their size (1987, 81). In addition, she suggests that the significance attached to an axe by the 'consumer' would have been directly related to the availability of raw materials in the area. No doubt access to such materials was one important factor in establishing control over the circulation of artefacts, particularly where this process was tied to specific power relations, but we should be wary of assuming that cost-benefit principles have a universal application. These problems are highlighted when we recall that some of the highest concentrations of non-local axes occur in areas which are especially rich in raw materials.

Chappell's study is more concerned with the relationship between morphological variation and the spatial patterning exhibited by these objects, but again her work emphasises discoveries of unusually large axes, or those which lack any evidence of reworking despite their distance from the source (Chappell 1987). Thus very large Group VI axes from Cumbria are interpreted as ceremonial items, and the largest and widest axeheads from Charnwood Forest (Group XX) are also considered as valuables. In some cases, for instance the relatively thick axes of Group VII, morphological variation is explained in terms of constraints imposed by the raw material. Where physical constraints are not apparent, these variations are attributed to 'stylistic' factors – epiphenomena which are never explored. Thus analytical significance is restricted to those examples which depart from the 'normal' pattern of dispersal and maintenance, and to cases where a more prosaic explanation cannot be found. Moreover, so little attention is paid to the question of context that it is difficult to explore the significance of such variation. Thus when Chappell identifies a subgroup of large axes found in the River Thames, she assumes that they were chance losses during trade. In her words, 'the sizes of these implements probably reflect . . . the sizes of axes generally carried by people using the Thames as a transport route' (1987, 339). She seems unaware of the very different means by which artefacts may have found their way into these contexts, nor does she ask why it is that stone axes of non-local, even Continental origin are found in unexpectedly high proportions in springs, bogs and rivers in Britain (Bradley 1990a, 66–7). The implication is clear. Whilst the morphology of these artefacts adds another dimension to distributional studies, it does not provide a sufficient basis for their interpretation.

In one sense, this discussion is too closely wedded to the data, so that a more basic question is never asked. Outside Ireland (Woodman 1978, 108–14) and Wales (David 1989, 248–9) Mesolithic axes were never polished, but they appear to have performed reasonably efficiently for a very long time. Why are polished artefacts so characteristic of Neolithic technology? It is certainly true that the polishing of axes can improve their mechanical performance: it can prevent the axehead from moving around in the haft, and the polishing of a cutting edge removes scars and ridges which may serve as incipient platforms, causing flakes to be detached during use (see Vemming and Madsen 1983 and Olausson 1983). But this cannot supply the entire answer to the question. It does not provide any reason why the entire surface of an axehead should have been polished, particularly considering that this process is laborious and time-consuming when compared with flaking. On the other hand, polishing brings out the distinctive character of the raw material in a way that simple flaking cannot do. It also affords a considerable degree of control over the form of the finished object. In this sense one of the principal changes of technology that define the beginning of the Neolithic attests a new concern with the elaboration of artefacts. *Style* may have been just as important as performance.

This argument is strongly supported by discoveries of Neolithic axes in Yorkshire (Manby 1979). Here there were at least three possible sources of raw material. The most striking of these was the local flint, which was certainly exploited on a large scale at sites on Flamborough Head. There are also major concentrations of imported axes in this region, particularly those of Groups I and VI. It is interesting that only about 20% of the axes found on the Yorkshire Wolds were made from the local raw material, and few of these were completely polished; many were only ground along the edges. This did not apply to non-local axes, which were ground and polished all over. In turn, this contrasts with the use of a third raw material found in the region itself.

In some ways the use of glacial erratics poses serious problems. Indeed, the fact that its full extent remains unmapped has been thought to discredit the whole idea of an 'axe trade' (Briggs 1976 and 1989) – a rather eccentric argument which could only be sustained in the absence of large production sites. In fact the existence of such erratics helps to define the characteristic features of this system, for here was a source of stone with similar properties to those imported from distant areas. The significant difference lies in the nature and extent of polishing. Axes made from local erratics were seldom polished completely. This has two implications. First, it suggests that the *origin* of the material was considered to be more important than its physical characteristics. This may be because exchanged items carried with them a history of relations between people. Secondly, the fact that axes made from materials with similar properties received different treatment according to their area of origin shows the extent to which such judgements were socially determined. They were not a response to practical problems encountered during use. The significance accorded to particular artefacts, as manifested in their treatment, depended more on their cultural biographies.

Another source of confusion in the British literature is the relationship between the movement of axes and the use of large earthwork monuments (Smith 1971; Houlder 1976). This confusion arose early on and happened because Wessex was one of the first areas in which imported axes were characterised. The result was a striking emphasis on the area around the great henge monument at Avebury. There is a major concentration of non-local axes in this region, but now that similar surveys are available for other areas it no longer exists in isolation. When it was first recognised, however, it seemed to suggest that Wessex in general, and the Avebury complex in particular, was the hub of a great trading network which covered the entire country (Stone and Wallis 1951, 132–3).

The emphasis on this small area was unfortunate for it also saw the first large-scale excavations of Neolithic monuments in Britain: the Windmill Hill causewayed enclosure and the later henge at Avebury itself (Smith, 1965). It was almost inevitable that the concentration of stone axes in this area should influence the ways in which both sites were interpreted, not least because the excavations and the stone axe survey were both organised by the same person: Alexander Keiller. From the 1930s onwards, there has always been a temptation to suppose that the axe trade was articulated through these sites.

The argument has taken many forms, with some authors interpreting these sites as redistributive centres or as the settlements of elites who controlled a monopolistic trading network. For example, Roger Mercer has argued that one function of the enclosure at Carn Brea was to control the movement of Cornish axes out of south-west England (1981b and 1986, 46–50). In addition, he contends that these artefacts passed through a chain of central places of similar character. At an empirical level, two observations certainly seem to be justified. Causewayed enclosures often contain an unusually high proportion of axes, of flint or other raw materials (Bradley 1982). Similarly, henge monuments, which rarely contain axes within their circuit, often lie in the centre of a distribution of exotic artefacts (Bradley 1984a, chapter 3). The complications arise when we seek to interpret these patterns.

Causewayed enclosures provide the perfect illustration of the problems involved in inferring exchange from the evidence of consumption. Much of the difficulty arises because these earthworks are not a unitary phenomenon. Different sites reveal quite distinct patterns of development towards the end of their history, and this may indicate how the ideas associated with them were drawn upon and interpreted in different ways. This point will be developed in chapter 8, but we are already in a position to suggest that the role of enclosures as a context for exchange was by no means straightforward.

As we have seen, like axe production sites, the enclosures in southern Britain could have been peripheral to the main areas of contemporary settlement, and many may have been used episodically. If they really were located near to social boundaries, they would have provided an arena where local groups could come together in the course of their movement about the landscape. The excavated material is particularly informative. The ditches contain a variety of formal deposits, and the pits often include a careful arrangement of pottery, axes and other artefacts. The faunal assemblages can be dominated by body parts which are commonly associated with feasting (Edmonds in press). At the same time, there is evidence that certain sites witnessed activities associated with the treatment of the dead. Taken together, these observations suggest that causewayed enclosures provided contexts in which it was appropriate to undertake rites of passage – conventional events which defined important thresholds in the life of the individual and the community (Edmonds in press; see van Gennep 1960). Although archaeologists have tended to limit their discussions of these pivotal events to funerary practices, death is just one of a series of occasions at which social categories may be brought into sharp relief. This has important implications for the notion of enclosures as monopolistic trading centres, especially when we remember how the circulation of artefacts plays a part in the classification of people.

Here we face something of a paradox. If these enclosures had served as appropriate contexts for exchange, what characteristic signatures would we expect to find in the archaeological record? At first sight it would seem most unlikely that they should be characterised by large quantities of non-local objects, yet these do occur at enclosures, often burnt, broken, placed in pits or associated with fragmentary human remains (Pl. 3.2). Such deposits provide evidence for a high level of consumption (Edmonds in press). We need not reject the idea that enclosures provided contexts for a variety of exchanges, but these finds are not consistent with their interpretation as trade or redistributive centres.

At the same time, it would be wrong to impose a spurious uniformity on this evidence, for the axes found in such numbers at causewayed enclosures include examples which had been made locally. Indeed, the siting of some of the enclosures on or near to sources of raw material suggests that this was an important concern. Verna Care (1982) has argued that the locations of chalkland enclosures were chosen in order to control long-established sources of flint and the movement of their products. This physical relationship is particularly obvious in Sussex where some of the enclosures are situated close to small groups of flint mines. Like the enclosures themselves, these mines were set apart from the main occupied areas (Gardiner 1990). Similarly, Carn Brea is located near to one of the main sources of stone axes in Cornwall (Mercer 1988, 47). A variant of this problem arises at Maiden Castle, one of the destinations of stone artefacts made in the south-west, for here flint axes were produced on the site itself. This is particularly striking now that field survey has demonstrated that axe making did not take place in the surrounding landscape (Edmonds and Bellamy 1991).

In the case of henge monuments and large stone circles, the evidence is different again. Axes are found occasionally, and those few that are discovered occupy significant positions within these sites. For example, a polishing stone was found with a human cremation just inside the bank of a henge monument at Llandegai, not far from Graig Lwyd (Houlder 1968, 218). Similarly, the axes from an early henge monument at Wyke Down in Dorset were confined to the entrance of the monument, an association also recorded on a small number of sites in Cumbria (Barrett *et al.* 1991, 101). At some sites it seems as if a convention existed that axes were not to be deposited inside these enclosures. The great timber circles found within the henges in Wessex must have required a prolonged period of woodworking, and yet axes are rare or even absent on these sites. Where the convention was breached, the result is equally surprising. Two of the axes found on the edge of the timber circle at Woodhenge were made out of chalk and could never have been used (Cunnington 1929, 112–13). The remaining fragments were of Cornish origin and, like one of the chalk axes, were deposited at the entrance of the monument (p. 77).

By contrast, axes are frequent finds in the areas outside these earthworks, where they may form part of more complex deposits, usually placed in pits. A high proportion of such axes are of non-local origin (see Barrett *et al.* 1991, chapter 3). It is uncertain whether some of these finds originated on settlement sites; the important point is that they had been deposited with some formality. The same most probably applies to the concentrations of axes recorded as chance finds in the vicinity of other Later Neolithic monuments. In each case we encounter the problems of interpretation that we discussed with causewayed enclosures. Large quantities of animal bones had been buried with some of the axes, and again these should evidence a high level of *consumption*.

Despite this emphasis on consumption, the practices undertaken at henge monuments may have played a part in structuring the production and circulation of artefacts. Some of these sites are again located close to sources of flint, and the distinctive structures inside them contain many features of exotic origin. The Grooved Ware ceramics which are such a feature of henge monuments carry a distinctive style of decoration which seems to have its source in the passage grave art of Ireland (Wainwright and Longworth 1971, chapter 6). Some of the styles of lithic artefacts found inside henges, in particular arrowheads, may also provide evidence of long-distance connections. It has been noted that the major regions linked by the Grooved Ware network are connected by sea or by important rivers, and it is certainly true that the largest henges are nearly always situated close to major waterways. This is not sufficient to demonstrate that the groups responsible for their construction and use were engaged in long-distance trade, or even that they exercised some form of control over materials travelling along the river network. But the possibility is intriguing and does deserve further research (Bradley 1984a, chapter 3).

Such evidence shows how far the significance of axes may have extended beyond questions of immediate utility. It seems likely that their symbolic content may also have changed over time. The argument no longer rests entirely on anomalies – on axes assigned a 'symbolic' role because of their size or because they were made out of raw materials that were not suited for practical tasks. Rather, it emphasises the circumstances in which they were deposited and the way in which their treatment seems to have varied according to their area of origin. We can even invert these 'arguments by anomaly' by suggesting that the production of apparently non-functional artefacts would have drawn upon the ideas with which axes were already associated. These may have derived from their habitual association with particular tasks or practices, and thus with specific sections of contemporary society.

The routine use or possession of axes may have played a part in maintaining social relationships, perhaps reaffirming distinctions drawn on the basis of age and/or gender. Yet the character and context of a number of these axes suggests that they may have been 'read' more attentively at certain junctures. It is when we explore the consumption of these artefacts – the conditions under which they were exchanged or deposited, and the purposes that such practices might have served – that we encounter

Plate 3.2 A stone axe in the filling of a feature inside the Etton causewayed enclosure, Cambridgeshire. Photograph: Francis Pryor.

major problems. The most serious of these concern the character and extent of control that different groups may have exercised over their production and circulation.

In our northern regional system the main problem to consider is the relationship between the emergence of a precocious tradition of single burial, and access to the objects and materials that were deposited with the dead. Had these been produced under local patronage, and, if not, under what circumstances did they find their way into this area? If some were obtained by means of long-distance exchange, were the networks through which they moved the prerogative of particular groups in society? Or can we suggest that access to exotica was one way of *creating* networks of authority and obligation? That is a long list of questions, but not one of them has received a satisfactory response because we lack the information needed to answer them. Although the region may have seen the development of workshops producing a restricted range of stone tools, we know very little about the character and chronology of artefact production in Yorkshire (Manby 1974, chapter 3; Manby 1988, 73; Hanson 1989). Even less is known about the development of stone axe production at Great Langdale, the main source of non-local axes in this region. As a result, we have little basis for exploring the relationship between production, exchange and broader patterns of use and deposition.

In the southern regional system, epitomised by the sequence in Wessex, the situation seems rather more promising, although that promise recedes the more closely the evidence is scrutinised. Here there is a broadly parallel trend from corporate to single burial, but grave goods are much less common. Instead, archaeologists have concentrated on the evidence of causewayed enclosures. As we have seen, that evidence is rather ambiguous since models which relate these sites to monopolies or trading networks cannot accommodate the large number of axes found there. Moreover, so little is known about the circumstances in which axes were made that existing patterns can be interpreted in very different ways. We have some information about the Sussex mines, but virtually nothing is known about the exploitation of other stone sources during the Earlier Neolithic. That places a severe restriction on research.

This introduces another problem, for we have no reason to suppose that flint and stone axes were imbued with the same ideas or that they circulated in the same ways throughout the Neolithic period. This is best illustrated by the changing chronology of the 'axe trade', for as causewayed enclosures became a regular feature of the social landscape in the south, there may have been a widening in the areas over which axes from highland Britain were distributed (Smith 1979). At about the same time, flint mining seems to have ceased in Sussex, although the mines in Wessex may perhaps have remained in use (Gardiner 1990). We need to understand the circumstances in which these changes happened, but here the archaeological literature is seriously deficient. The presence of non-local axes at causewayed enclosures in the south is thought to reflect the growing power of communities within the region, but the most important questions are hardly discussed. Why should they have obtained axes from other parts of the country? How was this process structured? And how did the influx of exotica affect the operation of the flint mines?

Although some of the detailed issues are different, the same problems afflict the study of the Later Neolithic. In this case, exchange figures prominently in the literature, no doubt because there is an increase in assemblage variation and a greater emphasis on exotica (Bradley 1984a, chapter 3; Darvill 1987, 85–6). As in the Earlier Neolithic, it is hard to tell how far large monuments played a part in structuring long-distance exchange. Of course there are important contrasts – axes are generally found outside henges rather than inside them, and in the south these earthworks occupied a more central position in the landscape – but such sites are still found near to local flint sources, and imported axes occur in formal deposits in their vicinity.

A major question to be addressed is the significance of the distinction between assemblages associated with Peterborough Ware and Grooved Ware respectively (Thorpe and Richards 1984). At once this problem recalls an observation made in our earlier discussion, for it seems that one of the differences between these two ceramic traditions concerns the nature of the associated axes. Those found with Peterborough Ware were usually made of flint, some of them from production sites on the Yorkshire Wolds, whilst those associated with Grooved Ware more often originate from sources in western Britain (Wainwright and Longworth 1971, 261; Bradley 1984a, 50). These distinctions may reflect differences in the practices with which the two assemblages were most closely associated (J. Thomas 1991, chapter 5), or they could evidence the existence of ranked spheres of exchange, in which axes of contrasting raw materials circulated in different social contexts (Bradley 1982). Moreover, the artefacts belonging to these two traditions may have carried rather different connotations from one core area to another.

Some writers consider that Peterborough Ware and its associations reflect the growing importance of prestige goods for the creation and maintenance of power. By contrast, Grooved Ware assemblages have tended to be associated more closely with a 'ritual authority structure', where relations of inequality were reproduced through references to the cosmos and the supernatural, and through control over ritual (Thorpe and Richards 1984). The distinction has probably been drawn too sharply, and in the case of the prestige goods model we have still to explore the purposes that the influx of complex artefacts served in particular social groups. Nevertheless, this model does highlight some striking contrasts between different regions. For example, it has been suggested that dominant groups in northern England maintained their position through the control of valuables (pp. 70–3). Some of these appear to have been locally made, perhaps under political direction, although this question has not been discussed in any detail. Among the types of artefact first found with the Peterborough tradition in the north are unusually elaborate flint axes, stone mace-heads and polished knives (Manby 1974, 83–101; Kinnes 1979). Equally important are a series of non-local artefacts coming into this system, in particular Cumbrian axes which seem to dominate the record at the expense of their locally made counterparts (Manby 1979). We have already discussed the complex relationship between flint axes, imported axes and those made from glacial erratics in this area; there are also important contrasts among the contexts in which they were consumed. The elaborate flint axes form part of the distinctive assemblage deposited in graves. The non-local axes, however, tend to be discovered in different circumstances, for example in pits with decorated pottery, some of it Grooved Ware (Manby 1974, 1979 and 1988).

We have already seen how closely Grooved Ware is associated with the larger henge monuments. In northern England these monuments occupy a peripheral position in the landscape, and the main examples are found away from the Yorkshire Wolds and closer to the routes through the Pennines by which stone axes are likely to have passed (Harding and Lee 1987). This is not a new observation, and a number of writers have observed how these henges have their counterparts across the mountains in the Cumbrian lowlands, where a few of these sites, and the larger stone circles, include finds of Group VI axes (Burl 1988). By contrast, the Yorkshire Wolds show only limited evidence of henge monuments, and in this area round barrows were more prominent features of the landscape, especially around the great cursus complex at Rudston (Fig. 3.3; see Manby 1988).

Grooved Ware is also associated with the largest group of flint mines in Britain, at Grimes Graves in East Anglia (Longworth *et al.* 1988, chapter 1). The main activity at this site took place towards 2500 BC when this style had achieved its widest distribution. One of the most interesting features of this complex is that it was making flint axes in an area that was already receiving imports from as far afield at Cornwall. At the same time, not all the products of Grimes Graves were axes; among the other types made there were knives of the same form as those originating in Yorkshire (Saville 1981). Again it seems as if changes in the axis of exchange may be reflecting much broader alignments in Neolithic society.

Unfortunately, it is much easier to identify such patterns than it is to interpret them. Outside Wessex, the distinction between these different traditions may have been drawn too rigidly, and once again there is a danger of extrapolating from well-documented cases at the expense of local variation. Such problems are both empirical and theoretical. At an empirical level, it seems likely that the Grooved Ware network came to incorporate artefact types that had originally been associated with Peterborough Ware (Bradley 1984a, 46–67). For example, Grooved Ware assemblages in the south sometimes include items that first appear as grave goods in northern England (Barrett *et al.* 1991, 101–8). This could illustrate the difficulty of maintaining the significance, associations and exclusive character of particular objects. At the same time, it is important to acknowledge a dimension to these exchange networks which is frequently overlooked. When we study such artefacts as maceheads or polished knives, we are describing the movement of *artefacts*. But with the exception of stone axes, most of the links uniting the Grooved Ware network exist at the level of *ideas*: ideas about ritual and ceremonial objectified in the form of monuments; ideas about the cosmos and its links with society encoded in ceramic art. Here the most important element is provided by long-distance links between *places* and *beliefs*, and not by the movement of artefacts from one area to another (Bradley and Chapman 1986). Grooved Ware is usually too badly made to have travelled far.

As with the Earlier Neolithic, problems of interpretation arise because these different elements are generally considered in isolation. It is hard to avoid the tendency that we described in chapter 1, of extrapolating from one class of data to suggest the nature of another. Thus the character of stone axe production has been inferred through analogy with excavated flint mines. This process has been taken even further in north-east England where the entire character of society, including the pivotal role assigned to control over status items, has been inferred from the evidence of burials alone (Thorpe and Richards 1984). Analyses of this nature often assume a direct relationship between production, circulation and consumption when it is precisely the nature of this relationship that is of interest to us. They provide no means of identifying those shifts in the roles and associations of artefacts that can happen as they move from one context to another. Nor do they allow for the possibility that the purposes served by the production and circulation of these artefacts may have changed over time. If we accept that their value and significance may have been open to manipulation, these relationships become a major focus for research. In place of such a unitary conception it may be more rewarding to look for the *thresholds* across which artefacts engaged in different roles. In order to do this, we need to study a number of complementary sources of information, contrasting these over the full extent of the system.

There is much to be gained from integrating dispersal patterns with evidence for the changing character of consumption across space and time. As we have seen in this chapter, such data pose a series of challenges to those models which have sought to explain the movement of axes in terms of everyday requirements. This is a theme to which we shall return in the final section of this study. Yet there is a further dimension which has still to be fully exploited. Whilst much has been written about lithic exchange systems, there have been few explicit studies of the conditions under which stone tools were produced. Nowhere is this problem more acute than it is in Britain.

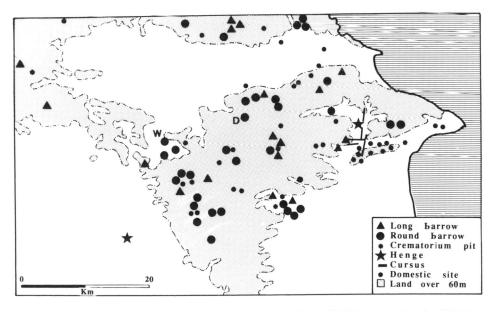

Fig. 3.3 Neolithic sites on the Yorkshire Wolds. D, Duggleby Howe; W, Whitegrounds (after Whittle 1988b).

If we wish to adopt a more integrated approach to the circulation of artefacts in prehistory, following their cultural biography from creation through to consumption, it is essential that the balance be redressed. This is why we decided to carry out fieldwork on the Neolithic quarries at Great Langdale.

II

AXE PRODUCTION IN THE CUMBRIAN MOUNTAINS

4

Tackling the problem at source

Studying production sites

In the first part of this book we presented a review of exchange studies in archaeology, with particular reference to one of the most sustained of all the programmes of research – the analysis of stone axes in the British Isles. Having concluded the previous chapter with a discussion of the shortcomings of that work, we must now concern ourselves with developing a rather different perspective.

We have seen how artefact *distributions* have always dominated our approaches to exchange (e.g. Earle and Ericson 1977; Clough and Cummins 1979 and 1988). To some extent this is because they lend themselves to quantification, but the development of exchange studies has already brought to light so many procedural difficulties that these methods are clearly insufficient in themselves; they involve the separation of a pattern from its context (Hodder 1982b). In chapter 1 we saw how work was now extending into other fields of archaeological enquiry. These are of undoubted relevance to many of the studies, but at present the one element that is under-emphasised in the literature is investigation of artefact production itself.

At one level there are obvious reasons for this reticence, for while production residues may be prolific, their sheer quantity tends to be discouraging. Nowhere is this more likely to be the case than in the study of flaked stone artefacts, for stoneworking is a subtractive technology which leaves enormous quantities of by-products behind, and these are effectively indestructible. It may be for this reason that British scholars have been so reluctant to work on axe production sites in the uplands, for here an enormous quantity of debris awaits investigation. The predeliction for flint mine excavation is partly explained because the shafts leave prominent earthworks behind them, setting at least some physical boundaries to their investigation.

Whilst this reluctance is understandable, it does mean that production sites are often the missing component in studies of exchange systems, especially those concerned with the movement of flaked stone artefacts. If we are to take a rounded approach to the circulation of artefacts in prehistory, following their cultural biography from manufacture through to consumption, it is essential that this imbalance be corrected.

Production sites have been on the margin of research in Britain, partly because so much emphasis has been devoted to monuments. In addition, they are generally located in the 'Highland Zone', which has remained an underresearched part of the country, compared with the lowlands. This imbalance can also be explained by the development of petrological analysis of axes, for nearly all the work carried out at stone sources in upland Britain has been designed to corroborate inferences derived from that programme of work, or to provide dating evidence for artefacts found in other parts of the country (Grimes 1979). It is no coincidence that one of the most considered studies of an 'axe factory' – Graig Lwyd – took place before the characterisation of stone axes was organised (Warren 1922).

Although certain studies of lithic production sites have made a serious contribution to our understanding of exchange, this work remains undeveloped. Moreover, all too often it reveals hidden assumptions that prevent it from realising its full potential. Many of the problems of sampling, analysis and interpretation have been discussed in a recent volume devoted to quarry studies (Ericson and Purdy 1984), but it is in the work of Robin Torrence (1986) on the obsidian quarries of Melos that they find their clearest expression. Her work represents a major advance in the development of a sophisticated methodology. If we question some of the approaches that she takes, this is only because she has set a standard for other work of this kind.

The most important problems concern the assumptions that underlie this study. Her approach is explicitly based on the notion of productive efficiency, employing Rathje's cost-control model to extrapolate from the organisation of production at the stone source to the broader economic framework in which activity was situated (see Rathje 1975). She works from the assumption that different levels of efficiency are related to different levels of social complexity. As she says,

> In order to understand how the extraction of resources and the manufacture of goods will vary systematically in relation to different types of exchange, it is necessary to examine the elements involved in competition for profits . . . As systems of exchange become more competitive and more profit-oriented, . . . one would expect that more types of behaviour which were increasingly efficient would be adopted. Consequently, the degree of efficiency exhibited during acquisition and production would increase with changes along the continuum from direct access to negative reciprocity.
> (1986, 40)

This approach is rather ethnocentric as it assumes the universal validity of modern economic principles. That is how her study can make a direct comparison between stoneworking methods among a series of human groups from Australian hunter-gatherers to the makers of gunflints in the modern world economy. A similar line of reasoning has been followed by Earle, who suggests that although the relationship between production and consumption is a complex one, 'different forms of production should correspond to different forms of exchange' (1982, 8). Such an approach is consistent with a 'typological' perspective: it is assumed that certain 'types' of economic system can be identified from the presence or absence of specific attributes. But even when we can recognise contrasts between different production systems, we have to ask whether it is permissible to use these as some form of evolutionary index in order to locate those examples that are imperfectly observed. Even if we can establish correlates for the ends of a hypothetical continuum, it does not follow that the 'missing' elements can be extrapolated directly by this means. The most that we can do is to characterise those systems that are driven by the profit motive and to isolate those that appear to deviate from it.

Few would deny the heuristic value of formal economic models as tools with which to think about archaeological patterns, yet such general correlations cannot tell us much about the nature of the societies that we are studying. Nor can they shed light on the historical conditions under which particular relationships between production and consumption came into being. As Hodder notes, we say little about the past when we state that a particular pattern fits, or does not fit, a particular regression line (1982b, 209). At worst, such devices lend support to the notion that costs and benefits are assessed in the same ways everywhere.

There are other reasons why we do not share Torrence's belief that we may be able to link different forms of specialisation with different types of society. Some of the problems are largely methodological. Certain of the dimensions that are most important to her kind of study may be archaeologically invisible at the source. This applies to the nature of access to the raw material, which plays an important part in Torrence's discussion. Was this carefully controlled? And how can we tell whether particular quarries had once been owned? The presence of non-local objects at these sites may be important here, but it is open to more than one interpretation (Purdy 1984). Control may also have been maintained by ritual or social conventions that would leave no trace at all – this is especially apparent from McBryde's work at the Mount William quarries in Australia (McBryde 1984). Similar problems have been identified in recent work on axe quarries in Highland New Guinea (Burton 1984a and b). Here control over where and when particular groups were allowed to work was effected by strong ideological proscriptions.

A second problem concerns the orientation of technological analysis. Torrence criticises studies in which little attempt is made to go beyond simple description, and her work helps to show *how* people approached the working of stone. Because that is an essentially subtractive process, we can shift our focus from the products themselves to look in more detail at the processes by which they were made. But how are we to use these increasingly detailed descriptions? There is no doubt that a study which seeks to measure efficiency, by recording such features as error rates, edge:weight ratios and the presence or absence of preparatory working, will make more sense of the debris from stone artefact production than a purely descriptive account (e.g. Sheets 1975 and 1978). On the other hand, technological characterisation, however subtle, will be able to supply little information unless other features of the raw material source are studied at the same time. It is unsatisfactory to extrapolate from just one kind of analysis when the opportunity exists for studying variations in several dimensions at once.

For example, we need to set the physical character of production against evidence for the criteria involved in selecting the stone. Similarly, it is worth investigating the techniques and tools employed in extracting that material. It is also important to consider how production was structured in spatial terms, for the ways in which people organise themselves in space are never arbitrary. Indeed, space provides one important medium through which they may assimilate basic ideas about the networks of social relations within which material production is situated (Bourdieu 1977; Moore

1986). We can extend this emphasis on spatial organisation by studying the manner in which stoneworking was structured in different areas. Combined with technological analysis, this sheds additional light on how production itself was organised. It may be possible to establish the decision-making processes that lay behind the creation of different artefacts, and the 'logic' that determined the manner in which particular activities were undertaken.

Once again the emphasis is on diversity rather than homogeneity: on analysis that studies different sources of variation at the same time. That is not an easy task in dealing with quarry sites, as Torrence's own work makes clear. In fact most studies of prehistoric stone quarries operate on a very generalised level of reconstruction, in which there is little emphasis on spatial or temporal variation. If 'there are a number of different workshops at a source, the data must be merged to form a composite picture of production' (Ericson 1982, 133). Of course there is a sense in which quarry sites contain only one kind of data – production debris – but this simplifies the issues to a point at which returns diminish rapidly. It is not prudent to characterise *the* nature and organisation of production, as uniformity cannot be assumed without investigation. Such a radical simplification of the archaeological record is often coupled with the study of surface samples, making it still more difficult to recognise any sources of variation and contrast.

Whilst the majority of quarry studies have been undertaken in other parts of the world, the same line of reasoning can be found in discussions of the stone sources used in Neolithic Britain. Excavation has been on an extremely small scale, but again the literature provides the impression that we already know how these sites were used. We must not assume that the conditions under which production was organised remained constant for as long as a thousand years, when the same period was characterised by changes in many spheres of social life.

Stone sources in Neolithic Britain

We have already mentioned some of the characteristics of the stone sources used in the British Neolithic, and have identified a gap in our information which stands in the way of any broadly based analysis. Flint mines have been investigated for many years, but characterisation of their products is still at a very early stage (Craddock *et al.* 1983; Bush and Sieveking 1986). The products of other stone sources have long been studied by petrologists, with the result that their changing distributions are known in detail (Clough and Cummins 1988). The production sites, however, have seen very little basic work. So great are the chronological, geographical and technological contrasts between the products of these two kinds of stone source that it would be quite wrong to extrapolate between them, using our detailed knowledge of a few flint mines to infer how highland axe quarries might have operated. The problem has to be tackled at source.

Our discussion of existing studies of production sites introduced other requirements. If we were to undertake a more broadly based study than the majority of our predecessors, we needed to work in an area which combined a high level of preservation with the maximum potential for internal variation and contrast. We would have to utilise several independent sources of data, including substantial deposits of working debris, extraction sites, flaking floors, and contexts in which it would be possible to obtain environmental evidence. In addition, it would be important to combine surface observation with the evidence of stratigraphy.

Although a large number of stone sources in Britain would repay investigation at some level, very few can supply sufficient of these elements. A basic requirement was a long history of axe production, combined with well-documented changes in the distribution of the products. Without these it might be difficult to discover sufficient dimensions of variation at the stone source or to relate the operation of these sites to the broader sequence in Neolithic Britain. That eliminated a few of the stone sources which seem to have had a short history of use, together with those that served a rather limited area. Only two of these sites, Mynydd Rhiw and Killin (Pl. 4.1), are known to be well preserved, and both have now been investigated, Killin by one of the writers (Houlder 1961; Edmonds and Sheridan in press). Although they operated at too small a scale for our present requirements, they still provide important material for comparison with our case study.

Among the stone sources that were in use over a long period or on a larger scale, several could be eliminated because of the nature of the raw material. Among these was the south-western source of Group I axes, which has been characterised as a uratised gabbro, epidiorite or greenstone. Like the products of other Cornish sources, these axes were of igneous rock which would have been worked by pecking, grinding and polishing, with the result that little but dust would have remained behind (Coope 1979). That left the claims of three major stone sources to consider. All had been

Plate 4.1 The stone axe source at Killin, Perthshire.

known for some time, and each had already seen at least small-scale survey and excavation. Moreover, each was situated in a region in which the broader pattern of settlement had already been investigated.

The earliest fieldwork had taken place at Graig Lwyd in North Wales (Warren 1922). Like the other sites to be mentioned here, the name really refers to a small region rather than a single place, and the rock used for making axes has more than one actual source (Royal Commission on the Ancient and Historical Monuments of Wales 1956, xli–lvii). Unfortunately, this complex was not sufficient to meet our need for internal variation, since the largest stone source has been removed almost entirely by a massive modern quarry (Pl. 4.2), whilst a much smaller subsidiary exposure at Garreg Fawr is disturbed by post-medieval sheepfolds. In fact, the chief sign of variation is provided by the report on Warren's early excavations. These revealed a small workshop floor beyond the limits of the parent rock (Warren 1922). The surface material spread over this area today confirms that the later stages in the production of large bifacial tools are strongly represented here. Whilst this may shed light on one part of the production process, it is no longer possible to follow the full sequence of activities in this complex.

The Tievebulliagh stone source in County Antrim, Northern Ireland, seemed to be more promising in this respect, although its full extent remains to be mapped and it is uncertain how many separate exposures of this rock were used for making axes (Jope 1952; Sheridan 1986). One particularly interesting outcrop is to be found on Rathlin Island, 5 km off the coast of Ulster, but again this has yet to be investigated systematically (Williams 1990). Tievebulliagh itself was subjected to very large-scale collection at the beginning of the century, when whole cartloads of roughout axes were

Plate 4.2 The stone axe source at Graig Lwyd, north Wales, seen across the Menai Strait. The site is in the centre of the photograph.

taken from the site (Knowles 1906). This must have entailed some disturbance of the archaeological deposits, but in fact the main problem here is that so much of the Neolithic complex seems to be buried beneath blanket peat. This may have secured its preservation, but it also means that any field investigation would be particularly difficult. There has been one small excavation on a deposit of axe-making debris at this site (Mallory 1990). There is also evidence that on Rathlin Island the later stages of axe production may have been carried out in a settlement some distance away from the stone source itself (Whelan 1934).

In this case it would have been feasible to mount an effective investigation, but this would have been expensive and possibly destructive. Environmental evidence is available from the surrounding peat (Mallory 1990, 27), and it is possible to investigate the relationship between the axes from this source and flint axes that were made not far away (Collins 1978). The location of one of the exposures on an island introduces important questions about access to the raw material, but in this case the data appear to be so fragmented that the issues raised in earlier discussion might never be resolved.

Fortunately, the Great Langdale complex supplied a far more satisfactory alternative (Pls. 4.3 and 4.4). As we have seen, this was apparently the largest producer of Neolithic stone axes in Britain. The separate components of this complex will be described in detail later, and at this stage it is enough to enumerate the features that convinced us that work in this region would meet our needs.

To recall our earlier discussion, we wished to investigate an axe-production

Plate 4.3 Pike o' Stickle seen from the west.

complex which exhibited the maximum internal variation, combined with strati-graphic depth. We also needed to work in a complex in which we could examine the methods of stone extraction alongside those of axe making and could relate any changing configurations in the operation of the industry to local environmental evidence. The Cumbrian stone source is unusually extensive and it soon became apparent that it called out for detailed investigation. The axe-making sites are widely distributed and range from places where very small quantities of the parent rock had been prised from the ground surface in order to make a few artefacts, to large-scale quarries that still survive as field monuments (Bunch and Fell 1949). In addition, there was also evidence for the existence of shallow extraction pits dug into the ground surface (Pl. 4.5; see Houlder 1979).

Such variations in the character of the stone sources were already known to extend to the artefacts found there. As at Graig Lwyd, some of the working floors seemed to be located beyond the limits of the parent rock, and one of these had been excavated (Clough 1973). It would be possible to examine any differences between the artefacts found on the sites, since large areas of stoneworking debris were exposed on the surface. Others clearly extended to a considerable depth, thus meeting the require-ment for stratigraphic evidence. In some parts of the source area stoneworking debris extended beneath blanket peat, and this should have ensured the preservation of any spatial patterning. Other archaeological deposits proved to be located within alluvial or colluvial sequences, raising the possibility of linking these finds of artefacts to the environmental record. The latter was a particularly exciting prospect in a region which

Plate 4.4 Pike o' Stickle seen from the north-east. The summit is at the top right of the photograph. Note the extensive peat bog behind the stone source.

had already seen an unusually large number of pollen analyses, many of them supported by a radiocarbon chronology. Given the possibility of combining these different strands of evidence, this was the area eventually chosen for fieldwork.

An introduction to the Great Langdale complex (Figs. 4.1–4.3)

The Cumbrian mountains occupy an area of nearly 500 km^2, projecting westwards from the Pennine range, which forms the main spine of the English uplands (Fig. 4.1). To the north, west and south, the Cumbrian mountains are flanked by fairly fertile tracts of lower ground, extending as far as the coast. This zone is between 7 and 20 km wide. To the east, the uplands of Cumbria merge with the foothills of the Pennines, although the two areas are largely separated by a major river valley up to 12 km across. The Cumbrian mountains include some of the highest peaks in England, pre-eminent among them Scafell Pike at an elevation of 978 m. The mountainous landscape is breached by a series of glacial valleys, which radiate out from the highest ground to the north, west and south. These include the main settled areas in this inhospitable landscape and provide the easiest routes into the main massif. They also contain the lakes that have given this region its popular name.

The source of epidotized tuff used for making stone axes occupies the central part of this region, and follows an arc that closely reflects the characteristic topography (Fig. 4.2; see Houlder 1979). This raw material has the same mechanical properties as flint, and can be worked in a regular and controlled manner, creating easily recognised debitage. The exposure has been traced in a narrow band over a distance of 19 km and is usually found at a height of between 500 and 900 m above sea level. Its sinuous

Plate 4.5 The earthworks of stone extraction pits at Great Langdale.

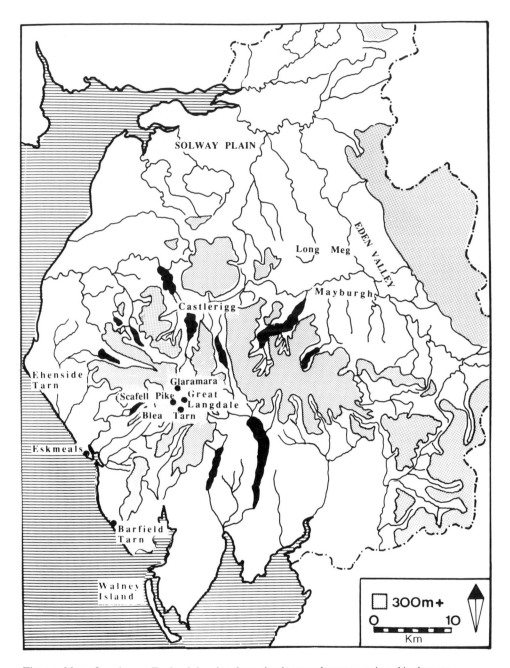

Fig. 4.1 Map of north-west England showing the main places and areas mentioned in the text.

course skirts some of the major valleys leading to the lower ground, and the main locations where the rock was worked seem to have been chosen for their accessibility from those areas. Despite their elevation, the sites on Scafell Pike may have been located for access from the coastal plain of west Cumbria. Those on Glaramara can be reached by way of Borrowdale, which could also provide a route to the northern part of the Cumbrian plain and to the Solway Firth. Similarly Langdale is well placed for access to the southern Lake District, the Pennine foothills and the Lancashire coastline. It is worth adding that no other points along the exposure of this rock would have been so easy to reach from the lowlands. At the same time, it is precisely in those lowland areas that we find the earliest archaeological and environmental evidence of settlement and land use.

It is important to define our terms of reference at the outset. The 'Great Langdale' complex is simply a shorthand term, enshrined in the archaeological literature, for a whole series of stoneworking sites in these mountains. The largest of these, and the first to be discovered, are at Great Langdale itself, but, as we have seen, axes were also made at other locations, in particular Glaramara and Scafell Pike, with more ephemeral working floors at other points on the same stone source. In the same way, the literature identifies this complex with axes of petrological Group VI, but again recent work has shown that this is too restrictive (R. V. Davis 1985; Fell and Davis 1988). Nearly all the axes assigned to Group VI did originate in Cumbria, the

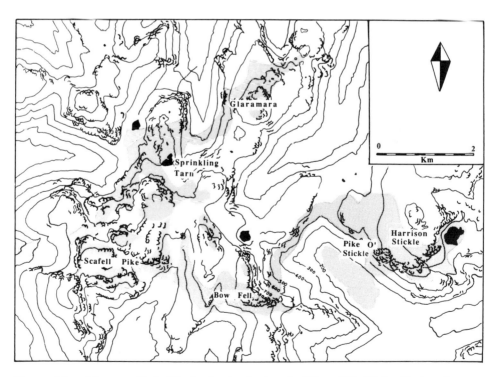

Fig. 4.2 Map of the central Lake District showing the deposit of Group VI tuff (after Claris and Quartermaine 1989).

exception being those artefacts made from glacial erratics. More intensive petrological analysis has shown that the parent rock also includes Group XI, as well as material of similar composition to Group VIII, which otherwise characterises Graig Lwyd (Fell and Davis 1988). Moreover, it seems as if the original definition of the Group VI rock may have been too tightly drawn, as samples taken from the axe-making sites match the composition of artefacts found in other parts of the country and described as 'near Group VI' (Evens *et al.* 1962 and 1972; Keen and Radley 1971; Woolley in Claris and Quartermaine 1989, 15–17). It is uncertain how many of these objects really originated in the Langdale area, but such work does suggest that the number of Cumbrian products in circulation may well have been underestimated.

Although some flaked stone artefacts were recovered in the early years of this century, the major influence on fieldwork at Great Langdale was provided by petrological analysis of axes found in other parts of the country. That directed attention to this area of north-west England, and as a result an extensive series of stoneworking sites were recognised around the Langdale Pikes, two mountains of volcanic origin, where the tuff used for making these artefacts was exposed over a considerable area. By 1949, a whole series of archaeological deposits had been identified on the high ground. The roughout axes recovered from them showed the characteristic features of the Group VI rock (Bunch and Fell 1949; Fell 1950).

Over the next thirty years a combination of chance finds and systematic field survey resulted in the discovery of similar material on, or close to, the same rock formation in other parts of the region. These did not rival the sheer quantity of stoneworking debris at Langdale itself, but this work did result in the discovery of the other major concentrations of material (Plint 1962 and 1978). Unfortunately, the publicity that these discoveries attracted soon resulted in a series of unauthorised excavations at the stone source and in the wholesale collection of roughout axes, very few of which can now be traced. Little of this material is securely provenanced and the disturbance that all this activity entailed also meant that some of the sites were seriously affected by erosion, in particular those on Pike o' Stickle, where extensive screes of debitage run right down the face of the mountain. This activity continues to the present day and threatens the remaining archaeological deposits on one of the most dramatic field monuments in Britain. For that reason we are obliged to be somewhat circumspect in our description of these locations.

On the other hand, the attention paid to the Cumbrian axe source also had beneficial effects. Two small excavations took place, one in a cave close to the summit of Pike o' Stickle (Fell 1950, 3–4) and the other on an outlying working floor at Thunacar Knott (Clough 1973). The latter work provided the only two radiocarbon dates from any parts of this complex, as well as important environmental evidence. Pollen analysts came to concentrate their work in the area surrounding the stone source, with the result that the basic vegetational history of this region is known in greater detail than in most parts of upland Britain (Pennington 1970 and 1975). Most important of all, the continuing erosion of the stoneworking sites, by tourists and by axe collectors, necessitated a more systematic survey of the archaeological material before plans could be instituted for the careful management of the sites. This was undertaken by the National Trust and the Cumbria and Lancashire Archaeological Unit and took place in 1984 and 1985; the results have recently been published (Claris and Quartermaine 1989). This survey was of crucial importance to our own work and little could have been achieved without it. We owe a great debt of gratitude to those who undertook this arduous task.

Their work showed that the quantities of stoneworking debris vary radically between the main locations, and the same certainly applies to the extent of the archaeological material exposed on the surface. Even excluding the south scree at Langdale, whose extent (12,000 m²) has been modified by recent tourist erosion, the sites in the vicinity of Langdale itself cover a considerably larger area (19,000 m²) than those on Scafell Pike (3200 m²) or Glaramara (160 m²). The same is true of the estimated flake counts, despite the difficulties of extrapolating from surface scatters to what lies beneath. A maximum of about 2400 flakes are exposed on the sites at Glaramara; in

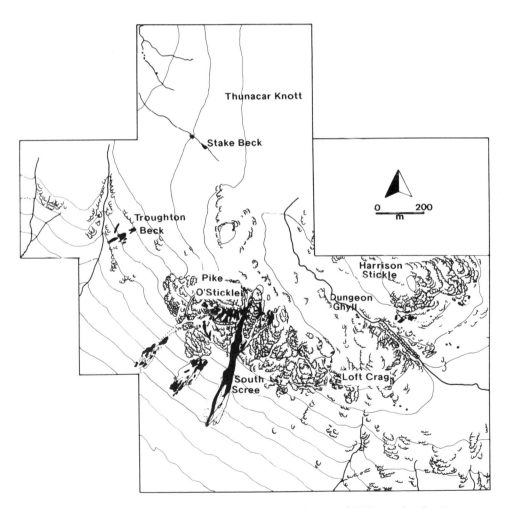

Fig. 4.3 Map of the Great Langdale complex, showing the main areas of debitage (after Claris and Quartermaine 1989). Contours at 50 m intervals.

Table 4.1. *The distribution of debitage at the three main stone sources in Cumbria*

	Glaramara	Scafell Pike	Great Langdale
Area of working debris:			
excluding South Scree	1%	14%	85%
including South Scree	0.5%	9.3%	90.2%
Number of surface finds	0.2%	3.8%	96%

the Scafell Pike complex the figure is about 38,000 and at Great Langdale it is no less than 950,000. The contrast is remarkable enough in itself, but it underemphasises the differences since it is only at Langdale that we find evidence of deep stratigraphy. Even so, there is a broad agreement between both types of estimate (see Table 4.1).

To a large extent these estimates mirror the distinctive nature of the surface evidence at these three locations. Glaramara and Scafell Pike are characterised by an appreciable number of small scatters of worked stone, located on level or gently sloping ground not far from the highest point on the mountain. Most of the concentrations at Great Langdale are more extensive and contain a much greater density of archaeological material. The majority of the finds come from inaccessible positions on a steep and rocky mountainside. There is no evidence of formal quarrying at Scafell Pike, where the stone seems to have been extracted by breaking up the material in a natural blockfield and then digging shallow pits or hollows in order to reach the tuff. Although these 'extraction pits' were badly disturbed by unpublished digging soon after their discovery, they seem to have been the main way of obtaining raw material in that complex, and several groups of these features have now been recognised. Only rarely do they contain sufficient debris for the manufacture of a significant number of axes. Indeed, some scatters probably reflect single episodes of axe production. The same impression is provided by the small scatters at Glaramara, where the tuff is exposed on the surface. Here again there is evidence for small-scale working of the rock, but no sign that it was obtained by quarrying. Still slighter scatters of debitage were identified along the rock source during the recent survey. Small numbers of broken roughouts have been recovered from a number of these sites, but here again it is likely that they represent little more than short episodes in which single implements were made. Some may even result from testing the raw material. No tools employed for extracting or working the stone have been found on these sites.

We must not exaggerate the contrast between such sites and those at Langdale (Fig. 4.3), for there are similar features in all three areas. On the plateau behind Pike o' Stickle, where Group VI tuff is exposed on or close to the surface, there are small scatters of worked stone very like those mentioned already, and where the raw material is exposed in the side of a ravine there are the earthworks of a series of small pits, not unlike those on Scafell Pike (Pl. 4.5). Other possible examples have been recognised in this complex, although they have been badly disturbed in recent years.

Apart from differences in the amount of archaeological material, the principal contrasts concern the methods of stone extraction that were being used at Langdale, and in particular on Pike o' Stickle and Harrison Stickle. At these locations the Group VI tuff is exposed in steep crags, not far below the summit (Pl. 4.6); it is also found in similar locations along the north side of the Langdale valley. A second major concentration of worked stone occurs where the mountainside is broken by deep gullies, containing enormous quantities of scree. There is no doubt that large amounts of raw material could have been obtained at these locations, either by prising it from the rock face or by collecting the larger pieces detached by natural erosion. A novel feature of these sites is that the rock faces themselves show evidence of intensive working. In each area they exhibit clear signs of conchoidal fracturing, reflecting the direct removal of stone. On Pike o' Stickle, it seems as if the rock had been consistently worked to a vertical face (Pl. 4.7). Here the sites are located on a series of narrow ledges, situated one above the other on the face of the mountain. It is these ledges which create the distinctive 'stepped' profile of the Pike. This is partly due to the way in which the rock is bedded, but the patterning of flake scars and distribution of screes of working debris indicate that this characteristic profile was maintained during the period of exploitation.

Elsewhere on Pike o' Stickle there is evidence for yet another approach to winning raw material (Pls. 4.8, 4.9 and 4.10). Here those extracting the rock seem to have exploited some of the natural lines of weakness running through the tuff. Narrow

Plate 4.6 View from Pike o' Stickle along the outcrop of tuff.

Plate 4.7 A Neolithic quarry at Great Langdale.

Plate 4.8 An artificial 'cave' at Great Langdale.

Plate 4.9 An artificial 'cave' at Great Langdale. The ranging pole indicates the highest extent of flake scars on the rock face.

fissures were opened out, creating a series of shallow caves or adits, whose artificial origin is clearly documented by the flake scars that can still be identified on their walls. One of these was excavated in the late 1940s (Fell 1950, 3–4). Such features contain a deep filling of debitage, and in a few locations modern erosion of the axe-making debris has exposed caves which are filled almost to the roof. These locations can only be described as *quarries* in the strict sense of the term, and they produce nearly all the evidence of tools used in this process. These artefacts consist of rounded pebbles made of granite or tuff, between 12 and 30 cm in diameter (Pl. 4.11). They show areas of intensive local battering; other examples are represented by detached flakes. These objects would have been too large for use in making artefacts, but they are ideally suited to the task of removing pieces of stone from the rock face. They do not occur naturally on the mountain and probably originated in streams or glacial deposits (Bradley and Suthren 1990).

Accompanying these quarries there are very large quantities of debitage, ranging in size from angular blocks which had evidently been detached from the rock face, to the characteristic debris of axe manufacture. This material is a major feature of the screes and forms the principal filling of the surviving quarries. It is known that this apron of debris extends a considerable distance down the mountainside, and it is possible that it could mask entire extraction sites. This raises a problem addressed in chapter 6. It would be impossible to retain the spoil extracted during work on the face of Pike o' Stickle since the quarries themselves are situated on narrow ledges on a 55° incline.

Plate 4.10 An artificial 'cave' at Great Langdale, still retaining most of its original filling.

Here one of the main groups of sites, those on Top Buttress, are located almost 200 m above a group on Central Buttress. In view of the flow of debitage downhill, how far can we associate the contents of individual quarries with the activities that originally took place there? The movement of artefacts down the mountainside makes it more difficult than ever to calculate the extent of the original workings and for this reason it is quite impossible to estimate the output of these sites. In fact our evidence shows a bias towards those areas in which the vegetation cover has been broken. Some locations still remain in which it is uncertain whether archaeological deposits exist below the surface.

The same problem applies to the sites on the more level ground behind the summit of the Langdale Pikes. Apart from the earthworks mentioned earlier, the main deposits lie buried beneath deep deposits of blanket peat and have only been exposed by accident where that cover is broken. To some extent this has happened through natural erosion, although other groups of material have been revealed in the footpaths that cross this area. It has been difficult to decide whether the distribution of these finds reflects a more general pattern, particularly as the water table in this area is normally too high to allow these exposures to be recorded.

So far this account has featured a variety of surface sites exposed along the course of the Group VI tuff. In fact there are other archaeological sites to consider in its vicinity. These generally occur on rather lower ground, away from the stone source and on the access routes leading down to the major valley floors. They have been discovered in three areas. Two are known on the route leading down from Scafell Pike by way of

Plate 4.11 A Neolithic hammerstone from Pike o' Stickle. Centimetre scale.

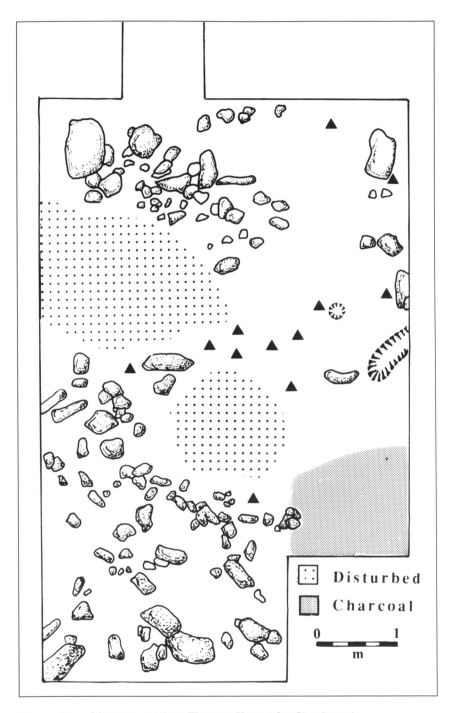

Fig. 4.4 Plan of the excavated site at Thunacar Knott (after Clough 1973).

Wastwater to the Cumbrian plain, where an important concentration of Neolithic sites is known (Cherry and Cherry 1983, 1984, 1985, 1986 and 1987a). Others occur on the southern flanks of Pike o' Stickle and Harrison Stickle, along the main paths leading down into the Great Langdale valley and from there to the southern Lake District, and still more have been found on the route leading northwards from the Langdale Pikes by way of Langstrath into Borrowdale. In every case the evidence consists of surface scatters well outside the known distribution of the rock used for making axes. The excavated site at Thunacar Knott probably belongs to this group, and here traces of structural evidence were revealed, including areas of stone clearance and a possible post hole (Fig. 4.4; see Clough 1973). All the debitage seemed to be associated with axe making, and charcoal found during excavation has given a radio-carbon date of 2850–3250 BC (BM 676). The location of this site in a more sheltered position some way from the stone source raises the possibility that this had been an ancillary workshop, doubling as a temporary camp.

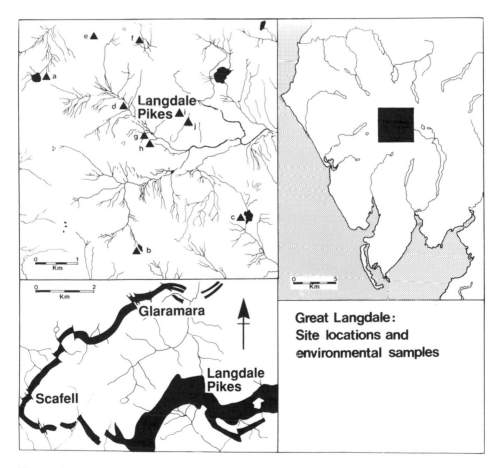

Fig. 4.5. Pollen sampling sites in the Great Langdale complex. a, Angle Tarn; b, Red Tarn Moss; c, Blea Tarn; d, Mickleden; e, Langdale Combe; f, Stake Beck; g and h, Mickleden medieval/post-medieval cairnfield; i, Thorn Crag; j, Dungeon Ghyll.

As we mentioned earlier, the site at Thunacar Knott also provided evidence of the contemporary environment, for like so many of the working floors at Langdale it was sealed beneath a deposit of blanket peat. This is particularly important, as one of the criteria which we used in looking for a suitable study area was the existence of a good environmental record. One peat sample has been analysed from Scafell (Pennington 1975, 80), but most of the published pollen analyses from the Cumbrian mountains were undertaken in the central area in which Langdale is situated (Fig. 4.5). They come from two complementary environments. First, there are analyses of the pollen found in the sediments of small lakes and tarns, including Blea Tarn, 3.4 km from Pike o' Stickle, and Angle Tarn, only 2.9 km away. Even nearer to the major group of Neolithic quarries were an infilled kettle hole in Langdale Combe only 1.8 km distant (Walker 1965) and another one located in Mickleden, the valley below the quarries (p. 80). All but one of these sites provide evidence for early disturbance of the vegetation, and work in Langdale Combe showed some signs of changes in the local landscape during the Neolithic period. Such detailed studies could also be integrated into the broader regional pattern of development, established through work in the major lakes and the Cumbrian lowlands.

The second type of environment to be sampled for fossil pollen is represented by ancient land surfaces like that at Thunacar Knott (Clough 1973); there is also a published analysis from a flaking floor on the mountaintop at Langdale (Fell 1954). The evidence from such sites should reflect events in a much smaller catchment area, but such samples do have the advantage that sometimes they can be related directly to archaeological evidence of human activity. That is perhaps the main importance of those working floors stratified in or under the blanket peat at Langdale, and it soon became apparent that it was worth paying special attention to finds of artefacts or lenses of charcoal identified in such locations.

We began by making a case for sustained investigation of an axe production site in highland Britain, and having reviewed the candidates we elected to work in the Great Langdale complex. We have now outlined the principal characteristics of the archaeological sites in that area as they appeared to us when we started this project. Even though the surface evidence had been surveyed to a very high standard, it seemed hard to know where to begin. We were embarrassed by the riches of this extraordinary area. The first stage in our research was learning how to use this material in a creative manner in order to approach the problems outlined in previous chapters. The next was to establish a workable methodology for recording the material in the field. Exactly what did we wish to know? and how far would we need to accommodate our broader objectives to working in such a hostile landscape? These were the questions that we addressed during our preliminary reconnaissance in 1985. In the following chapter we describe the working methods established during that initial season and some of the ideas which first emerged at that stage.

5

Establishing a methodology

Earlier chapters offered a justification for working at a Neolithic axe production site in Britain and set out our reasons for selecting the Great Langdale complex for this purpose. Having described the wide variety of surface evidence that confronted us when we started, we must now turn to the crucial problem of linking that material to our specific objectives.

The reader will have gained some impression of the sheer extent and variety of the surface deposits on the sites making up this complex, and also of the vicissitudes that so much of that material had undergone. Some had been disturbed by illicit excavation and was moving downslope in massive screes; other assemblages lay on the ground surface where they had been exposed by peat erosion or brought to light by footpaths. How, if at all, could such material be put to use?

As we mentioned in chapter 4, our first season's work in this extraordinary landscape was concerned with exactly this problem. It is all too tempting to discuss the details of a research design as if it were fully formed from the outset, but this is rarely the case, for growing familiarity with an archaeological phenomenon inevitably brings new issues to the surface. In fact our preliminary reconnaissance was exactly that: an initial phase of fieldwork in which we tried to come to terms with an extraordinary data set. Whilst some of the questions that we wished to ask were already formulated, it was not always obvious quite how we were to answer them. We needed to work out which approaches to recording the archaeological material were likely to be productive, given the various biases that it had undergone. We also needed to temper the purity of our more abstract conceptions by the experience of working in such a hostile landscape, where fatigue, foul weather and a high water table raised at least as many problems as the archaeology itself.

Existing studies of production sites were helpful in two respects, for they gave an impression of the usefulness of different sampling techniques and provided an opportunity to identify certain pitfalls in advance. It was important to break down the great mass of data into its constituent parts if there were to be any chance of identifying chronological variation. At other sites this had been revealed through overlapping episodes of working, through changes in the choice of raw materials or through stratigraphic evidence (Purdy 1984; Singer and Ericson 1977), but at Langdale the sites were dispersed over such a large area that these phenomena might be recognised only in exceptional cases. In any event it was equally important to identify synchronic variation in the character of extraction and production.

The first step was obviously to investigate the integrity of the surviving deposits in order to come to terms with the distortions brought about by erosion and by the impact of several decades of collection and unauthorised excavation. The situation was particularly complex at Great Langdale, where the most extensive sites are found on precipitous slopes, and form the point of origin for great screes of debitage, hammerstones and broken roughouts. The development of screes provides a classic instance of size sorting (Wood and Johnson 1980), and in such a mountainous region this process can completely transform the character and structure of an archaeological assemblage. Any sampling strategy had to take this factor into account. Moreover, what have been described as separate 'sites' may sometimes form parts of a much more general spread of material, exposed where the vegetation cover has been broken. It was essential that we were able to model the character of the screes in different areas. In this way we could infer the general structure of concealed deposits where only a small proportion was exposed.

That was why any sampling strategy needed to be closely linked to the character of the material in this complex. It was important to establish the limits of variation in a number of different dimensions, before we could decide where more detailed investigation should take place. The features of interest included: the selection of the raw material and the character of stone extraction; the nature of the reduction sequence(s); and the spatial organisation of production. In turn, variations at this general level would help us to select those sites where more detailed investigation might be justified. At Langdale, Glaramara and Scafell Pike each scree or horizontal spread of material with more than 200 flakes was examined. Sample frames, each one metre square, were located in the centre of the exposure, and where debitage seemed to be associated with signs of *in situ* extraction, samples immediately adjacent to the tuff outcrop were also examined. In the case of material incorporated in screes, biases caused by downslope movement were assessed using multiple samples at 10 m intervals down the longitudinal axis of the deposit (Fig. 5.1). This provided invaluable data on the differential movement of debitage created at specific stages in production. Thus we were able to distinguish exposures where the overrepresentation of material from the later stages of axe making was due to natural processes from others where it seemed to reflect the original activities on the site. The following attributes of the debitage were recorded for each sample: measurements of length, width, thickness and weight, flake morphology, the presence or absence of dorsal scars, weathering patterns, platform preparation and the nature of the terminations on individual pieces. We also considered where material could be refitted. Note that at this stage such work was not expected to reconstruct the production process in any detail: our main objective was to consider how far these samples revealed a homogeneous assemblage.

As a number of studies have shown, size measurements are not always enough to assign stoneworking debris to different stages in a production sequence. This point will be considered in detail later, but for present purposes it can be stressed that the combination of attributes recorded during this preliminary fieldwork provided a reliable indication of the range and character of the activities represented at each exposure. On technological grounds the surface material could be attributed to four activities: (a) quarrying; (b) testing/initial preparation of the rock; (c) mass reduction; and (d) thinning. The most striking observation was that whilst the term 'factory' may be wholly inappropriate, virtually all the debitage did result from making axes. This observation was borne out by examining the broken or rejected implements that could be found on these sites. Because of the activities of collectors, we could no longer assess the integrity of the sample that remained, and this made it impossible to study the typology and standardisation of those artefacts. Even so, all these examples were weighed and measured, and the character of the working, including the extent and sequence of flaking, was recorded. We also noted whether they had been made from flakes or blocks, and the reasons why they had been rejected.

Such work could not extend far into the upland plateau behind the Langdale Pikes, where only limited amounts of archaeological material were exposed. Here the old ground surface was covered by a layer of blanket peat. This problem was addressed by the excavation of four transects of test pits, each one metre square and spaced at 50 m intervals. The main transect ran parallel to the known extent of the Group VI outcrop and was supplemented by three further transects, offset from it at right angles (Fig. 5.2). The layout of these test pits was constrained by the excessive depth of peat in the central part of this zone, and here no work was possible. Even so, this limited operation did have two important results. There was little evidence of extensive scatters of working debris. Production seems to have been limited to the more level ground immediately above the major screes and extraction sites. In addition, it showed that a subsidiary band of tuff outcropped behind Pike o' Stickle and this too had been exploited (Fig. 5.3; cf. Claris and Quartermaine 1989, 3). Pits in the vicinity of

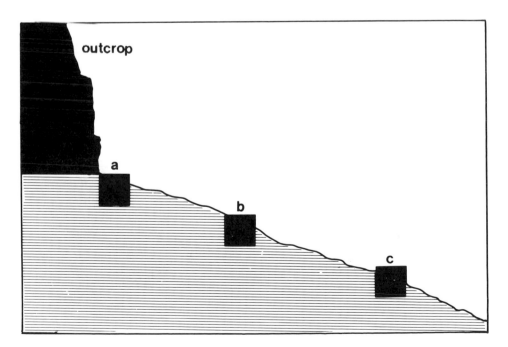

Fig. 5.1 The recording system for debitage in the scree deposits.

Dungeon Ghyll demonstrated that raw material was being extracted and worked in this area, confirming the impression given by the surface earthworks. In view of the smaller scale of the sites at Scafell and Glaramara, a similar exercise was not attempted there, nor could such work be carried out in the vegetated areas on Pike o' Stickle without causing serious damage to the natural environment.

Experimental studies (Tables 5.1–5.4)

One further line of enquiry was followed throughout the analysis of surface samples: the experimental replication of axes. This technique had been used successfully in other studies (Burton 1980; Cleghorn 1982; Olausson 1983; Vemming and Madsen 1983), and here it could provide information on several levels. The creation of flaked stone tools made it possible to determine the character and frequency of different classes of debitage generated during successive stages of production. This equipped

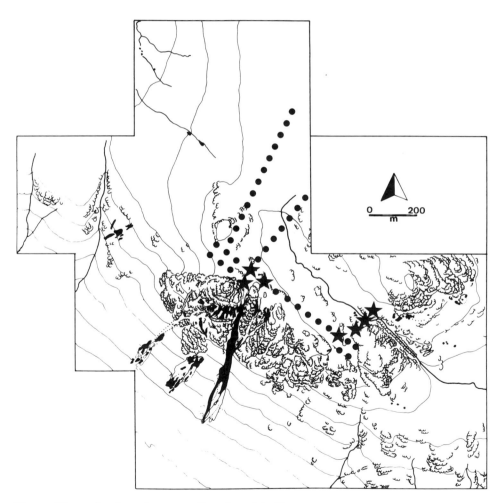

Fig. 5.2 The results of test pit survey at Great Langdale. The stars indicate the concentrations of debitage.

Table 5.1. *Flake categories created during experimental roughout production*

Category	Description	Reduction sequence stages
A	Massive flakes, with irregular edge morphology	Preparatory trimming and shaping of raw material
B	Large invasive flakes, thick in section Irregular edge morphology	Primary shaping of roughout through invasive alternate flaking, which establishes guiding ridges for subsequent removals across both faces
C	Broad, squat flakes, thick in section	Mass reduction
D	Long, invasive flakes, thin in section, often with curving profile ('thinning flakes')	Final shaping and thinning of roughout
E	Small thin platform chips, thin in section, often with curved profile	Platform preparation prior to removal of thinning flakes, or final shaping and trimming of roughout edge
F	Small angular platform chips, often with large platforms and a marked triangular section	Platform preparation prior to primary and secondary working; may also be generated during later stages

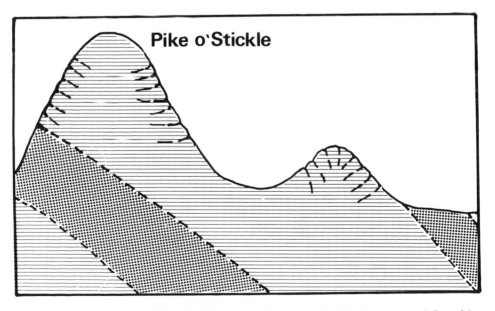

Fig. 5.3 Geological section of Pike o' Stickle, showing the outcrop of tuff on the steep south face of the mountain and the subsidiary outcrop on the plateau to the north.

Table 5.2. *Quantitative characteristics of the flakes created during experimental axe production*

Expt	Raw Mat Wt	Axe Wt	Debitage Wt	No. of Flakes	Axe:Deb. Weight Ratios	Form
1	3950 gm	640 gm	3310 gm	212	5.17	Block
2	4330	710	3621	170	5.10	Block
3	4550	660	3894	196	5.90	Block
4	3543	721	2822	195	3.91	Block
5	4365	703	3662	202	5.20	Block
6	4621	680	3941	221	5.79	Block
7	3506	647	2895	201	4.41	Block
8	3850	730	3120	188	4.27	Block
9	3688	692	2996	207	4.32	Block
10	3005	685	2320	163	3.38	Block
11	2785	620	2164	139	3.49	Flake
12	2605	643	1962	153	3.05	Flake
13	3041	694	2347	160	3.38	Flake
14	2251	706	1545	120	2.18	Flake
15	2060	581	1379	127	2.02	Flake
16	2098	678	1420	156	2.09	Flake
17	1979	666	1313	126	1.97	Flake
18	1732	595	1127	113	1.89	Flake
19	2713	642	2071	130	3.22	Flake
20	2547	686	1861	132	2.71	Flake

us to recognise quite subtle distinctions in the spatial organisation of working. It could also show the extent to which variations in the raw material (and thus in the method of extraction) would affect the ways in which it had been used. So much importance is attached to measuring error rates and standardisation in studies of prehistoric quarry sites (Torrence 1986, chapters 3 and 7) that it was essential to know how far those features resulted from differences in the form in which the raw material was obtained.

There was another side to the question. It was just as important to discover which methods *could* have been used to make an artefact as it was to establish which were actually selected. It is clearly important to understand *how* the production process was structured in a given context, but we also need to discover *why* it took the form it did (see Lemonnier 1986). For that reason, it was important to distinguish between the form of a flaked stone tool and the means by which that form was realised (Edmonds 1990). Different technological strategies can be followed in the production of a single type of artefact. Faced with the task of creating a particular object, an artisan works within the limitations imposed by the nature of the raw material. Within those constraints, however, he or she may choose from a number of options as to how to proceed (Young and Bonnichsen 1985; Pelegrin 1990; Edmonds 1990). Each option may be characterised according to the potential that it offers for controlling the form

Table 5.3. *The frequency of flake classes created during experimental axe production*

Expt	Form	A	B	C	D	E	F	Totals
1	Block	3	23	30	38	55	63	212
2	Block	2	18	26	35	41	48	170
3	Block	2	28	36	33	42	55	196
4	Block	1	17	31	37	49	60	195
5	Block	2	21	37	42	41	59	202
6	Block	3	24	39	40	49	66	221
7	Block	3	19	28	39	44	68	201
8	Block	1	16	33	37	40	61	188
9	Block	2	22	30	41	43	69	207
10	Block	2	18	24	36	39	44	163
11	Flake	0	10	13	31	44	41	139
12	Flake	1	14	18	40	42	38	153
13	Flake	1	15	13	36	39	56	160
14	Flake	1	9	14	28	36	32	120
15	Flake	0	17	15	32	35	28	127
16	Flake	2	24	28	29	38	35	156
17	Flake	1	16	12	36	32	29	126
18	Flake	0	12	8	29	37	27	113
19	Flake	1	15	10	36	40	28	130
20	Flake	1	18	16	27	37	33	132

Table 5.4. *The results of experimental axe polishing*

Axe	Original Wt	Polished Wt	Wt Loss	Time taken (hrs)	Material used
1	640 gms	510 gms	130 gms	9.21	Tuff block
2	710	622	88	8.53	Tuff block
3	660	612	48	8.06	Tuff block, flaked facets
4	721	664	57	7.57	Tuff block
5	703	668	35	7.38	Tuff block
6	620	584	36	7.16	Tuff flake
7	643	592	51	7.24	Tuff flake
8	694	648	46	6.55	Tuff flake
9	579	537	42	7.07	Tuff flake, flaked facets
10	706	679	27	6.10	Tuff flake
11	536	492	44	7.50	Tuff natural
12	604	587	17	7.03	Tuff natural
13	618	592	26	24.02	Flint
14	656	621	35	25.17	Flint
15	714	687	27	23.09	Flint
16	681	665	16	22.19	Flint

of the artefact, and the extent to which it allows the stoneworker to anticipate and avoid mistakes.

This observation has two important consequences. If different pathways can be followed in transforming raw material into an artefact, our knowledge of lithic technology allows us to identify them from the waste, even in the absence of refitting. This distinction is important when we are studying a large production site, for there is always the temptation to establish a single, generalised reduction sequence. Experimental replication provides a way of identifying variations in the suite of decisions made in the production process. In fact this work allowed us to trace those paths in detail, and each could be examined in terms of the different levels of control and forward planning that they required.

A total of twenty axes were made out of the Langdale tuff. The raw material came in a variety of forms and sizes: ten axes were produced from large angular blocks, five resulted from the preparation and removal of large flakes from cores, and five more were made out of large flake 'blanks' struck directly from the rock face.

All the debitage created during these experiments was recorded, and as each axe was being made, problems such as excessive hinge fracturing, angle correction, or difficulties in achieving mass reduction were noted. Each flake struck from the parent material was given a number which indicated its position in the reduction sequence. At certain points the work generated large quantities of small chips and flakes, and since these could not be numbered individually, they were weighed. Changes in the character of the hammers used were recorded at the same time.

These experiments allowed us to make a number of observations. They made it possible to identify several general categories of debitage which correlated with specific stages in the reduction sequence (Fig. 5.4). These could be recognised on the grounds of size, mass, thickness, profile and edge morphology – an important consideration since tuff does not have a clear natural cortex. To some extent these categories followed a logical sequence: very large flakes reflected preliminary trimming, thick squat flakes resulted from shaping and mass reduction, and thin and often curved flakes reflected the final thinning and shaping of the axe. In addition, two categories of chips could be identified. Those with small butts and a similar profile to the larger thinning flakes tended to be created during the final phase of working, either in the preparation of striking platforms or as deliberate removals during trimming. Those platform chips with larger butts were generally thicker and triangular in section, and these occurred as by-products at a number of different stages in the reduction sequence; they might also be detached during the removal of larger flakes. In addition, it was noticed that 'lips' were sometimes created on the proximal edge of the flakes. These were usually associated with the small platforms and low flaking angles that characterised material detached during the final finishing and shaping of an axe. This scheme provided one basis for 'reading' the character of the surface finds at Langdale.

The next issue to consider was the quantity of debitage which resulted from working the material in these different forms (Fig. 5.5; Table 5.2). The experiments were intended to produce axes of a consistent size, and so it soon became apparent that a smaller mass of stone was wasted when these artefacts were made from flakes. The quantity of debitage was also lower in this case. This was easily explained, as the production of axes from blocks raised two practical problems: the need to maintain a good working angle between the face and the striking platform; and the difficulty of shaping and reducing the mass of the roughout axe. Working from a block rather than a flake made it more difficult to establish the symmetry of the artefact in plan and section. This was because more material had to be removed from large blocks in order to create a roughout, and the process involved detaching flakes from surfaces which occurred at widely different angles from one another. The use of flakes for the same purpose meant that less mass reduction was needed as one began with a piece of rock whose cross-section was closer to the intended form. That is why the production of axes from flakes involved a higher ratio of thinning flakes to shaping and mass reduction pieces than the axes made from blocks (Tables 5.2 and 5.3).

There was a further problem in making axes from blocks. It seemed that flaking across the major axis of the blank was not sufficient to reduce the mass; it was also necessary to detach long flakes, using the cutting edge as a platform. As a result, the patterning of scars and ridges on a number of the flakes differed from those detached in the other experiments, where lateral flaking and more limited working of the cutting edge were usually sufficient to attain the desired form. It also emphasised the importance of achieving a symmetrical cross-section. This was more difficult than

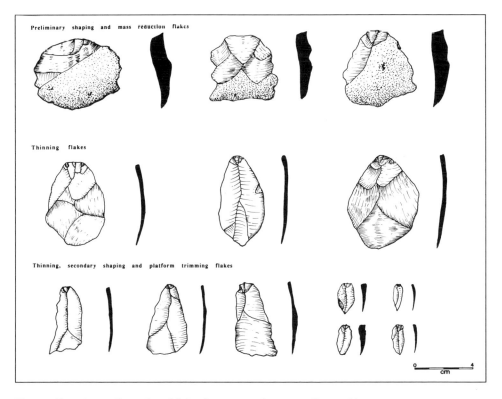

Fig. 5.4 Experimentally produced flakes from successive stages of axe making.

creating a regular outline in plan, and increased the chances of miss-hits or of breaking the roughout, especially on blanks with a variable angle between the face and the platform. Again this proved to be more common when axes were made out of blocks, and it accounted for the slightly higher incidence of hinge and step fractures recorded in the experiments.

Having created the roughout axes, it remained to complete them by the laborious process of polishing (Table 5.4). This was not in evidence at Great Langdale itself and, as we have seen, is more likely to have taken place at settlement sites. Polishing was not an operation that required much skill, but it was time-consuming. Ten of the axe roughouts went through to this final stage, together with two unmodified pieces of naturally fractured tuff. Five of the roughouts had been made by working down angular blocks, whilst the other five were produced from large flakes. Two axes in each group were reflaked along the sides to create the kind of facetting that characterises some of the Cumbrian products.

All the polishing experiments were undertaken on a slab of millstone grit, to which sand and water were added. Those axes made from blocks of tuff took consistently longer periods of time to polish and involved the removal of more material than those made out of flakes (Table 5.4). This was because it was harder to achieve a symmetrical cross-section in working down a block. Moreover, this process often resulted in miss-hits and hinge fractures that needed to be erased during polishing. There were fewer such errors to remove from the roughouts made on flakes, for here shaping and trimming had been easier to manage because the angles between the dorsal and ventral surfaces were more consistent.

Lastly, the provision of side facets did not involve any significant increase of weight loss or time. The same was true of the creation of polished axes from unworked fragments of tuff, but this process had the disadvantage that at no stage would it have been possible to assess the quality or suitability of the stone being used. This is an important point since many studies of stone tool procurement assume that raw material is only 'tested' prior to artefact production. In fact the act of producing an object involves a more continuous process of monitoring; those working the stone have to act upon the conditions created by earlier removals. Indeed, this process can be extended through technological procedures that anticipate tasks that occur at a later stage in the sequence (Pelegrin *et al.* 1988; Edmonds 1990). As we shall see, the extent to which such steps are taken may be an indication of changing attitudes to production.

The results of these experiments were important in two ways. They placed our analysis of the surface exposures on a more secure foundation. At the same time, they allowed us to explore the relationship between specific technological tasks and their material signature in the debitage – an understanding that was to prove invaluable in analysing the material from excavation. Moreover, these experiments emphasised the importance of determining the form in which the raw material was obtained. For that reason they required a closer scrutiny of the ways in which rock was selected and extracted.

In chapter 4 we drew attention to some striking contrasts between different sites located along the stone source, from the use of material incorporated in natural screes or obtained on or close to the ground surface, to the creation of vertical quarries. To some extent, this can be explained on the basis of geology and topography, but a different approach is needed if we are to establish why particular locations were selected in the first place. It is clear that at Great Langdale working was unevenly distributed along the outcrop, and some of the sites with the greatest amounts of archaeological material were in the most inaccessible locations. At the same time, others showed little sign of use. It seemed important to ascertain how far these variations were due to differences in the nature of the tuff.

In her study of the obsidian quarries on Melos, Torrence ranked the individual sources in terms of their potential for sustained exploitation (1986, 171–81). This ranking depended on the extent of these outcrops, the nature of the raw material and the ease with which it could be extracted. A similar approach was taken to the sites at Langdale. This involved experimental working of the stone at different points along the outcrop. Each location was evaluated in terms of its accessibility, the extent of the stone source and the quality of the raw material. In the event there seemed to be little relationship between the areas best suited for exploitation and the actual scale of the

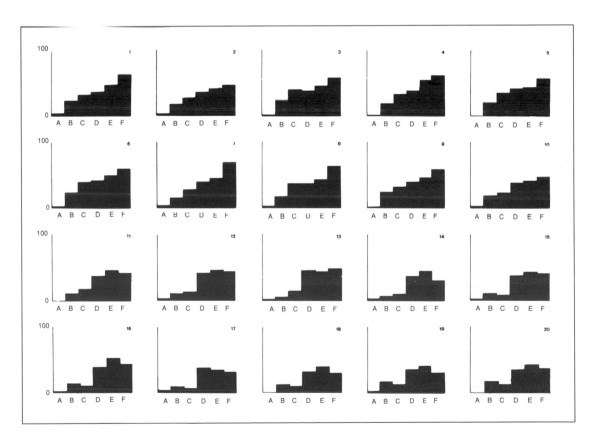

Fig. 5.5 Details of the debitage from experimental axe production. The letters refer to the types of flake defined in Table 5.1.

Table 5.5. *Uniaxial tensile strength of rock samples from the main sources of Group VI tuff in Cumbria*

Location	Mean tensile strength (MPa)	Standard error	Standard deviation
Great Langdale complex:			
Dungeon Ghyll	36.7	1.2	3.9
Middle Gully	34.2	3.2	9.0
East Middle Gully	37.0	1.9	5.9
Harrison Stickle A	35.8	2.9	8.3
Harrison Stickle B	35.9	1.7	4.1
Harrison Stickle C	37.2	1.7	4.1
Loft Crag	39.3	1.8	7.2
Top Buttress	42.0	2.1	5.6
Great Langdale complex	*37.4*	*0.8*	*6.5*
Other Cumbrian sites:			
Scafell Pike A	34.5	1.1	3.9
Scafell Pike B	33.0	1.1	4.4
Glaramara	27.3	1.1	3.7

archaeological deposits found there (Bradley and Ford 1986). Inevitably such a study suffered from the subjectivity of the estimates that it used, but this disadvantage was overcome by recourse to materials science. Through the kindness of Dr Philip Meredith of the Rock Physics Laboratory of University College London, it was possible to measure the uniaxial tensile strength of samples of the tuff taken from different locations at Great Langdale and Scafell Pike (Bradley *et al.* 1992). These included samples from both the simpler and more complex extraction sites, as well as locations at which no archaeological debris could be seen. For the most part this work showed little difference between the tensile strength of raw material taken from these separate outcrops, but it is clear that the stone at Great Langdale was better suited to axe production than its counterparts at Scafell Pike and Glaramara. In the same way, some of the best stone was to be found in the quarries at Top Buttress, but material of almost equal quality was worked on a much smaller scale at the more accessible outcrop on Loft Crag. Overall the tensile strength of the rock bore little relation to the amount of evidence for stoneworking at the different sites (Appendix, Table A.1). Whilst other physical parameters could be explored, the results of these tests suggest that the selection of the stone sources was not determined entirely by the mechanical properties of the raw material. The mean values for samples from eleven locations along the Group VI rock source are given in Table 5.5.

A further perspective on the extraction sites is provided by a detailed study of the quarries. Here large blocks and massive flakes had been detached directly from the rock outcrop. Indeed, on a number of sites it seemed as if the parent rock itself had been worked on alternate faces (Pl. 5.1). The success of this approach depends on maintaining a consistent edge on which to work, and this may be one explanation for the stepped profile of the quarries on Pike o' Stickle. This would also have allowed the use of fire-setting; since heat rises, this method depends on the existence of a vertical quarry face. The technique is documented in the ethnographic literature (Collins 1893), but there were two particular reasons why its appearance at Langdale would be of special importance. It would provide another indication of a higher level of invest-ment in working the rock at these locations, and at the same time it might also mean that deposits of burnt wood and stone, suitable for absolute dating, could be recovered by excavation. In this case our work was aided by Dr David Sanderson of the Scottish Universities Reactor Centre, who examined a series of samples taken from the rock face in and around the quarries. These were analysed for thermoluminescence, not as a means of dating but as a locational device: had the rock been subjected to fire-setting, the values could be expected to be low, whilst unburnt rock would give much higher readings (Fleming 1979). Dr Sanderson's work showed that the low readings *were* associated with the two quarries that he sampled, thus providing some limited support for the suggestion that fire-setting had been used there. As we shall see in chapter 6, in each case this inference was to be supported by excavation.

We have also commented on the presence of imported hammerstones at these quarries and their rarity elsewhere in the Great Langdale complex. Again they may

Plate 5.1 Evidence of flaking on the rock surface at Pike o' Stickle.

provide indications of a higher investment of technology at these locations, but since they had been brought to the quarries from outside they might also shed light on the connections between those sites and settlement in the wider landscape (Bradley and Suthren 1990). Were the quarries associated with hammers that originated in a number of separate regions? Or were individual extraction sites associated with imports from only one source area? Clearly such questions would have implications for the social context in which these sites had operated. For this reason, as part of our evaluation of the surface evidence, samples were taken from a whole series of well-provenanced hammerstones and submitted to Dr Roger Suthren of Oxford Polytechnic for petrological examination (Bradley and Suthren 1990).

Lastly, it was already apparent that pollen analysis in the vicinity of the quarries might help to locate these sites in their contemporary landscape and could provide another way of linking activity at Langdale to the pattern of settlement in the lowlands. For the most part, suitable samples would only be obtained during excavation of the stoneworking sites, but at Langdale Combe (Pl. 5.2) Walker's work in the early 1960s had already revealed an important environmental sequence in the filling of a former kettle hole (Walker 1965). The upper part of his pollen core extended from the Elm Decline, which dates to about 3800 BC in Cumbria, to the first growth of blanket peat in this area. He identified a major episode of land use in the period following the Elm Decline, and noted that this was associated with a layer of sediments containing charcoal. This material was never dated, but since it had such important implications for our own work, the relevant deposits were exposed by hand excavation in 1986

Plate 5.2 The position of the environmental column from Langdale Combe.

(Fig. 5.6) and a fresh series of charcoal and pollen samples were collected by Dr Roy
Entwistle. Their significance is considered in chapter 7.

Preliminary observations

With the completion of this sampling programme, we were able to begin interrogating
the data. At this stage the most direct questions were aimed at the debitage itself. Had
all the sites witnessed the same activities? Were some associated with certain ways of
working the rock rather than others? Were there significant variations in the character
of the reduction sequence followed at different sites? And were all the stages of axe
production represented at each location? Such questions were of vital importance if

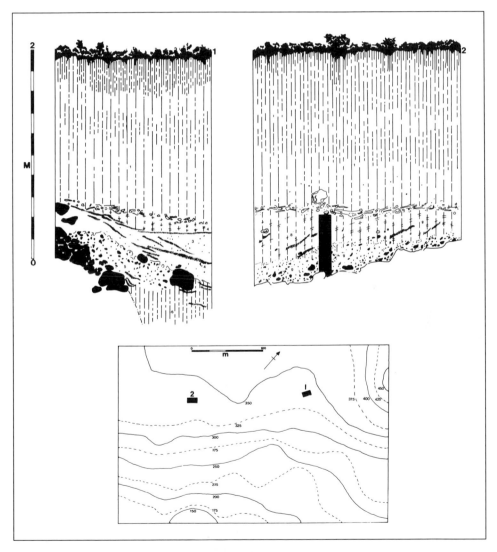

Fig. 5.6 Location plan of the excavation in Langdale Combe, and section of the deposits showing the
position of the pollen core.

we were to understand how axe production was organised. The other analyses added detail to our emerging interpretation and helped to pick out suitable candidates for excavation.

Given the sheer extent of the Group VI rock source, it is impossible to provide a full account of the observations made at every site; those who wish to examine the information in greater detail are referred to Mark Edmonds' doctoral thesis, which forms the site archive (Edmonds 1989). In this section we shall provide a short digest of those observations, backed up by tables A.1 and A.2 in the Appendix which summarise the results of these analyses. To a certain extent a framework was provided by the detailed field survey undertaken by Claris and Quartermaine (1989). From this we could identify three distinct classes of site. It may be helpful to consider these at the outset, before turning our attention to instances where the outlines are less clearcut.

We can start by considering those locations at which there was field evidence that the rock had been obtained on or close to the ground surface. Two particular areas were selected to illustrate the geographical spread of this technique, Scafell Pike and Dungeon Ghyll, where there were shallow features interpreted as stone extraction pits.

The plateau below the summit of Scafell Pike contains a large number of small scatters of worked material, arranged in eight concentrations. In some cases the nature and quantity of the debitage were consistent with the production of little more than a single axe, but elsewhere larger quantities of material clustered in shallow hollows, excavated through an area of fractured and partially cleared blockfield in order to reach the tuff. The earthworks that resulted seemed to reflect a combination of prospection and stone procurement, but always on a small scale. The debitage from these locations showed some emphasis on the earlier stages of axe making, although waste from later stages was also present. Some of the axes were made from blocks. Moreover, the character of the waste suggested that working in this area was undertaken without much control or forward planning. There was very little evidence for the preparation of platforms, and the incidence of hinge fractures and other flaking errors was relatively high. In addition, the flakes displayed a wide range of thickness values. On some sites we could identify assemblage profiles that suggested the spatial differentiation of activities, so that the earlier stages of axe production appeared to be represented in one location and the later stages in another nearby, but in all cases the scale of the operation was very limited. Taken overall, the surface samples from Scafell Pike suggested a relatively unstructured approach to stoneworking. There is little indication that the producers anticipated crushing, hinge fracturing or irregular removals, and there is no evidence for the implementation of recovery strategies.

The sites close to Dungeon Ghyll at Langdale form a particularly interesting group and include a number of shallow earthworks, one of which was later excavated. This time the surface debitage suggested a clear emphasis on the preliminary stages of axe manufacture. Many of the flakes had no scars on their dorsal surfaces, and on morphological grounds were likely to have been generated during quarrying, testing or the initial reduction of crude angular blocks. The material from a test pit 25 m upslope from this complex added considerable detail to the picture. The assemblage was skewed towards by-products from the early stages of working: preliminary shaping and mass reduction. A high proportion of the flakes had irregular terminations, and the material exhibited a wide range of thickness values. This group lacked significant evidence for the preparatory trimming of platforms or the correction of flaking angles.

Although much more activity seems to have taken place at Dungeon Ghyll, the character of the assemblage is not unlike that at Scafell Pike, where shallow extraction pits are also represented. In each case the work was undertaken in a fairly *ad hoc* manner, resulting in similar technological characteristics among the debitage. The main difference is that the entire production process seems to have been carried out at Scafell Pike, sometimes at separate locations within each cluster of sites, whilst the earlier part of that process was overrepresented in the samples from Dungeon Ghyll. It shares that characteristic with a number of other locations where less is known about how the rock was extracted, in particular South Scree and Loft Crag, both at Langdale. A similar spatial arrangement is suggested by surface samples from Central Scree.

A second group of sites, already identified in our initial reconnaissance, were located off the Group VI source and usually on lower ground. The excavated site at Thunacar Knott was one example (Clough 1973), but the finds could no longer be traced. The most suitable material for analysis came from the Langdale Pikes, where small sites of this type were located alongside Stake Beck to the north of the quarries, and below Thorn Crag and Harrison Stickle to the south.

The clearest evidence was provided by three sites beside Stake Beck. In each case, analysis of the debitage showed that the assemblages were skewed towards flake classes generally associated with the later stages of roughout production. There were many flakes with scars on their dorsal surfaces, together with characteristic mass reduction and thinning flakes. A high proportion of the flakes also displayed hinge and step terminations. The fact that so few of them showed signs of platform preparation meant that this was a reflection of technological practice and had not been caused by the choice of raw material. The flakes showed a wide range of thickness values, again suggesting that little effective control was exercised in working the stone. It seemed as if this material resulted from the working of partly finished roughouts or large angular blocks, brought to the site from the stone source.

Two assemblages exposed by footpath erosion below Thorn Crag were sampled in a similar manner and again seemed to be skewed towards the later stages of roughout manufacture. In this case, large quantities of small chips and flakes were recovered on the surface. As at Stake Beck, it was apparent that little effective control was being exercised in the production process, nor had any attempt been made to cope with the risk of breakage. There were few traces of preliminary preparation of the raw material, and the thickness values for the flakes extended across a wide range. In addition, the samples included a high frequency of irregular flake terminations. The material found along another footpath below Harrison Stickle was of a very similar character. Again, the surface assemblages revealed an emphasis on the later stages of the production process, although a slightly wider range of flake classes was represented. In this case there was also a relatively high proportion of irregular terminations, and little evidence for the preliminary preparation of striking platforms before the flakes were removed.

Each of these sites is on lower ground than the quarries, along routes leading down into major valleys. Their distinctive assemblage seems to complement those from some of the extraction sites, where the earlier stages of axe production are over-represented. In both groups the level of technological expertise was low and the error rate was high. It is tempting to describe these places as 'roughout finishing sites', although this may not have been their only function. In any case the nature of the debitage suggests that the artefacts leaving these sites would have been relatively crude and irregular. There are almost certainly more of these working floors to be found, because they tend to be located in areas with a continuous vegetation cover.

The third group of sites identified in early reconnaissance are the major quarries. As we have seen, their position on such steep slopes makes it difficult to be sure that the surface material was generated on the spot and is not the overflow from activity further up the mountainside. For that reason particular attention was paid to the sites at Top Buttress on Pike o' Stickle, where large amounts of debitage could be found beneath overhanging rocks or inside artificial caves. Here conchoidal fractures on the rockface attested the direct removal of large flakes. In such places the archaeological record had a very distinctive composition. All the stages of axe production seemed to be present, and there was a low incidence of hinge and step terminations. The range of flake thicknesses was unusually narrow, and a relatively high proportion of the flakes had seen preparatory platform trimming, mostly the removal of crests. All these features suggest that a high degree of control was being exercised during manufacture. This has two implications. First, it suggests a relatively high level of efficiency in the use of the raw material; the preparation of platforms and the use of controlled flaking would reduce the likelihood of breakage or hinge fractures. Secondly, it may indicate a similar level of standardisation in the manufacturing process itself – most people may have been attempting to follow the same sequence of actions in the production of roughouts. This contrasts with the sites considered earlier, where the pattern of working around a piece of stone was far more haphazard.

Sufficient of these roughouts still remained at Top Buttress for this approach to be taken further. These artefacts had been made from both large flakes and angular blocks, although the axes made from flakes predominated. In many cases these roughouts had been trimmed and finished to such an extent that they closely resembled their intended (polished) form. Most of the breaks were across the blade of the axe and would have resulted from striking an incorrectly angled blow along the side of the artefact; alternatively, the blow could have been too forceful.

These assemblages contrast sharply with all those considered so far. This is hardly surprising in view of the extraction method. More control and precision were exercised in flaking, and the increased use of flakes for making axes suggests that less material was wasted. Apart from the final act of polishing, all the stages of production were represented at the stone source, and the finished products followed a largely consistent reduction sequence. The same can be said of the extraction method itself, since the quarry faces had been prepared, maintained and worked in a systematic manner. It seems as if every part of the production process – from stone extraction to final trimming – was undertaken in a manner which anticipated the stages that were still to follow. This evidence is not confined to Top Buttress, but it is peculiar to the Langdale Pikes and is not found in the Scafell Pike or Glaramara complexes, or in the still smaller working floors elsewhere in central Cumbria. At Great Langdale itself there are less well-preserved sites where the same procedure seems to have been adopted, notably the much smaller exposures at East and Middle Gully, not far from the top of the crag.

There remained a number of other sites in which the debitage shared only certain characteristics with the material described so far. All were located at Langdale. There are two main reasons for this divergence: the use of detached pieces of Group VI rock obtained from screes or blockfields; and an 'intermediate' class of quarry site at which the working procedures were more wasteful than those evidenced on Top Buttress.

In the first case, the main problem was the presence of large pieces of Group VI tuff detached from the main outcrop. This happened in two areas. First, we considered the sites found in the blockfield below Harrison Stickle. These fragments no doubt originated in the main outcrop, but had fallen down the mountainside. The main evidence that they had been worked was provided by an unusual feature of some of the debitage in this area, which included a high percentage of flakes with a heavily patinated dorsal surface. The sheer number of these pieces meant that they could not have been detached directly from the Group VI outcrop, as the extent of the weathered surface on these flakes was greater than the total area of the rock face which could have been worked. The high frequency of pieces with this characteristic feature suggested that a major emphasis was placed on the earlier stages of axe production, although some tertiary debris was also present.

A second example occurred on Pike o' Stickle where major groups of worked material at Central Buttress and Central Scree were found well below the level at which the Group VI tuff outcropped. This cannot have happened because debitage had spilt down the mountainside, since all the stages of axe production were evidenced together at these locations; material transported within the screes would have undergone size sorting, and this did not happen here. It seems more likely that detached blocks of tuff were being worked *in situ*. Further evidence that this material had been worked on the spot was the complete absence of the hammerstones so common on Top Buttress; if any objects had found their way downhill, they would surely have included nodules the shape and size of footballs. The axe roughouts discovered on Central Buttress and Central Scree had been made from angular blocks of Group VI tuff, and the debitage was rather different from that discovered further up the mountainside. There was less evidence for the preparation of striking platforms and a higher proportion of step and hinge fractures. To some extent these patterns recall the material found below Harrison Stickle.

The other group was represented by some of the sites on Harrison Stickle itself. Here the situation is rather obscure. As we have seen, some of the working sites made use of detached blocks of tuff, but there were other locations where rock was obtained by quarrying the rock face. In four places this could be demonstrated by the presence of conchoidal fractures like those at Top Buttress, and in one instance the exposure had been undercut in a similar manner. A few hammerstones are also recorded from Harrison Stickle, but these are poorly provenanced. All the stages of axe making were represented at these quarries, but with rather more emphasis on the earlier stages of production and a much greater incidence of hinge fractures. In this respect, the material recalled the finds from the nearby blockfield.

Another group of sites shares rather similar characteristics. These were at Troughton Beck, towards the western edge of the Great Langdale complex. Here the debitage was found in a series of major screes, but their points of origin against the Group VI tuff were obscured by thick vegetation. All the stages of axe manufacture were represented, and at the tops of the screes, where this material had undergone least disturbance, large quantities of platform trimming chips and flakes were found, suggesting that axes were made in the immediate vicinity. In addition, the frequency of large flakes without dorsal scars provides indirect evidence that the rock was obtained on the spot. The debitage from Troughton Beck was characterised by a high frequency of hinge terminations; there is no evidence that striking platforms were prepared before the flakes were removed, which again seemed to indicate a lack of control or precision in working the stone. It is in this sense that such material is 'intermediate' between the finds from the extraction pits and those from the quarries on Top Buttress, for even where all the stages of axe making were represented, the amount of control exercised in stoneworking was relatively low. There was little evidence for the more systematic approaches seen on those quarry sites. It seems likely that the raw material was exploited in an *ad hoc* manner.

We began by stressing the dangers of treating axe production sites as a homogeneous entity and emphasised the importance of looking for internal variations in the data. This analysis of the debitage found in the surface assemblages certainly suggests that more than one approach to axe making was followed at the sources. These patterns become still more revealing when they are set against variation in other fields.

There were important contrasts in the ways in which stone was extracted in the three principal areas of central Cumbria, and some of these do seem to reflect significant differences of geology and topography. On the other hand, certain techniques *could have been used* but were not adopted. At Glaramara and Scafell Pike much use was made of raw material obtained from blockfields, although the nature of the crags and ledges in the Scafell area means that the preparation of large quarry faces would have been quite practicable. The same is true on a smaller scale when we consider the evidence from the Langdale Pikes. Here we find both quarries and open-cast workings, yet many of the areas with suitable raw material do not seem to have been used at all. Although there is considerable evidence of stone extraction at Top Buttress, parts of the same outcrop between Middle/East Gully and Loft Crag do not appear to have been exploited. This is particularly surprising, considering that many of these unused areas are easier to reach than Top Buttress itself, raising the intriguing possibility that the choice of extraction site was determined by factors other than topography and geology.

These patterns can be compared with the evidence of spatial organisation provided by the surface finds from Scafell Pike and Langdale. On Scafell Pike, many of the scatters are of limited extent, but in some cases there seems to have been a distinction between those areas where stone extraction was taking place and others where roughout axes were finished. Here the distinctions are by no means clearcut and the sites themselves are small. At Langdale, however, there is a much more dramatic contrast between places such as Top Buttress, and the sites clustering about the head of Dungeon Ghyll. In the first case all the stages of axe production took place at the stone source, but in the latter area there was a greater emphasis on the primary stages of manufacture, and little evidence for the finishing of roughouts. A similar, if less obvious contrast exists between the sites on Top Buttress and those on Harrison Stickle, and this is important because of the way in which it cuts across any distinctions in methods of extracting the stone, suggesting that the spatial organisation of production was not determined by the manner in which the raw material could be obtained.

If the contrasts between different assemblages at Scafell Pike are rather limited, those found in the Langdale complex are more dramatic. Sites like those at Stake Beck, or below Thorn Crag and Harrison Stickle, are some distance from the Group VI outcrop, and each lies on one of the major routes leading away from this area. In these cases we find a far greater emphasis on the final stages of roughout production, and

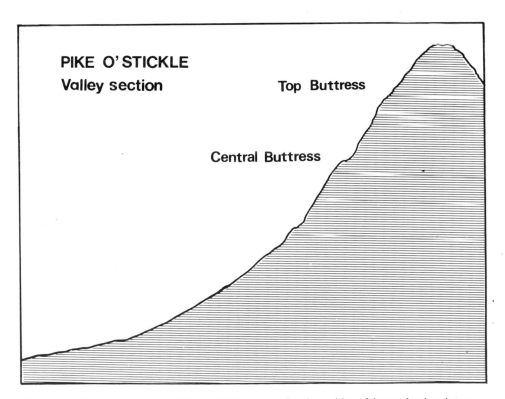

Fig. 5.7 Profile of the south face of Pike o' Stickle, comparing the position of the production sites on Central Buttress and Top Buttress.

it is tempting to associate them directly with those extraction sites containing a disproportionately high frequency of primary waste.

To sum up, the evidence described above goes some way to suggest that stone procurement and axe production in Cumbria were far from undifferentiated phenomena. There were striking variations in a number of fields, and it was particularly interesting how few of these differences could be explained in terms of the geology or topography on individual sites. We seemed to be seeing traces of at least two different forms of organisation, both of which were directed towards manufacturing the same product.

But there were ways in which that analysis was inconclusive. It was based entirely on surface finds, and however striking some of this patterning might appear it needed to be confirmed by more carefully selected samples obtained in excavation. A still more serious drawback was that this information existed in a chronological vacuum. Were these different ways of organising production employed alongside one another, or were they used in succession? And if they did possess an element of sequence, when did the changes occur? Unless those questions could be answered, we would have no means of relating our observations at Langdale to the broader cultural sequence elsewhere in England. That was why it was so important to look for stratified sites where we could obtain evidence of sequence and absolute chronology.

On the other hand, the results of this detailed survey did suggest one idea concerning the pattern of development at Langdale. We have seen how difficult it was to analyse the surface material on the steep flanks of Pike o' Stickle, where so many of the sites are found. This was because little of the material won by quarrying the rock could be retained on the narrow ledges where it was worked – it tended to flow downhill. For precisely that reason the sequence of stone extraction *must have proceeded in the opposite direction*; otherwise it would have been both inefficient and dangerous (Fig. 5.7). On that basis, the working sites at Central Buttress and Central Scree should be earlier in date than those near the summit of the mountain. That hypothetical sequence matches the important distinction between two of the principal methods of making axes: the rather rudimentary stoneworking techniques found on the lower slopes, and the more standardised methods used in the quarries on Top Buttress.

Such an argument is provocative, but it is not conclusive, and for that reason it needed testing by excavation. The results of that research – the final stage in our fieldwork – are described in the following chapter.

6

Test excavations at Great Langdale

Sharpening the focus

The last chapter highlighted some of the problems encountered when research is based on surface sampling alone. Similar problems arise in Torrence's work on Melos (1986). Quantitative and qualitative comparisons between assemblages can only serve as a basis for recognising the extremes of variation. Such distinctions disappear if these observations are brought together to describe production sites 'as a whole'. In doing so, we make the implicit assumption that all patterning is contemporary. At the same time, surface samples do not provide a sufficient basis for determining the precise character of the reduction sequence or sequences within a particular assemblage. Characterisation necessarily remains at a general level. A more detailed frame of reference can come only from stratified contexts.

We have also considered some of the practical problems that were encountered in sampling the surface assemblages. These had a direct impact upon the location and character of the excavations that were carried out in 1987. The Great Langdale area is one of the most popular parts of the Lake District and attracts a vast number of visitors every year, who come to enjoy the spectacular scenery. Paradoxically, it is their activity which poses the greatest threat to its survival. This is an environment which can easily be damaged by erosion, and so it was essential that any excavation should be on a very small scale, particularly on the steep flanks of the mountains. At the same time, the rugged topography which made this area so attractive to walkers and climbers put serious restrictions on our own activities. The excavated sites were located at heights of between 500 m and 700 m: indeed, those on Top Buttress appear to have been the highest excavations carried out in England. The equipment needed for this work had to be taken up to the sites and the excavated artefacts were brought down the mountain at the end of each day's work. The time spent travelling to and from the sites limited the period that could be devoted to excavation, just as the practical difficulties of transporting so much stonework set limits on the quantities that could be recovered. Bad weather posed further problems, and for much of the time these sites were above the cloudline.

Such restrictions are mentioned because they set limits on how much work could be contemplated. In fact this was beneficial, for it focussed our attention on the issues that most needed investigating and ruled out the apparent luxury of speculative excavation. These circumstances also explain a decision that arose from the surface survey described in chapter 5. On the basis of those analyses it became clear that the sites at Scafell Pike and Glaramara had close counterparts at Great Langdale itself, where the full range of activities recognised in this complex seemed to be represented in one manageable area. This made the planning of our work rather easier, and we decided that all the excavations should take place there.

At this point we should recall the main questions that we hoped to address through excavation. We needed to explore the variations in technological practice which seemed to be evident in the surface material. This included both the character of working and its spatial context. Only when we could specify how particular assemblages differed from one another could we start to ask why. We also needed to test the idea that much of the observed variation resulted from changes through time. These had to be demonstrated stratigraphically, as well as through radiocarbon dating.

This approach necessitated the recording of a wide range of attributes on the excavated material. The significance of many of these has been discussed elsewhere, but others were recognised as important on the basis of experiment (Burton 1980; Cleghorn 1982; Torrence 1986). The results of these analyses are summarised in Appendix Tables A.1 and A.2. These studies were not designed to cover every dimension that might ordinarily be considered. Thus little attention was paid to the utility of the by-products beyond recording the presence and character of retouch on individual flakes. It was more important to consider the character of *production*.

In the previous chapter we introduced the idea that the process of stone tool making can be seen as a sequence of decisions and actions; choices are made concerning the steps that can be taken in creating a particular artefact. Such action is usually context-specific. The full significance of this idea is often lost when we talk of reduction sequences (Collins 1975). The process of flaking is subtractive and, in strict terms, it is linear. Yet the act of making an artefact is seldom so straightforward, as studies of ceramic technology have shown (e.g. Roux 1990). It is a more integrated process, involving the perception of the desired object, negotiation of the practical conditions obtaining at a particular step, and anticipation of conditions that may arise later in the sequence (Pelegrin 1990; Edmonds 1990).

These lessons have been brought home most dramatically through the refitting of assemblages, which restores material arranged in a linear sequence to its three-dimensional state. This is generally undertaken where the number of production episodes is small and the assemblage is of modest size. The technique is wholly impractical in circumstances where conjoinable pieces are mixed in with several tons of debitage. In this case episodes of production may be difficult to separate.

The scale of the deposits at Langdale necessitated a broader approach. Whilst we could not come close to the level of descriptive detail achieved by refitting the excavated material, our analyses were intended to record the degree of emphasis placed on particular techniques. It is here that experiments had an important part to play, for they allowed us to explore the significance of a wide range of attributes. This made it possible to recognise not only the different tasks represented in a given assemblage, but also the different approaches taken to the same task. How much attention was paid to the preparation of platforms, and what form did this take? What level of precision was exercised in the positioning of blows during manufacture? What evidence was there for control over the form of flakes detached during production? To what extent did the producers anticipate and cope with particular problems? And what could be said about the manner in which they worked around a piece of stone? As the surface evidence suggested, there were many options to consider.

The selection of sites for excavation depended on a combination of judgement and chance. Five of the seven areas selected for closer study were chosen on the basis of surface survey, combined with the results of remote sensing. Two further sites – both of them very small – were discovered during the 1987 field season and were examined before they were destroyed by erosion (Fig. 6.1).

A number of sites seemed to reflect a rather summary approach to stoneworking.

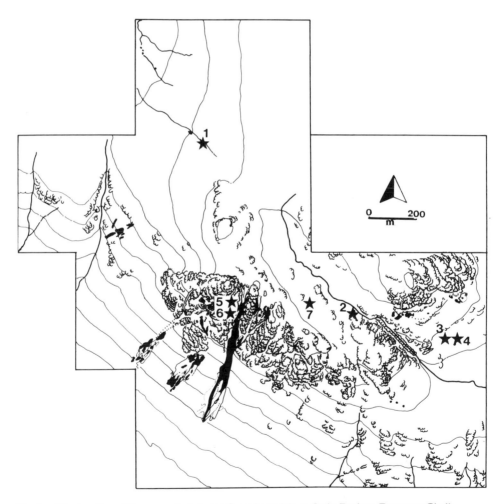

Fig. 6.1 The location of the excavated sites at Great Langdale. 1, Stake Beck; 2, Dungeon Ghyll; 3, Harrison Stickle, trench 4; 4, Harrison Stickle, trenches 1–3; 5, Top Buttress site 95; 6, Top Buttress site 98; 7. Loft Crag.

Three of these were chosen for more detailed study. These were the 'extraction pits' at Dungeon Ghyll and two sites away from the outcrop, at Stake Beck and below Harrison Stickle. Their locations highlight the main routes to the lower ground, one to the north and the other to the south. Our selection of a suitable extraction pit was guided by Chris Gaffney's resistivity survey, which suggested that it had been sufficiently shallow to allow careful excavation without the need for shoring. The choice of the more distant sites was rather simpler, since the edges of both the examples selected were already being damaged by erosion. The site at Stake Beck offered further potential, since it was stratified within a mineral soil buried below blanket peat. This meant that any spatial patterning might be well preserved. Equally important, it could allow us to relate the archaeological material to a series of pollen samples taken from the same location. Both the salvage excavations were at sites of similar character. One lay close to our trenches below Harrison Stickle, where it was threatened by footpath erosion, whilst the other – a small knapping cluster – was found protruding from the blanket peat to the north-west of Loft Crag.

The other approach to working the stone was epitomised by two of the sites below the summit of Pike o' Stickle. Here the surface data had suggested a different approach to production. Site 98 was situated on a narrow ledge, whilst Site 95 was an artificial cave on a second ledge, 5 m vertically above it and close to the upper limit of the Group VI outcrop. These two sites were selected for several reasons. Both had shown an unusually low level of thermoluminescence, consistent with burning during the last few millennia. This might suggest that fire-setting had been employed there. At the same time, there was reason to believe that each of the sites retained its original archaeological deposits. Site 98 included a heavily worked boss of overhanging rock, which would protect this material from any overflow of working debris running down the hillside. Similarly, the cave could not have filled up by that means. In the case of Site 98, there was the added advantage that it was known from photographs taken in the 1940s that the deposits had been covered by at least 1.5 m of debitage, before they were dislodged by unauthorised excavation; what remained had once formed the lower levels of a deep stratigraphy (C. Fell pers. comm.). Similarly, the gap between the floor and ceiling of Site 95 was only 50 cm, yet flake scars could be found on all the surfaces of the cave, suggesting that a considerable deposit might have formed *in situ* (Fig. 6.2). There was one final reason behind the selection of these particular quarries. The structure of the screes on Pike o' Stickle as a whole indicated that work must have progressed up the face of the mountain through time. For that reason it was essential to select sites near to the top of the exposure of tuff, for they would have to be among the latest in date.

Dungeon Ghyll, Site 148 – primary phase (Fig. 6.3)

Perhaps the most informative of all these sites was the extraction pit above Dungeon Ghyll. Here the excavators experienced some difficulty, for it soon became apparent that the surface earthwork – the feature whose profile had been revealed by resistivity survey – belonged to a secondary phase of activity in an extensive area of stoneworking. Some hint of this had been provided by the quantity of material encountered in the test pit survey, but this was on too small a scale to alert us to the problem. The feature identified on the surface as an 'extraction pit' proved to be a recut of a larger open-cast working, surrounded by a bank of upcast, one of a more extensive spread of features identified in recent survey. In order to relate the excavated evidence to our initial hypotheses, we shall consider the two main phases of activity on the site at separate points in this chapter.

This feature was expected to be about 50 cm deep, and it was planned to examine it in half section. As the true position became apparent, only half the original area could be excavated, and for safety reasons not all the deposits could be removed down to the natural bedrock. All the material was recorded on a 50 cm grid. The natural tuff was horizontally bedded and it was evident that those working the rock had followed its course back from where it outcropped in the gorge above Dungeon Ghyll. The primary phase of working was represented by contexts 3, 6, 9, 10, 11 and 14. Here we found evidence for the extraction of large quantities of stone from a massive open-cast working. The raw material had been prised out of the ground in the form of large angular blocks. Where a piece had proved too tenacious, it was left behind. Charcoal was completely absent from these deposits, and it seemed most unlikely that fire-setting had been employed. Many of the large angular pieces of rock displayed single flake scars from testing the raw material, whilst others had been worked more

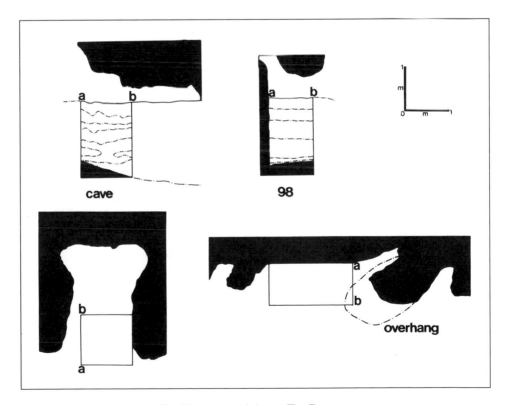

Fig. 6.2 The location and profile of the excavated sites on Top Buttress.

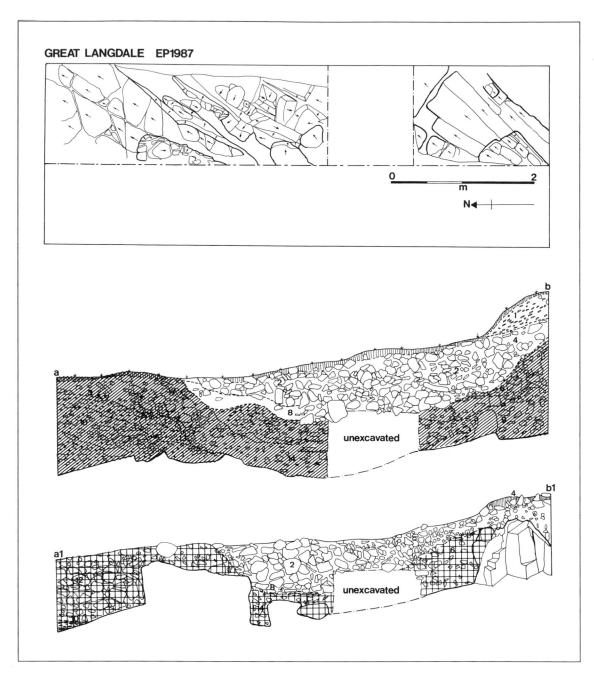

Fig. 6.3 Plan and section of the excavated site at Dungeon Ghyll. The section drawing is shaded to highlight the contexts belonging to the first phase of stoneworking.

extensively before they were broken or discarded. Both had happened with some frequency.

Flaking debris was found throughout these deposits, and particularly in contexts 10, 11 and 14. It is clear that the bulk of this assemblage reflects the earlier stages of production. To some extent this is because raw materials were being tested, but the frequency of flakes with scars on their dorsal surfaces suggests a wider range of activities. Both flakes and broken roughouts attest an *ad hoc* approach to stoneworking (Fig. 6.4), and only 0.15% of the material showed signs of retouch. Many pieces had been worked along only one edge before they were discarded. Some of the hinges, lumps and irregular angles had been hammered repeatedly, but little attempt was made to remove these flaws by working from another platform. Further characteristics add detail to this picture. Few of these platforms were facetted, suggesting that the flakes were detached without much preparation and that flaking did not alternate between opposing faces of the raw material. Little control was exercised over the point of impact, with the result that the flakes show a high frequency of hinge fractures. There are few of the flakes associated with later stages of the reduction sequence. Not many of these have prepared platforms, and a large number were heavily crushed.

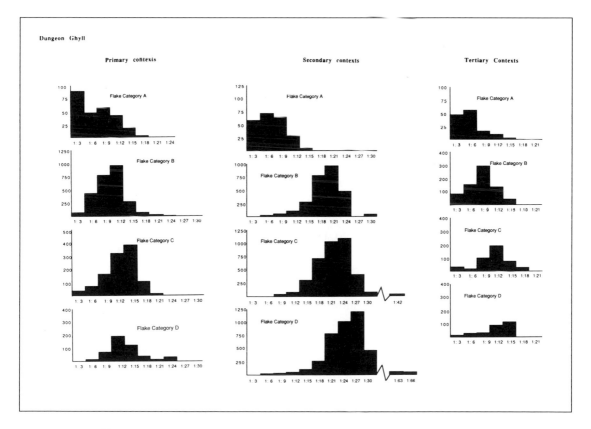

Fig. 6.4 Summary of the excavated material from Dungeon Ghyll, according to the flake categories defined in Table 5.1. The ratios are of flake length to platform width.

There is little to suggest that attempts were made to cope with the risk of breakage or with the development of unworkable flaking angles. This is also reflected in the character of the roughouts. They show little sign of regular alternating flaking; nor is there any indication that the dorsal ridges on these artefacts had been used for controlling flake removals. Those examples which had broken shortly before completion showed an emphasis on establishing symmetry in plan but not in section. The same features are echoed by a lack of symmetry among the flaked blocks from these contexts.

In this case, excavation lent support to the observations made during surface survey. Although the 'extraction pit' itself belonged to a secondary phase, the evidence from the open-cast working suggested that blocks of tuff were extracted in a very rough and ready manner. Stoneworking was inefficient and wasteful, and the earlier stages of axe making were overrepresented among the debitage. In its turn that posed another problem: where did the later parts of that process take place?

Our second objective was to test our claim to have identified 'roughout finishing sites' from the surface finds some distance away from the stone source. Two major excavations took place, at Stake Beck and below Harrison Stickle. Part of another site was salvaged in a footpath in the latter area.

Stake Beck (Fig. 6.5)

The site at Stake Beck was located beside one of the main footpaths linking Borrowdale with the Langdale Fells. At this point the path ran alongside the small stream (Stake Beck) which runs down towards Langstrath. The archaeological material exposed in the path is roughly 200 m from the site of Thunacar Knott, which had also been exposed by peat erosion. That site was excavated in 1969 and 1970 (Clough 1973).

Two trenches were cut into the peat to the south of the footpath, but in only one of these were the archaeological deposits removed. All the debitage was stratified in a layer of sediment, probably of alluvial origin (context 7), sealed by blanket peat (contexts 8–10). The environmental sequence on this site is discussed in chapter 7.

The site had two major components. Its limits were marked by a series of blocks or slabs of rock that occurred naturally in the immediate area. Several of these were stratified within context 7 and did not lie directly on the rock surface, suggesting that they may have been moved from their original positions. This could well result from clearing an area of boulders, and certainly they marked the limits of the distribution of archaeological material on the site. It is not clear whether they had performed any structural role, and none showed traces of damage or modification. Taken together, they formed an arc about 3.4 m in diameter.

Inside this arrangement of slabs and boulders was a dense spread of archaeological material. The outer part of this area contained a distribution of large flakes, some of which extended amongst the boulders, whilst the internal area contained five separate clusters of smaller pieces, almost certainly dumps rather than deposits resulting from *in situ* activity. Similar concentrations seem to have been found in excavation at Thunacar Knott (Clough 1973), but this cannot be checked until the finds from that site have been traced. Charcoal belonging to four species (*Corylus avellana*,

Pomoideae, *Quercus* and *Salix* or *Populus*) was collected from the surface of the working floor at Stake Beck and provided a radiocarbon date of 3410–3730 BC (OXA-2181). All the species were represented by young wood, apart from *Quercus*, which was probably between twenty and seventy-five years old. This determination provides a *terminus ante quem* for the site itself and should be compared with a date of 2850–3250 BC for charcoal found amongst the flakes at Thunacar Knott (BM 676). There is a second date for charcoal from Thunacar Knott (3140–3680 BC), but this must be discounted as its stratigraphic context is unknown.

As predicted from the surface finds, this area saw more emphasis on the later stages of axe production. Although a percentage of the excavated material is consistent with the primary working of tuff, the amount is disproportionately small compared with the frequency of shaping and trimming debris (Fig. 6.6). This suggests that stone was brought to the site as large blocks and partly finished roughouts. It is likely that the large concentrations of debris occurring in both trenches result from the dumping of

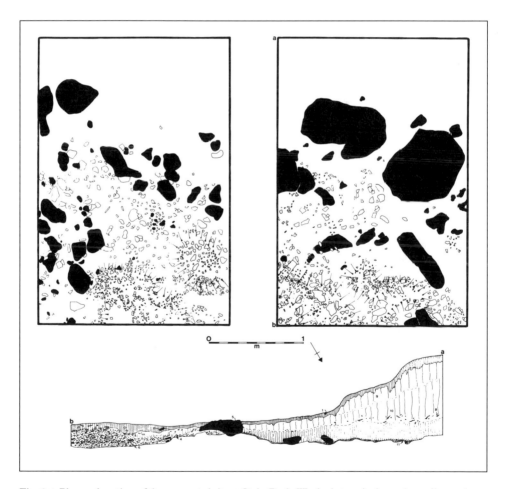

Fig. 6.5 Plan and section of the excavated site at Stake Beck. Worked stone is shown in outline and unworked stone in black.

material. Scatters generated during *in situ* working tend to spread over a wider area and do not form the distinctive 'cones' in which the flakes occur here. This is particularly interesting given Schiffer's distinction between primary and secondary refuse (1987, 58–64). Although many factors influence the movement of refuse from one location to another, potentially hazardous material such as lithic debitage may be removed from activity areas in order to reduce the chances of injury (Hayden and Cannon 1983, 157–60). In other words, the nature of these deposits suggests that sites on rather lower ground may have served as temporary camps. This possibility is strengthened by the occurrence of sixty-three retouched pieces among the waste (0.8% of the total). Again this suggests that activity was not confined to the production of axes. It is worth adding that this excavation also produced a broken flint blade which must have been introduced to the area.

In technological terms, this assemblage raises some interesting questions. Although material was probably being brought to the site, it seems to have been worked in a fairly summary manner. There is little evidence for the trimming of platforms before the flakes were removed, a fact which to some extent accounts for the high frequency of irregular terminations. In each flake category the striking platforms tend to be fairly large, indicating that little concern was felt to position the point of impact. Platform trimming and final shaping flakes are rather uncommon here, although these may be overlooked when material is moved to a secondary location. Again this influences the flake length:platform thickness ratios, which tend to be low. Cleghorn (1982) argues that this ratio provides a useful index for the level of skill of the producers. We concur

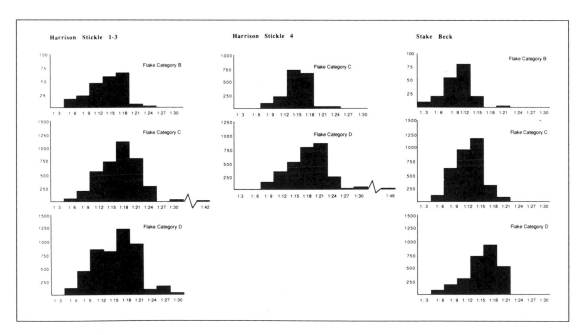

Fig. 6.6 Summary of the excavated material from Stake Beck and Harrison Stickle according to the flake categories defined in Table 5.1. The ratios are of flake length to platform width.

with that view, but rather than serving as a measure of innate ability, as he suggests, this ratio may provide an indication of the extent to which the stoneworkers were concerned with the possibility of failure, or with control over the form taken by the final product. The same argument applies to the ratio of flake thickness to length.

In most respects the results of this exercise were consistent with our original hypothesis, although the existence of structural evidence was completely unexpected. The raw material had apparently been introduced as roughouts or large blocks, and stoneworking possessed a rather summary character. In most cases the later stages of axe making were overrepresented. The presence of a small amount of retouched material may provide one indication that places on the lower ground had doubled as temporary camp sites. Although this area is exposed to the elements today, it could have been below the Neolithic tree line (see below, p. 138).

Harrison Stickle (Figs. 6.7 and 6.8; Pl. 6.1)

We can usefully compare these observations with the results of work on two other sites. Both were located on a break of slope below Harrison Stickle, and again they were probably more sheltered during the Neolithic period. They had both been cut by the main footpath linking Langdale with the valley which runs towards Lake Windermere. The larger of these was investigated by three small trenches running from the lower edge of a blockfield towards the path, where a substantial number of flakes could be seen in section. These trenches revealed an abrupt change of level in the bedrock which had not been apparent from the surface topography, and Trench 3 included the edge of a feature of uncertain origin cutting into the mountainside. Its filling included

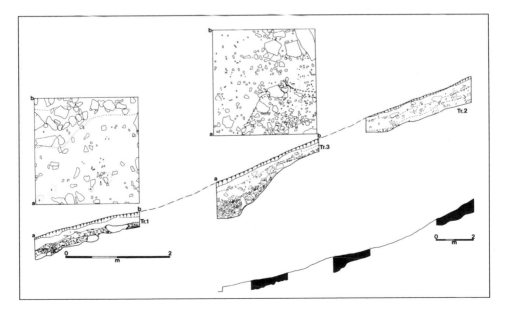

Fig. 6.7 Plan and section of Harrison Stickle trenches 1–3.

a small amount of debitage (Fig. 6.7). Virtually all the archaeological material was found in the cuttings closest to the footpath. It would take large-scale excavation to tell whether this 'platform' was an artificial feature, but in any case it certainly formed the focus for Neolithic activity. Detailed study of the flakes across the excavated area confirmed that they were *in situ*, for they did not show the sorting by weight that identifies eroded material. The main deposit of debitage was in the lowest of the three trenches where it was directly associated with charcoal. This belonged to four species: *Betula*, Pomoideae, *Quercus* and *Salix* or *Populus*. The oak was mainly between twenty and thirty-five years old, whilst the other species had a maximum age of about twenty-five years. Together they provided a radiocarbon date of 3525–3780 BC (BM 2625).

The debitage from this site indicates a similar range of productive tasks to those undertaken at Stake Beck (Fig. 6.6). There is the same emphasis on the later stages of axe production, and it seems likely that material was introduced to the site in the form of large, partly worked blocks. Again the ratios of flake length to platform thickness are relatively high. Given the frequency of platform trimming chips, this suggests more emphasis on preparing the edge of a block before flakes were removed. The incidence of this practice seems to increase through the reduction sequence, suggesting a corresponding increase in the level of preparation once a rough form had been achieved. In the earlier stages of the reduction sequence, the position of scars and ridges on many of the flakes was distinctly irregular. This contrasts with their position on thinning and shaping pieces, suggesting that a clear routine of alternate flaking did not emerge until the end of the production process.

These distinctions are interesting considering that the site is situated away from workable outcrops of stone. Although the raw material may have been tested during its selection, extraction and preliminary working, the movement of blocks to a secondary location took place before much attention was paid to the possibility of

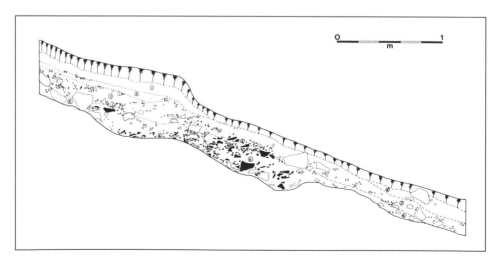

Fig. 6.8 Section of Harrison Stickle trench 4. Worked stone is shown in black.

failure. Until the thinning stage the stone continued to be treated in a fairly summary fashion. The occurrence of large numbers of thinning and shaping flakes at this site supports the idea that the final finishing of axes was undertaken with a relatively high degree of control. Many of these pieces bear dorsal ridges which run down from a central platform crest, indicating the careful positioning of the percussor. The incidence of hinge and step fractures on individual flakes is lower than it is at Stake Beck; indeed, it is also lower than the frequencies recorded in surface samples from both these sites. A smaller trend can be seen in the flake thickness:length ratios, which are slightly higher than those at Stake Beck. In common with the latter site, a small proportion (0.15%) of the excavated material showed signs of retouch.

The second site below Harrison Stickle was immediately upslope from trenches 1–3 in the side of the same path (trench 4). Here large quantities of debitage had been collected in a natural hollow (Fig. 6.8; Pl. 6.1). The assemblage was tightly focussed within the trench, suggesting that this material had been worked in the immediate vicinity. Again there was no evidence of size sorting to suggest that it had accumulated through erosion. The concentration of debitage was directly associated with charcoal of four species, *Betula*, Pomoideae, *Corylus avellana* and *Salix* or *Populus*, all from wood under twenty-five years old. These provided a radiocarbon date of 3530–3780 BC (BM 2626).

In most respects this assemblage matches that found in trenches 1–3 (Fig. 6.6), and

Plate 6.1 Neolithic debitage exposed by footpath erosion on the flank of Harrison Stickle.

exactly the same proportion is retouched. On the other hand, it is interesting that the debitage shows an even greater emphasis on the last stages of production. Most of the debris reflects the final process of trimming, thinning and shaping, as if crude roughouts were being 'finished' here. Once again the ratios of flake length:platform thickness and flake thickness:length tend to be relatively high. As with the material from trenches 1–3, this assemblage suggests that the later stages of working saw a higher level of preparation and control. Although the group appeared to be distinct from the other 'sites' in the area, this may reflect the separation of different stages in the manufacturing process.

So far we have suggested that at Dungeon Ghyll large blocks of tuff were extracted from an open-cast working, tested for quality and often rejected. Those that were used were prepared in an extremely summary fashion and taken away from the site. That interpretation is supported by the character of the three assemblages excavated away from the stone source, for here there is evidence that the later stages of axe making are significantly overrepresented. A detailed reconstruction of the debitage from these sites, combined with analysis of the surviving roughouts, shows that the material may have reached them after preliminary working of a rudimentary character; indeed, in many cases angular blocks of stone were introduced before any attempt had been made to fashion an axe. There were striking differences between some of these sites – a significant proportion of retouched pieces at Stake Beck; a higher standard of finishing on Harrison Stickle – but at least the broad outlines were those predicted in our surface evaluation.

Loft Crag, Site DS 87 (Fig. 6.9)

Some of these processes are graphically illustrated by the results of our other salvage excavation, on a small group of worked material eroding from under the peat to the north-west of Loft Crag. Excavation revealed a tight cluster of worked stone. As with the cones of debris recorded at Stake Beck, it seemed unlikely that this was an *in situ* knapping cluster, particularly since there were so few small chips, spalls and platform trimming flakes.

The different classes of waste reflect all the stages of production apart from initial shaping and mass reduction; indeed, all the flakes bear dorsal scars, indicating earlier removals that are not accounted for in this collection. The material was not plentiful and covered a very limited area – features which made it suitable for an attempt at refitting.

This material appears to have been generated during the production of two axes – one from a crudely flaked block and the other from a partially flaked roughout. This explains the relatively high frequency of the finer, curved thinning flakes in the assemblage as a whole. Material in this category was produced on two occasions, whilst debris from earlier stages of reduction is represented only once. The products appear to have been very crude. In outline they were roughly symmetrical, but they showed little symmetry in cross-section. Not only does this group recall some of the small scatters on Scafell Pike: it reflects in miniature one of the basic approaches to the extraction and working of stone in the complex as a whole.

Dungeon Ghyll – secondary phases (Fig. 6.10)

We must now turn to the other production sequence suggested in our preliminary studies, and to do this we can begin by discussing the second phase of activity in the open-cast working at Dungeon Ghyll. This was represented by contexts 2, 4 and 8, which were separated from the earlier levels by a thin soil horizon. At the northern end of the trench the distinction was also revealed by a different degree of compaction against the face of context 11. It seemed that these features marked the limits of a pit dug into the central section of the existing excavation. When the loose blocky material filling this pit subsided, it left the distinctive hollow visible on the surface today. It had been this secondary feature whose outlines were traced by resistivity survey.

Our interpretation is supported by the character of the debitage, which appears to reflect a different approach to stoneworking (Fig. 6.4). The frequency of different flake classes suggests that all stages in the production process are represented. Indeed, differential patination on a number of blocks and broken roughouts indicates that the raw material had been obtained by reworking some of the stone discarded during earlier use of the site.

This phase saw a marked increase in the degree of platform preparation and in the preliminary trimming of edges prior to flaking, even on material removed during the primary and secondary stages of the reduction sequence. The flake thickness:length ratios also reflect this change. Thinning flakes travel further across the face of the roughout and there is a general decrease in the frequency of hinge and step terminations. The roughouts found in this context bear out these distinctions. They are far more regular and are symmetrical in section and plan. The waste flakes are easy to group into technological and morphological classes, adding weight to the idea that production was characterised by highly structured routines, quite different from those

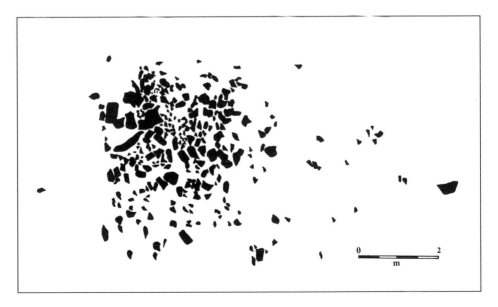

Fig. 6.9 Plan of the knapping cluster on Loft Crag.

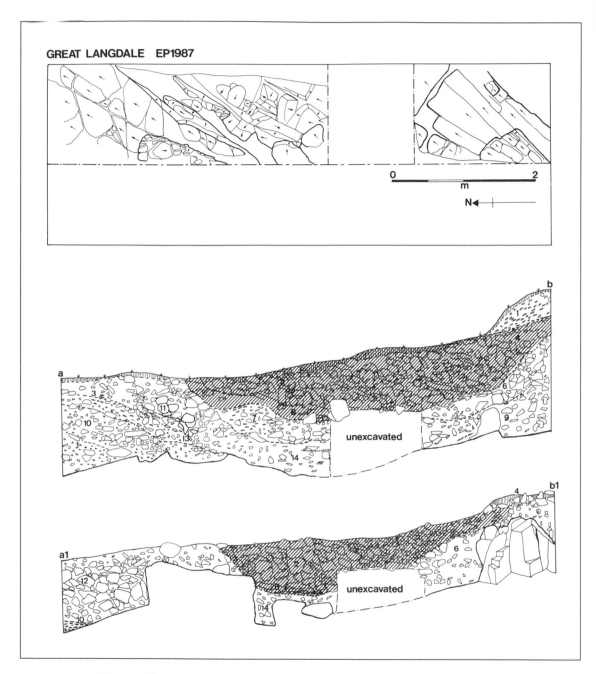

Fig. 6.10 Plan and section of the excavated site at Dungeon Ghyll. The section drawing is shaded to highlight the contexts belonging to the second phase of stoneworking.

employed during the first phase of activity on the site. Only 0.001% of this material was retouched. In addition, hammerstones occurred in these contexts, but not in earlier horizons.

The southern end of the excavation included a further layer of stoneworking debris, separated from the filling of the recut by a thin layer of silt containing small pieces of charcoal, identified as *Calluna vulgaris* or *Erica*. This provided a radiocarbon date of AD 330–440 (OXA-2178). In technological terms the flaked material resembles that found in the primary levels of the site, and in the light of this date it seems probable that it had been displaced during later land use.

At Langdale itself the evidence from the recut pit has most in common with the results of excavation on Top Buttress, close to the summit of Pike o' Stickle. Two sites were excavated here, but before the results of this work are summarised, we must say rather more about the way in which it was carried out. The sites were situated on narrow ledges on one of the steepest parts of the mountain (Fig. 6.2). This was one of the most inaccessible locations in the entire complex. There was no clear access, and passage to and from the sites involved climbing along a number of precipitous ledges. This meant that the material retained for analysis had to be transported to the top of the crag before it could be taken away. Since we wished to examine a substantial sample of the finds from every context, purely practical considerations dictated that excavation should be on a very limited scale (Pl. 6.2). Moreover the very problem which we had identified in the extraction of the tuff also affected the conduct of this work, since it was necessary to retain the spoil within a very restricted area and to

Plate 6.2 Excavation against the quarry face on Top Buttress.

prevent it from falling downhill. Unauthorised digging had already shown that unless this could be managed effectively, disturbance of the ground surface would lead to serious erosion (cf. Claris and Quartermaine 1989).

Top Buttress, Site 98 (Fig. 6.11; Pl. 6.2)

The first excavation to consider was on Site 98, one of a number of large quarries situated on the south face of Pike o' Stickle. It consisted of a substantial deposit of waste flakes, hammerstones and broken roughouts which spread away from a sheer rock face to form a considerable scree. The archaeological deposits were known to have been much deeper until some of this material was dislodged in hunting for axes (C. Fell pers. comm.), and conchoidal fractures could be recognised on the surface of the outcrop to a height of 2–3 m above the remaining deposits of debitage. Because this material was so mobile, the eastern part of the excavation was located beneath a large overhang, which had been worked from two directions. By doing so we could reduce the chances of collecting material derived from sites on higher ledges.

In order to minimise any possible damage, a limited area, measuring only 2 × 1 m, was excavated against the rock face, and the debitage was removed in 10 cm spits. Each of these levels contained between 5000 and 10,000 flakes, making the implementation of a sampling strategy essential. Approximately 1000 pieces from each context (10%–15% by volume) were retained for analysis, together with a bulk sample designed to assess variations in the density of chips, fragments and flakes which were too small to measure. This amounted to 5% of the volume of material in each spit.

The work revealed a deep sequence of deposits, although there was no reason to suppose that they had taken long to form (Fig. 6.11). The site seems to have witnessed alternating episodes of quarrying and stone axe production. Large amounts of charcoal were found throughout the profile, suggesting that fire-setting had been employed in the preparation and working of the rock face. Analysis of this material shows that branches of birch and young oak were brought to the site for the purpose. Although the site was excavated in 10 cm spits, little analytical detail is lost by combining the results from each pair of spits. Although this makes no difference to the number of pieces to be studied, it does reduce the need for excessive repetition in describing the genesis of these deposits.

They could have formed quite quickly. The distinctions that can be drawn between the different stratigraphic levels are entirely technological. Considerable volumes of debris from quarrying and stoneworking can be generated over short periods. On the other hand, it is possible to talk of different episodes in the development of the profile. Debris at the base of the section reflected all stages in the production of stone axes. Given the step-like profile of the mountain, it is possible that the raw material for this episode of production was obtained on the ledge below Site 98.

This initial phase was followed by a horizon in which debris from quarrying predominated (levels MN–KL). Large angular blocks and massive broken flakes provided evidence for the removal of material directly from the rock face. It is not surprising that it was at this level that the first substantial deposits of charcoal were

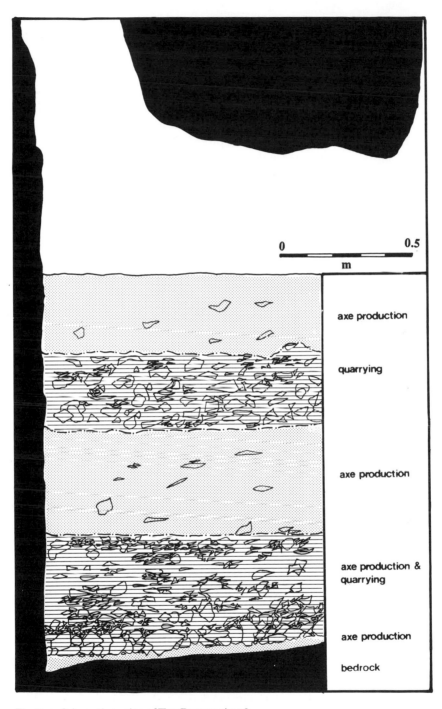

0   0.5

m

axe production

quarrying

axe production

axe production & quarrying

axe production

bedrock

Fig. 6.11 Schematic section of Top Buttress site 98.

found, suggesting the use of fire in the preparation and working of the outcrop. Most of the larger pieces of stone carried flake scars indicating testing and initial preparation, and all the biggest flakes were broken. They had probably been abandoned because of errors or miss-hits during quarrying.

These two horizons encompass the main sources of variation seen on the site as a whole. All the stages of the reduction sequence were represented, and it would appear that both flakes and blocks were exploited for making axes. The clearest indication that a particular horizon reflected production, rather than extraction, was provided by the large quantities of small chips and trimming waste. The varying density of these pieces throughout the profile echoed the changes suggested by other classes of debris. They occurred in particularly high densities at the base of the section, then decreased in level MN, only to increase again in level KL. This suggests that to some extent the winning of material from the rock face overlapped with the production of axes.

Above this level, horizons IJ to GH contained little evidence for intensive quarrying. Instead, the debitage reflected axe making. Here again the volume of small chips and flakes was particularly high. This gave way to a major episode of quarrying between horizons EF and CD, and larger blocks and flakes were again mixed with flaking debris towards the top of horizon CD. The upper levels of the site (AB) appear to mark a greater emphasis on axe production. This was the final phase of exploitation for which any evidence survived.

The technological characteristics of the worked stone support our interpretation of the sequence (Fig. 6.12). Thus the finds from layers with large amounts of quarry debris show the widest range of platform sizes. This is to be expected given the size of some of the mauls and hammers used to extract the rock – some of these tools were found in the excavation. Similarly, the frequency of irregular flake terminations tends to be higher in these levels than in deposits associated with axe production.

Those contexts in which axe manufacture appears to predominate exhibit a very different set of characteristics. They also contrast with those observed in the 'finishing sites' at Stake Beck and below Harrison Stickle. Here the level of control and precision was appreciably higher. This is evidenced by the ratios of flake length to platform thickness and flake thickness to flake length. Every category of flake shows a high incidence of platform trimming, suggesting that even during the preliminary stages of shaping and mass reduction, care was being taken to minimise the risk of crushing or hinge fracturing along the edge of the roughout. This was true whether axes were made from blocks or from flakes. As one might expect, these horizons contained large quantities of trimming and preparation debris. This emphasis on careful preparation is reflected in a low frequency of hinge and step fractures, especially among the primary and secondary flakes.

Many of the flakes in these two groups also have facetted platforms. Together with the patterning of the dorsal ridges, this suggests that a clear routine of alternate flaking was followed. This is also true of the debitage from later stages of axe making, but the fact that it is present throughout the sequence may indicate a highly structured approach to stoneworking. From the outset attempts were made to establish symmetry in the plan and section of the roughouts. This is supported by the character of the ridges and scars on the dorsal surface of many flakes. A large number of them have a dorsal ridge that originates at a central crest on the platform edge, which implies a high level of accuracy in positioning the point of impact. At the same time, the frequency of blade-like flakes with dorsal scars cutting across their long axis from both directions suggests a greater emphasis on establishing a symmetrical cross-section. Similarly, the incidence of thinning flakes with laterally opposed dorsal scars shows that at this stage flaking often meant removing material right across the face of the roughout. Only 0.04% of the finds from Site 98 showed any sign of retouch.

On this site (and on Site 95) there is no difficulty in assigning flakes to different stages in the production process, since the majority are 'typical' examples. In other words, even the waste shows a relatively high level of standardisation, suggesting that recurrent routines were followed. The data from Site 98 reflect a concerted effort to anticipate and avoid errors from the start of the reduction sequence. More important, they also suggest that the producers had a clear idea of the intended form of the polished axe, and attempted to realise it through flaking.

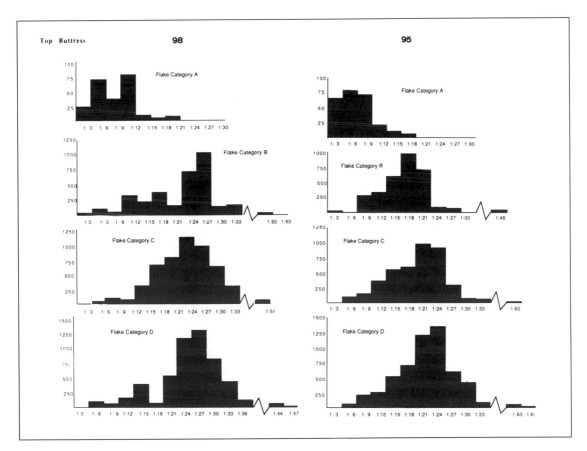

Fig. 6.12 Summary of the excavated material from sites on Top Buttress according to the flake categories defined in Table 5.1. The ratios are of flake length to platform width.

Top Buttress, Site 95 (Fig. 6.13)

The last site to be excavated was situated on the ledge directly above Site 98. This consisted of a small cave, whose walls and ceiling carried conchoidal scars from the removal of large flakes. The cave mouth was 50 cm high, and the floor and ceiling sloped down towards the rear, following the natural bedding of the tuff. This floor was littered with a substantial quantity of debitage, suggesting a similar range of material to that encountered on Site 98. Here we had to contend with even greater limitations of space, for the opening of the cave was only a metre wide. This left very little room for manœuvre. In the event, excavation had to be confined to an area 1.3 m square. The material was removed in 10 cm spits, and sampled on the same basis as on Site 98.

Again it seems likely that extraction and production took place on the site and that axes were made from both flakes and blocks. In this case, however, the profile did not show the same pattern of alternating episodes. The principal deposit of quarrying debris overlay a small lens of charcoal on the true floor of the cave (PQ–MN). Like the lowest level of Site 98, that floor showed signs of conchoidal scarring. Larger fragments of stone characteristic of quarrying occurred at other levels in the stratigraphy – notably in horizon GH – indicating that extraction continued here after this initial phase. Since it was not possible to extend the excavation to the rear wall of the cave, we could not rule out the possibility that similar debris had been pushed further back into this feature.

One of the main contrasts between the two profiles on Top Buttress is the way in which each suggested a different sequence of episodes. Site 98 showed alternating episodes of quarrying and axe production, but with little evidence that these were spread over any length of time. At Site 95 we can propose a rather different development. Technological analysis suggests that between horizons KL and GH all the stages of production were undertaken in the cave itself. Here the high volume of small chips and fragments, and the horizontal bedding of the flakes, evidenced a more gradual build-up of production debris. Substantial lenses of charcoal, like those at the base of the profile, may indicate that fire was used in the preparation and extraction of the stone.

The episodic nature of this activity is suggested by another feature. In contrast to Site 98, larger quantities of soil occurred within this profile, although it did not extend in homogeneous layers across the trench. Instead, small cones of soil were observed on top of the layers of horizontally bedded flakes, and usually these were sealed by similar material. It may be that it had dripped through the roof in solution, precipitating out on the floor of the cave. Although it is difficult to determine the length of time needed for such deposits to form, it does seem likely that the sequence of activity had been punctuated by short intervals of disuse.

The pattern of *in situ* working appeared to be interrupted at a depth of 80–90 cm from the surface, at the top of spit GH. At this point the knapping debris was overlain by material of a very different character. Although every stage of axe production was represented, more of the flakes had been broken or crushed, suggesting that they had been heavily trampled; this level was more consolidated than the others and contained very little charcoal. Clearly axe production continued on the site, but the evidence of

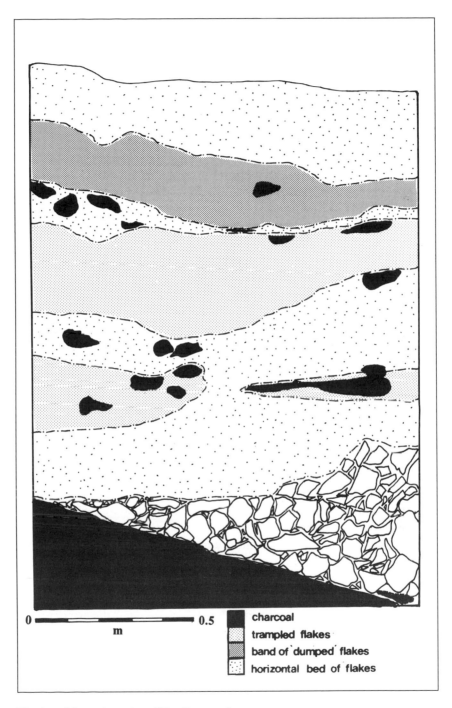

Fig. 6.13 Schematic section of Top Buttress site 95.

trampling suggests that the rate at which the deposits developed may have changed. Either the intensity of activity in the cave increased, or, as seems more likely, there was a decrease in the rate at which the debris was generated.

This horizon of trampled material was overlain by another layer of horizontally bedded flaking debris. Again all the stages of axe production were present, and the recovery of substantial quantities of small chips and flakes provided evidence of working in the immediate vicinity. At the same time, substantial amounts of charcoal reappeared at this level, suggesting the use of fire to extract the raw material.

Perhaps the most significant break in the sequence occurred at a depth of 50–60 cm (horizon CD/EF). Here the band of horizontally bedded material was sealed by a layer of jumbled and poorly sorted debris sloping down towards the back of the cave. It seems as if this level accumulated very rapidly. Its origin may be explained by the results of technological analysis. The larger classes of mass reduction and thinning waste predominate, and there is a marked decrease in the frequency and volume of the smaller pieces thought to indicate *in situ* working. Rather than being a location at which production took place, the cave became an area in which stoneworking debris was dumped. This may not mean that material was carried to the cave over any distance since the rock face above the narrow ledges showed signs of conchoidal fracturing.

This distinctive deposit was covered by a horizontally bedded layer of waste, which in turn was sealed by a mineral soil about 20 cm thick. Rather surprisingly, this layer (horizon AB–CD) provided evidence for a return to *in situ* working after a period in which the cave had been used as a dump. On the other hand, it is possible to detect a change in the nature of the debitage. Although working certainly took place inside the cave, the smaller proportion of preliminary shaping and mass reduction flakes suggests that now it provided a convenient location at which to work material that had been extracted elsewhere.

The main period of use of Site 95 is bracketed by two radiocarbon dates. The earlier sample came from a depth of 130–140 cm and contained charcoal of four species: *Betula*, Pomoideae, *Quercus* and *Salix* or *Populus*. The oak had been between twenty and seventy-five years old (mostly between twenty and thirty-five), whilst the other species were no more than twenty-five years old. Together this material provided a date of 3370–3690 BC (BM 2628). The other sample was of very similar composition and came from a depth of 40-50 cm. The charcoal belonged to four species – *Betula*, *Corylus avellana*, *Quercus* and *Salix* or *Populus* – and the age distribution was exactly the same, except that the hazel charcoal came from wood not more than twenty-five years old whilst some of the beech charcoal had the same age range as the oak. The resulting radiocarbon date was 3100–3500 BC (BM 2627).

In technological terms the material from the cave has much in common with the debitage from Site 98 (Fig. 6.12). The proportion of retouched material was even lower (0.02%) and hammerstones were found in both excavations. Variations in the size of the striking platforms in the lowest levels, in spit GH and at the top of spit EF, are likely to result from the fact that both extraction and production took place here. The finds from other contexts suggest that similar levels of control and precision were exercised in flaking the tuff and that all the stages of axe production were undertaken in the same location. Again the debitage suggests that recurrent routines were being followed; this was particularly apparent from the material found in spits KL–GH. In addition, the patterning of the scars on the dorsal surface of flakes suggests that attempts were made to correct mistakes. When heavy hinge fracturing or crushing occurred on an edge, reflaking from a different angle, often the opposite edge, was employed.

There is one further point of comparison between the cave and Site 98. This is suggested by a photograph taken in the 1940s, before this area was disturbed by private collectors (C. Fell pers. comm.). It shows a large scree of debitage masking the face of Site 98. Such a deposit must have been created by the movement of material from above, and for this reason at least the final stages of activity at the cave should have been later than those on the ledge below.

Summary

This chapter began with a series of questions concerning variability within and between the assemblages at Great Langdale. It should be apparent that these excavations supply at least some of the answers. Let us complete our account of that work by summarising its main results. Their significance, and the changing role of Langdale in its regional setting, will form the subject matter of chapter 7.

Our first need was to determine how far the results of surface evaluation would be supported by detailed analysis of debitage from stratified contexts. On the whole the results of excavation were consistent with those first impressions, although in several cases they added unexpected detail to that outline. At Dungeon Ghyll they showed that our surface samples had identified only the earlier of two quite different phases of activity, and at Stake Beck they brought to light a number of retouched flakes that had not been predicted from our earlier reconnaissance. The presence of structural evidence in both of these areas was even more surprising. Apart from these observations, the work tended to confirm the distinctions recognised at an earlier stage of the research.

It now seems quite impossible to subsume all the patterns into one synthetic category: to characterise *the* nature and organisation of axe production at Great Langdale. In fact analysis of the material recovered during excavation supports the impression formed during surface sampling that exploitation of the stone source was structured in at least two different ways. Whilst the nature of the products seems to be the same in all deposits, that cannot be said for the means by which they were realised.

The main contrast is between an essentially informal way of working, in which little attempt was made to anticipate technological problems, and one in which a far more structured and precise routine was followed. One approach resulted in the creation of crude, frequently asymmetrical roughouts, often with deep scars and irregular hinges on their surfaces, whilst the other seems to have been directed towards the production of axes that closely resembled the forms that they would take after polishing. This distinction is mirrored by the evidence for two different ways of organising the work. In one case the different stages of axe making took place at separate locations; in the other, every stage in the process happened at the stone source. There are certain links between the two ways of making axes and the methods of extracting the raw material, but these technological distinctions are not sufficient to account for all these contrasts, and to some extent they may be an artefact of change through time. That view was first suggested on the basis of observations among the rock sources of Pike o' Stickle, where the process of extracting the stone most probably moved up the mountainside with time. Somewhat unexpectedly, this idea found decisive support in the results of excavation at Dungeon Ghyll, where the first major stage of activity resembled that at Stake Beck, Harrison Stickle and to some extent Central Buttress, whilst the reuse of that location involved the same working methods as those used at Sites 95 and 98. It is important not to exaggerate these contrasts, however, for the radiocarbon dates from different sites overlap with one another, and the latest of all comes from Thunacar Knott, provisionally interpreted as a 'roughout finishing site'.

This final stage in our fieldwork was intended to characterise activity at the stone source using a number of different kinds of information. Armed with these results, we could begin the task of exploring the significance of the changes that took place in Cumbria. Yet if we are to follow the line of argument developed in the first section of this study, this process of interpretation must involve a widening of focus. However detailed the analyses reported in this chapter, they are only descriptions of one broad class of data, and in themselves they are not enough to suggest why the character and organisation of working underwent such a radical change. We can only understand the developments that took place at the stone source by considering them in their broader context. We begin that process in the following chapter.

7

Great Langdale in its regional context

Introduction

We concluded the previous chapter with a short summary of the main results of the excavations at Great Langdale and related these to the working hypotheses formed during surface survey. Those results were encouraging, but there is a sense in which they might seem to have taken us away from the more general issues with which we started. In this chapter we begin to work outwards from Great Langdale again, first by attempting to set activity at the stone source in its wider economic and social setting and then by relating the history of these sites to the changing character of activities in the Cumbrian lowlands. Once this has been accomplished, we can pick up many of the broader issues discussed in earlier sections, tracing the changing significance of Langdale axes across the country as a whole and using that experience to draw some lessons for the study of exchange systems in general.

Interpreting the sequence at Great Langdale

The first stage in this process is to consider the wider significance of those findings. We can begin by stressing again the extent of the spatial and chronological variation identified in a complex that had once been interpreted as a homogeneous entity. It is also clear that few of the variations observed at the stone source had their roots in geological or topographical conditions. Naturally, the methods used to extract the stone depended on the orientation of the bands of tuff – it would be impossible to establish a vertical quarry face where the raw material was fractured and horizontally bedded – but this was *not* the sole determinant of the manner in which production was undertaken. Raw material with effectively the same mechanical properties is found from Troughton Beck to Loft Crag, a distance of more than a kilometre, but over that range the nature and intensity of extraction varied markedly, and the character of roughout production also changed. In some areas there were exposures of accessible and good-quality stone which had never been exploited (Bradley and Ford 1986); yet these outcrops must have been passed in order to reach quarry sites that presented major problems of access.

The same point can be illustrated by the evidence from Dungeon Ghyll, where there was a significant change in the ways in which the stone was being worked *at a single site*. This only emphasises the point that some of the variation must have been due to changes in the mode of working through time. We made the same point in our account of the surface finds from Pike o' Stickle: the wider range of values for the flakes on Central Buttress may indicate that the debris which was generated there differed from that created in the quarries higher up the mountain. Whilst this cannot be proved, the fact that a number of quarried benches and ledges on the side of Pike o' Stickle are sealed by scree emanating from above suggests that extraction and production progressed up the mountain with time. This argument is strengthened by the radiocarbon dates that indicate that Site 95 was used at a later date than the 'finishing sites' at Stake Beck and Harrison Stickle. Thunacar Knott remains a problem, however, as the finds from that site have been misplaced.

We can recognise variations in three distinct aspects of the data. Although the nature of the finished products remained largely unchanged through time, the means by which they were realised appears to have altered quite dramatically. We have already recognised the contrasts between an essentially *ad hoc* form of working in which little attempt was made to cope with the risk of irregularity or breakage, and another in which a more structured routine was followed. This marks a change in the level of control and precision exercised during production, and to some extent in the efficiency with which the raw material was used. More attention was paid to preparing the stone and anticipating and correcting errors, with the result that far less of the raw material was wasted. This also suggests that the production process was perceived rather differently.

The same changes can be recognised among the rejected roughouts from this complex. Those from Dungeon Ghyll reveal a striking contrast between the primary and secondary levels of the site (Fig. 7.1). The examples found in the earlier layers were often irregular and had been worked in an extremely summary fashion. On the other hand, even those made from blocks in the secondary levels of this site showed a greater emphasis on creating symmetry in both section and plan, as well as a closer adherence to a pattern of alternating the working face, even during the preliminary stages of manufacture. Whilst these features recall the character of the technology in evidence on Top Buttress, the finds from the earlier deposits at Dungeon Ghyll recall those from Stake Beck, Loft Crag and the two 'finishing sites' below Harrison Stickle. There seems to have been a shift towards a far closer realisation of the intended form of the axe during 'roughing out'. Our experimental evidence reveals that this would have had significant implications for the amount of effort invested in polishing these artefacts. The time and energy required to undertake this work should have decreased during the local sequence, whilst the shift towards defining the axe's form at an earlier stage suggests a corresponding change in people's perceptions of the object itself. It surely reflects the emergence of clearer morphological classes: in short, a more explicit concern with the *form* of the axe.

Distinctions can also be drawn in terms of the spatial organisation of production. Where it was only loosely structured in technological terms, the different tasks tended to be dispersed around the landscape. This can be seen at many of the sites on Scafell Pike, at Dungeon Ghyll, on the edges of South Scree and in the excavated site at Stake Beck. It may also have been the case below Harrison Stickle, although here the character of stoneworking could have changed towards the final stages of the reduction sequence. This need not reflect the development of a 'production line' approach, since the distances between these separate locations can be considerable.

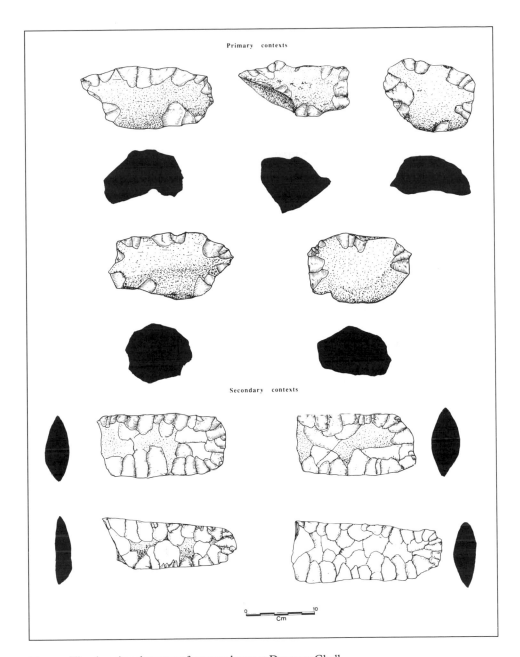

Fig. 7.1 The changing character of axe roughouts at Dungeon Ghyll.

By contrast, those sites with evidence for a different approach to stoneworking also occupy a quite distinctive setting. The most dramatic are located on Top Buttress, where all the stages of axe production were undertaken in the same place. Their remote position poses an interesting problem of interpretation. We have shown that the mechanical properties of the rock were little different from those in other parts of the complex, yet it seems that those making the axes sought out especially inaccessible locations. Their position towards the summit of the mountain is undoubtedly spectacular and commands an unparalleled view over the surrounding country (Pl. 7.1). In a sense it would have been efficient to perform all the stages of axe making in such places: this would reduce the bulk of material to be carried over the crag and would mean that unsuitable pieces could be eliminated before they had been transported any distance. Yet there are two major flaws in this argument. In the first place there was no need to have created this problem at all, since equally suitable rock was available in far more accessible and hospitable locations. At the same time, this distinctive way of organising production was also found in places where there were no problems of access whatever, in particular the secondary levels of the open-cast working at Dungeon Ghyll, and a similar site exposed by our test pit just above the top of South Scree. All display a similar technological profile to Top Buttress on Pike o' Stickle.

There may be a less mundane reason for this arrangement. Perhaps it was the very remoteness of a number of these sites that added to their importance. These formal, maintained quarries allow the delimitation of working areas in a way that would hardly be possible among the more disparate spreads of boulders and natural scree that seem to have been exploited at an early stage in the sequence. Once the quarries were established, conscious distinctions may have been drawn between the places in which the axes could be made by particular groups. If such groups undertook repeated trips to the area for the purpose of producing artefacts, this process may have been accompanied by specific notions of where it was appropriate to work. In addition, some of these locations would not have been easy to discover by chance; it was necessary to know exactly how to reach them. We shall return to this question when we consider the sources of the hammerstones brought onto these sites from the lowlands.

Taking these arguments together, it seems likely that Scafell Pike, Glaramara and Great Langdale saw different patterns of development. If we can extrapolate from the sequence established in our fieldwork, all three areas *could* have been in use from an early stage; candidates at Langdale itself include South Scree, the original open-cast working at Dungeon Ghyll and possibly the sites at Loft Crag and Troughton Beck. With the passage of time, it seems as if it was the Langdale complex that became the principal source of raw materials. Although all too little is known about activity at Glaramara, the deposits on Scafell Pike reveal a very informal approach to procurement and production, and here the work was undertaken on a rather small scale.

This has serious implications for the relationship between the axe production sites and the broader processes of exchange, for the shifting character of axe making at Great Langdale may be echoed by the large number of Group VI products that were exchanged eastwards across the Pennines (Manby 1965 and 1979). It may be no accident that of the three main production area in Cumbria this is the one which would be best placed to serve the settlement zone that lies close to the routes through the high ground into Yorkshire. We shall return to this point in a later chapter, but for the moment it only emphasises the importance of studying these sites in relation to their wider hinterland.

The environmental sequence in Cumbria

The first stage in that study is to consider the environmental evidence from the Langdale Fells and from the lowlands of Cumbria (Fig. 7.2). We have already seen

Plate 7.1 Aerial photograph of the Langdale Pikes looking east towards Lake Windermere and the foothills of the Pennines. Photograph: Bob Bewley. Crown copyright reserved.

how the principal production areas seem to have been located for access from the major valleys. At the same time, the sheer scale of the central massif means that communications *across* the high ground may have been restricted. For this reason such areas must be considered separately.

The first region to discuss is the coastal plain, particularly the well-researched area to the west of the Cumbrian mountains, where extensive field survey has taken place (Cherry and Cherry 1983, 1984, 1985, 1986 and 1987a). Here the environmental and archaeological records are in close accord, although our information still lacks much fine detail. The coastal strip seems to have been used intensively from the later Mesolithic period onwards. Flint scatters are common but tend to follow the shoreline fairly closely, especially in the earliest phases, but we know all too little about the character of domestic sites. The Mesolithic occupation of the coastal region south of Ravenglass has been examined in detail, and excavation has brought to light some structural evidence thought to indicate fairly long-term occupation (Bonsall *et al.* 1989). Although this area could well have sustained year-round settlement, it is not possible to prove this. This coastal zone is one area which lacks the Mesolithic/ Neolithic hiatus so typical of the British sequence, and there is little to separate the carbon dates for the 'Mesolithic' occupation site at Eskmeals from the earliest date for the waterlogged site at Ehenside Tarn, which is assigned to the 'Neolithic' period on the basis of its artefact assemblage (Darbishire 1873). The futility of such divisions is apparent when we realise that the structural evidence from both sites is really rather similar; if anything, the later site left more ephemeral traces. Apart from finds of pottery, almost the only feature to distinguish these two occupations was the presence of Group VI axes at Ehenside Tarn.

This minimal view of the Mesolithic/Neolithic transition is supported by the environmental data from the coastal zone. These provide fairly strong evidence for human interference with the vegetation cover some time *before* the Elm Decline, which traditionally marks the beginning of the Neolithic period (Pennington 1970 and 1975; Annable 1987, map 9). In fact the distribution of such early clearance horizons in Cumbria is mainly on the coastline.

At one level this simply emphasises the artificiality of the period division, and on present evidence it seems possible that cereals were available during a period that was otherwise 'Mesolithic'. Similarly, some of the Neolithic clearances were no more obvious than those attributed to the Mesolithic population. To some extent these distinctions may be an artefact of pollen analysis itself – for example, at Barfield Tarn, where lake sediments were analysed, there was a level of cereal pollen associated with charcoal and eroded soil, but this was probably recognised because the samples were taken next to the settled area (Pennington 1975, 76). Otherwise the one clear trend in the environmental evidence is that the areas first settled at this time show a history of continuing clearance during the Later Neolithic. This interpretation is supported by the distribution of diagnostic flintwork (Annable 1987; Edmonds 1989).

It seems likely that much the same sequence applies to activity to the south of the Cumbrian massif, where the evidence is derived largely from the results of pollen analysis. These take a substantially similar form. Again there are signs of pre-Elm

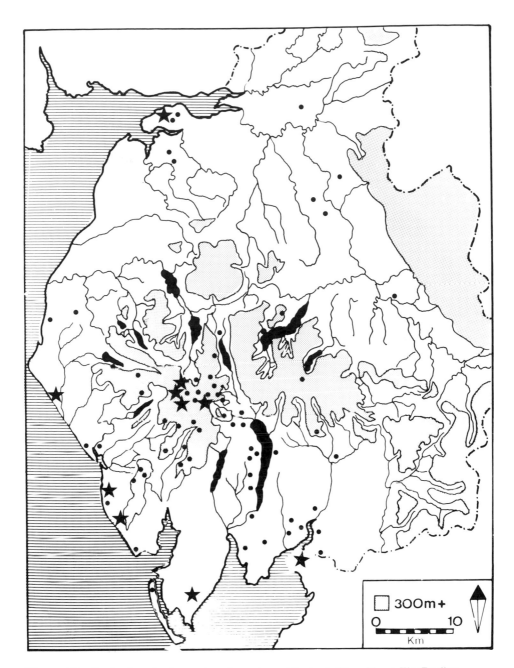

Fig. 7.2 The distribution of pollen analyses in north-west England. Sites with pre-Elm Decline disturbance are indicated by stars.

Decline activity near to the coast and occasional discoveries of cereal pollen (Powell *et al.* 1971). The chronological sequence also appears to be comparable, but this area has yet to see a sustained programme of fieldwork, and we lack many surface finds.

One reason for stressing the early beginning of human activity around the shoreline is that it contrasts with the environmental history of the other major area of productive lowland, the Eden Valley to the north-east of the mountains. The sequence from the sites so far studied in this area indicates that the vegetation cover remained unchanged until the mid fourth millennium BC. At Abbot Moss episodes of forest reduction are dated to about 3500 BC and a similar development may be represented at Moorthwaite Moss (Annable 1987, 21–2). This general outline seems to be supported by more recent work (J. Innes pers. comm.). Unfortunately the archaeological sequence comes mainly from the limestone hills on the edge of this area, where surface finds of Mesolithic and Neolithic date are both represented (Cherry and Cherry 1987b), and we do not have sufficient information from the lower ground. The earliest monuments, however, could be of the same age as the first clearings in the pollen record.

We must now compare these patterns with the evidence from the upland areas, where nearly all the archaeological material is related to axe production; there is no indication of settlement in this region until a developed phase of the Bronze Age (see Annable 1987, maps 56a and 58). Here there is some difficulty in working out the altitudinal range covered by early activity. With very few exceptions, the valley floors and the margins of the lakes do not seem to have been used at this time. This is suggested by Pennington (1975) because the only types of vegetation to show disturbance during the Neolithic are those that would have colonised the higher ground. The pollen analysed by Walker (1965), from a kettle hole just south of Pike o' Stickle, certainly supports this hypothesis. On the other hand, there is room for argument about the location of the tree line. Much of the highland area is supposed to have been forested to a height of about 750 m (Pennington 1975), but this general picture is in conflict with the results of detailed analyses which suggest a much thinner vegetation cover at sampling sites between 500 and 550 m above sea level. At Red Tarn Moss, for example, only 30% of the pollen from a mineral soil beneath the peat was of arboreal origin (p. 82), and in our own work at Langdale Combe the percentage of tree pollen just before the Elm Decline was almost exactly the same; in this case another 16% was contributed by shrubs. In the sequence at Stake Beck the proportion of tree pollen was between 13% and 28% and shrubs contributed between 8% and 19%. Similarly, in the mineral soil preserved below the flaking floor close to Loft Crag trees accounted for only 9% of the pollen, whilst shrub pollen contributed another 25%. Taken together, these estimates suggest that the 'finishing sites' at Langdale would have been much nearer to the tree line.

If the Cumbrian mountains provide little evidence of disturbance taking place in the valleys, the same cannot be said of the evidence from the higher ground. Here it seems as if activity had started before the Elm Decline, and at Blea Tarn, only 2.8 km from some of the extraction sites at Langdale, minor clearances of this kind have been identified (Pennington 1970 and 1975). These are earlier in date than any occurrence of Group VI axes so far, but reconnaissance around the edges of the tarn in 1985 failed to find any artefacts which might have shed light on this question. Most of the upland clearances are contemporary with the Elm Decline or belong to rather later stages of the Neolithic sequence. They share the common characteristic that they show some thinning of the upland vegetation and often evidence the expansion of grassland on the higher ground. In a few cases these samples are associated with finds of charcoal, suggesting that vegetation was being burnt (Pennington 1970 and 1975, p. 79). The duration of these episodes is very hard to estimate, but almost all of these areas were eventually consumed by blanket peat. Although many analyses have been carried out in the uplands, such episodes of early land use are apparently confined to the central Cumbrian mountains between Langdale and Scafell, where this evidence is best represented in the area around Great Langdale itself (Higham 1986, 35).

It was in order to shed light on these processes and their relationship to the axe production sites that pollen samples were collected from three stratified contexts. The longest sequence was that from Langdale Combe and is calibrated by two radiocarbon dates. It extends from the Elm Decline, at an estimated date of 3800 BC, to the base of the blanket peat, which is dated by a birch twig to 450–700 BC (OXA 2179). At least two, and perhaps as many as four, episodes of clearance had taken place during this sequence. The third and most intensive of these was associated with a layer of alluvial sediments resulting from soil erosion. This contained pieces of birch charcoal, from wood under twenty-five years old, and is dated to 1750–2050 BC (OXA 2180). By that time axe production had ceased, but two less intensive clearance episodes, each involving a reduction in shrub pollen, had already taken place. These most probably result from Neolithic activity, and the first occurred just after the Elm Decline. The principal trees at Langdale Combe had been birch, alder, oak and hazel, and the earlier parts of this sequence saw a gradual expansion in the proportions of grasses and heathland plants.

The other sequence was at Stake Beck. Here a series of pollen samples were taken from sediments which also contained the 'finishing site' mentioned earlier. The percentage of tree pollen averaged only 18%, although it was higher towards the upper and lower limits of this sequence. The main contributors of pollen were the same as those at Langdale Combe, and here again grasses and heathland plants were prominently represented. The sequence was of uncertain duration but certainly included the period in which the 'finishing site' had been in use. It revealed a regular alternation between periods of more open conditions and phases in which the vegetation cover had increased. Each of these 'clearance' episodes was marked by a deposit of microscopic charcoal, a sample of which was identified as oak, hazel, Pomoideae and poplar or willow. These charcoal deposits seemed to indicate that the vegetation was being modified by burning, perhaps on a regular basis.

Very similar conditions were evidenced at a third site. At Site DS 87, near to Loft Crag, two samples were collected from directly beneath the dump of knapping debris. Again they were associated with quantities of microscopic charcoal. In this case the main trees were alder and oak, but, taken together, they account for only 9% of the identifiable pollen. Hazel was abundant in both these samples, and in common with the other sites, grasses and heathland plants were strongly represented. Comparable results came from pollen analysis below Thorn Crag (Fell 1954) and at Thunacar Knott (Clough 1973), but here the samples cannot be dated so closely. In every case this work indicates a landscape well suited to seasonal grazing, and on both sites with evidence of Neolithic artefacts open conditions were probably maintained by firing the vegetation.

Axe production and land use

How far is it possible to bring these different sources of evidence together? In many ways the contrasts revealed by pollen analysis recall the patterns of land use in the same areas during the historical period. The important difference between the lowlands, with their evidence of cereal pollen, and the uplands, where a more limited range of vegetation was modified by burning, is reflected by early place names. The lowland sites occur in regions where these names describe farms that were occupied all year round, whilst the other samples come from the higher ground where the names refer to topographical features or to the summer settlements known as shielings (Higham 1986, figs. 7.4 and 7.5; cf. Whyte 1985). The fact that these distinctions could have been so long lived is hardly surprising when we remember the distinctive topography of this area.

In fact the Cumbrian mountains may once have been more hospitable than they are today, for beneath the blanket peat that mantles so much of this area are mineral soils which supported grassland and heathland suitable for extensive grazing. The fact that so much of that area is under snow during the winter means that land use could only have been seasonal, and the few grains of cereal pollen identified from Stake Beck and the uppermost levels of our sequence in Langdale Combe were no doubt transported by the strong winds in this area. At different times there have been reports that the remains of small stone buildings could be observed beneath the peat in exceptionally dry summers (T. Clare pers. comm.), and one was recognised and surveyed near to Langdale Combe in 1986. This was certainly earlier than the peat, but otherwise it cannot be dated, although it could well be connected with the major clearance episode dated to the Earlier Bronze Age. Its size and ground plan recall similar buildings in the uplands which seem to have been used in summer (see Bradley 1978, 60–3).

The environmental evidence from Cumbria shows that the central uplands were being used before the extraction of Group VI tuff had begun, and the pre-Elm Decline clearances at Blea Tarn have been assigned to the Mesolithic period. Finds of this date have yet to be recorded by fieldwork, but this is probably a matter of archaeological visibility: very little of this area is ploughed and most of the Mesolithic ground surface is beneath the blanket peat (see Wymer 1977, 331). There is evidence that similar areas in the Pennines were used by hunter-gatherers in the summer months, when the vegetation was burnt in order to modify the food supply for human and animal consumption (Jacobi *et al.* 1976; Stonehouse 1988).

Such seasonal activity may provide the most plausible context for the first discovery of the Group VI rock. This point needs careful discussion, for tuff of the same composition was being used in the coastal settlements of this period, but analysis of these finds reveals that it had been obtained in the form of small pebbles (Cherry and

Cherry 1983, 1984, 1985, 1986, 1987a). These could have been collected from the streams originating in the Cumbrian massif. Most likely the parent rock was discovered by following these streams back to their source. If so, this would explain the location of what seem to be the earliest workings at Langdale. Dungeon Ghyll, Troughton Beck, South Scree and Loft Crag would all have been found by this method, and the same might be true of Scafell Pike and Glaramara.

We have already seen how one of the earlier sites was associated with intermittent firing of the vegetation. There is some reason to suppose that the earlier phases of stoneworking at Langdale were 'embedded' in a wider cycle of summer land use. Most probably this involved the pasturing of animals, but similar environmental effects can be connected with hunter-gatherers (Mellars 1976). At all events this evidence is most apparent in the uplands surrounding the stone source.

At this point we should recall the characteristic technology practised at Dungeon Ghyll, Stake Beck and below Harrison Stickle. This was wasteful and inefficient. There was no attempt to use this material to the full, especially at Dungeon Ghyll where stone rejected during the first phase of working was reused in a later period. Little attempt was made to avoid errors, and the techniques of roughing out the axes do not imply that their intended form was an important consideration at this stage in the production process.

Perhaps the clearest demonstration of these points is provided by the spatial organisation of production, for in general only the earlier stages of the reduction sequence took place at the stone source, after which crude roughout axes, blocks of stone or even large flakes were taken away. Most of these must have gone to a series of sites on the lower ground, along the routes leading out of the mountains, although a few flaked blocks could have been removed from the area altogether; that would account for the discovery of such pieces at Blea Tarn and in Langstrath, although all were chance finds. With that exception, the later stages of production seem to have taken place at locations like Stake Beck. Even here, the working methods did not make effective use of the raw material. Nor did they show any explicit concern with the final form of the axes. The presence of broken roughouts emphasises the shortcomings of this system, for it would have been more efficient to eliminate flaws in the raw material before taking the trouble to carry it down the mountainside.

In fact it seems quite likely that such considerations were never paramount, simply because axe making was not the only activity taking place here. The choice of these locations may be significant, for they are found at a lower altitude than the stone source. Although the height of the tree line still remains in doubt, it is likely that these locations would have been much more sheltered than they are today, and certainly more sheltered than the rock outcrop itself. Two of our excavations revealed some structural evidence at these locations; again the same may be true of the more disturbed site at Thunacar Knott (Clough 1973). Their character could only be defined by large-scale excavation, but already it seems possible that one site saw a significant amount of stone clearance and that another occupied a platform in the hillside, possibly of artificial origin. The debitage from our excavations lends support to the idea that these 'finishing sites' had doubled as temporary bases for hunting or summer grazing. Stake Beck, Harrison Stickle and the primary levels at Dungeon Ghyll had a higher proportion of retouched material (0.8%, 0.15% and 0.16% respectively) than other excavated contexts at Langdale. The equivalent figure for the secondary levels at Dungeon Ghyll was 0.001%, and in the two quarries on Top Buttress it was 0.02% and 0.04%. The sites with the highest proportions of retouched material are all located close to streams.

In most respects these patterns contrast with the ways in which axe making was organised at the quarries, which seem to be a rather later development, but there is no reason to suppose that traditional patterns of land use had changed. At sites like Thunacar Knott some of the axes may still have been made in the course of summer grazing, and in Langdale Combe, burning of the upland vegetation reached its peak during the Earlier Bronze Age, long after artefact production had ended.

On Pike o' Stickle, axes were made by very different methods. All the stages of production took place at the stone source, errors were anticipated, avoided or corrected, and a much more regular routine was followed. The form of the finished artefact was conceived from the start of the process, and stylistic considerations appear to have been more important. Less time was lost in making roughouts which could never be used, and unsuitable examples were no longer taken away from the stone source. Moreover, the care that was shown in axe making is reflected by a decrease in the number of errors that had to be corrected during polishing. As a result, less time needed to be devoted to this final stage of manufacture, and output could have increased.

These changes in the character and organisation of production are mirrored by very striking changes in the locations at which it took place. There were also changes in the way in which the raw material was obtained. Extraction was no longer conducted in the rather informal manner evidenced during the earliest phase at Dungeon Ghyll, and greater technical expertise was invested in quarrying the raw material. This involved the first use of fire-setting in this complex and also required a range of stone artefacts for detaching the rock. Both had logistic implications. The fuels used for fire-setting – birch, hazel, oak and Pomoideae – were those species that dominate the pollen record, but they would still need to be collected for the purpose, sometimes in the form of large branches. Moreover, the hammerstones, which were often of considerable size and weight, would have to be brought up from the valleys. Excavation on Top Buttress suggested that a regular, highly structured routine was being followed, from quarrying right through to the final stages of axe making. Rather the same impressions are provided by work at Dungeon Ghyll, where material discarded during an earlier phase of stone extraction was brought back into commission.

One way of interpreting this development is to suggest that during the later part of this sequence people may have been visiting the stone sources for the express purpose of making axes. No longer were the productive stages dispersed around the uplands, and there are signs that efforts were being made to increase output and to minimise the loss of raw material.

On the other hand, there is a point beyond which 'practical' interpretations lose their force. We have already seen how people had elected to quarry the rock on remote ledges in the mountainside, when stone with the same mechanical properties could be obtained with greater ease, and in far more accessible locations. It seems as if people had chosen to make axes in places where it would be feasible to control access to the raw material. As we have seen, these exposures could hardly be discovered by chance, and those working the material would have required a detailed knowledge of how those locations were to be reached around the face of the mountain.

Finally, there is one further reason for supposing that such considerations were of major importance on these sites. In chapter 5 we mentioned that the hammerstones found there in such large numbers were sampled for petrological analysis, with the intention of determining their areas of origin in the lowlands. These artefacts proved to be of two main compositions – granite and tuff – but each would have been suited to just the same range of tasks. However, they need not have been found together in the same source areas, for the granites can have come from only a limited segment of the lowlands, most likely the west Cumbrian plain, whereas the tuff is distributed much more widely (Bradley and Suthren 1990). Moreover, on the quarry sites them-selves, their distributions overlap to only a limited extent, suggesting that people coming from different parts of the surrounding area may have worked on different sections of the rockface (Fig. 7.3). Again this indicates that by this stage in the development of the Great Langdale complex, individual quarries could have been controlled by particular communities or groups within them. In short, the sources of the axes were not generally accessible.

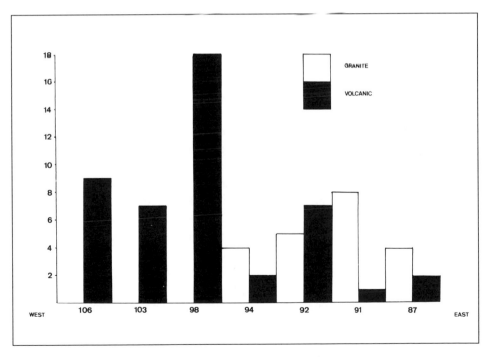

Fig. 7.3 The petrography and distribution of hammerstones from sites along a transect across Top Buttress.

Axe production and the Cumbrian lowlands

The final stage in this discussion involves the processes that took these axes into the Cumbrian lowlands, where they were completed by polishing. As we have seen, we know very little about the character of settlement sites in these areas, apart from the information provided by pollen analysis. This suggests the existence of clearings throughout the coastal plain and also in the Eden Valley, and provides evidence that some of the occupants of those areas engaged in the small-scale cultivation of crops, although this may have been subsidiary to the keeping of livestock. If domesticates had been taken to the mountains in summer, we should consider the possibility that on the return journey they may have acted as beasts of burden. This would be a convenient way by which the axes could have been transported.

The evidence that axes were polished on settlements in the lowlands is almost entirely circumstantial, and the only place where this can be accepted without question is at Ehenside Tarn, where roughouts, polished axes and grinding slabs were all found together with structural evidence (Darbishire 1873). Otherwise the case depends on associations between a similar range of artefacts (Manby 1965). This is not enough to establish the existence of settlement sites, although it is certainly true that all the examples that have been suggested are peripheral to the uplands.

These arguments are greatly strengthened when we consider the distribution of the axes themselves. They take three basic forms: the roughouts so typical of the stone source, and the so-called 'Cumbrian' and Variant' forms (Fell 1964; Manby 1965).

Apart from those found at the production sites, there are several concentrations of roughout axes in Cumbria, and few examples outside the region (Fig. 7.4). They occur in two main settings. The first group are found around the lower limits of the valleys leading to the production area, where the distribution of finds may be partly a product of the modern centres of population at Ambleside and Keswick. The others are found at more scattered locations along the coastline and in the Eden Valley. The major difference between these two zones of findspots is that polished axes predominate in the latter areas (Fig. 7.5), but closer to the stone source they occur in similar numbers to the roughouts. The changing proportion of those two types identifies the region where polishing must have taken place as lying between 12 and 20 km from the area of origin. That estimate is consistent with the locations where Manby (1965) has identified possible grinding slabs. It also identifies the area in which polished and roughout axes are found together in possible hoards, although virtually nothing is known about the detailed contexts of these discoveries (Fig. 7.6; see Annable 1987, 335–7).

The other two groups of axes are usually thought to comprise quite separate classes, the Variant axes (Fig. 7.7) being of smaller proportions than the classic Cumbrian type (Fig. 7.8; Fell 1964; Manby 1965), but close examination of these objects reveals that the difference is due to reworking. The Variant axes are the result of modifications made to these objects after their original production. That being the case, their distributions raise certain points of interest. The Cumbrian axes that remained close to the form taken by the original roughouts are the only type found within the central

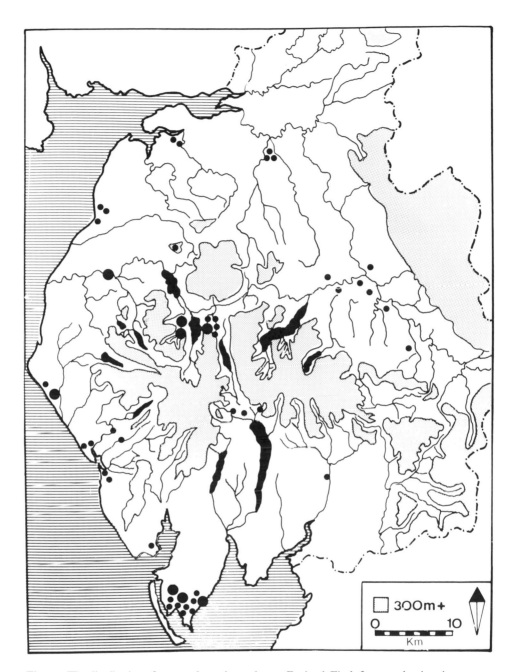

Fig. 7.4 The distribution of axe roughouts in north-west England. Finds from production sites are not included.

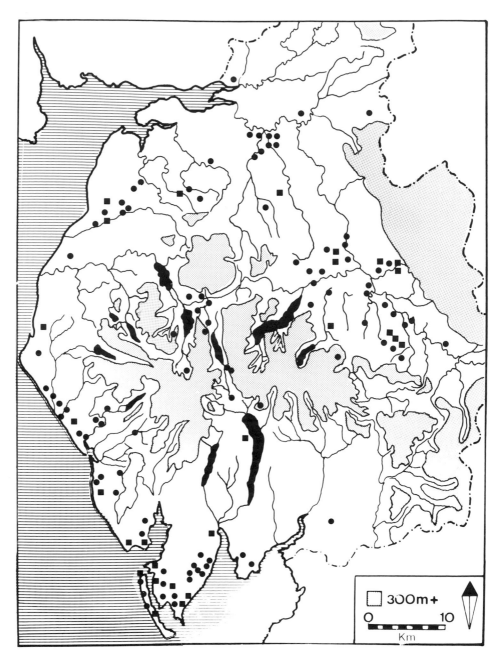

Fig. 7.5 The distribution of Cumbrian and Variant axes. Cumbrian axes are indicated by circles and Variant axes by squares.

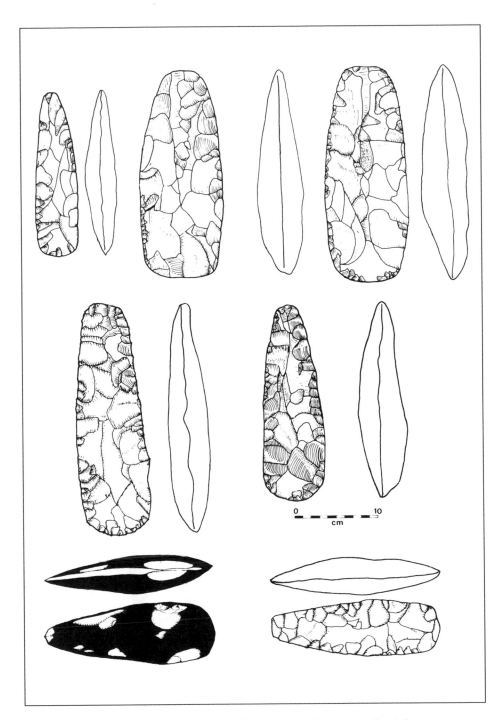

Fig. 7.6 A possible hoard of polished and unpolished axes from Portinscale, Cumbria.

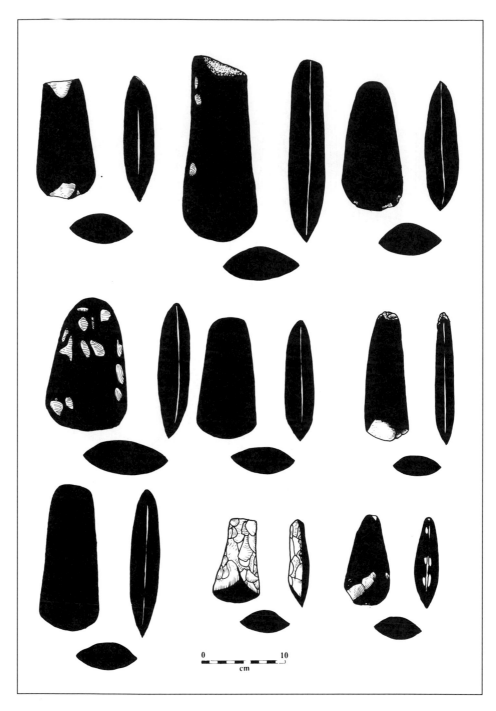

Fig. 7.7 Examples of Variant axes from north-west England.

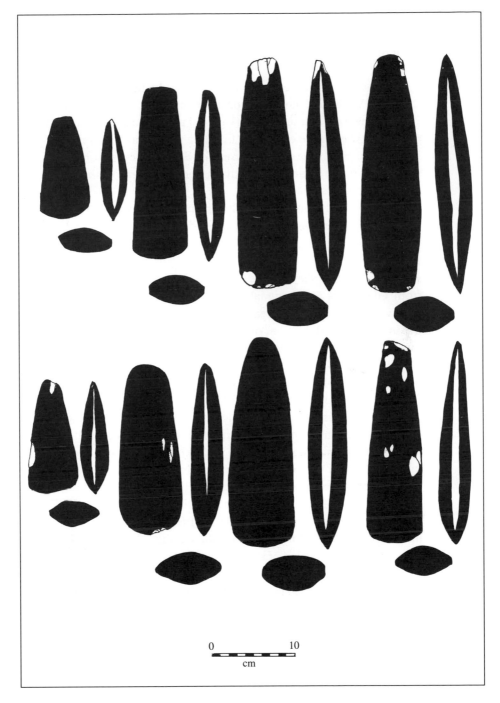

Fig. 7.8 Examples of Cumbrian axes from north-west England.

massif, where they account for both the clusters of polished artefacts mentioned earlier. All the Variant axes, however, occur well away from the high ground, and most of them at a distance of at least 25 km from the source area (Fig. 7.5; see Annable 1987).

We have seen that the Group VI products cluster in two main parts of Cumbria, in the Eden Valley and along the coastal plain, but the settlement history of these areas is rather different. Although both were occupied during the Mesolithic, the main focus of activity was on the coast, and this area maintained its importance throughout the Neolithic period. The evidence from the Eden Valley is more limited, but at present it seems as if it was settled most actively from the later fourth millennium BC. This is of interest for several reasons.

The most likely source of supply for sites on the coast of west Cumbria would have been Scafell Pike, which can be reached from Wastwater. We do not know the period of operation of this stone source, but it has most in common with the simpler group of sites at Langdale. At any event, axe making at Scafell Pike was always on a limited scale. The Eden Valley, on the other hand, would more probably have been supplied from Glaramara and Langdale. As we have seen, the sites on Glaramara operated on a very small scale, whereas the evidence from Langdale points to an increase in the intensity of production, or rather, a change in its character. To some extent this may reflect the growing importance of the Eden Valley, but it could also be a product of the long-distance contacts that could be established through that region, for it occupies a pivotal position in relation to some of the major routes across the Pennines.

In the same way, both of these lowland areas do contain monuments of Neolithic date (Figs. 7.9 and 7.10). The interpretation of these sites will be pursued in chapters 8 and 9, but at this stage it is worth noting how a contrast arises during the late fourth millennium BC. Despite the long history of settlement on the Cumbrian plain, the area contains only three possible long cairns, two of which are found to the south of the Cumbrian massif. By contrast there are six of these sites in the Eden Valley, four of them within a quite limited area (Fig. 7.9) (Masters 1984). Their precise dates are still uncertain, but should not be later than 3500 BC. A similar contrast is apparent if we consider the distribution of stone circles in Cumbria (Fig. 7.10). These virtually ring the high ground, but again the density of such sites is rather greater in the Eden Valley than it is towards the coast (Burl 1976, chapter 4, and 1988; Waterhouse 1985). The contrast is even more striking when we consider the distribution of the broadly contemporary henge monuments, for all of these are associated with the Eden Valley (Burl 1976). Moreover, some of the monuments associated with the latter area were built on a larger scale than any others in the region. Like the largest stone circles, they should belong to the Later Neolithic period.

The presence of such monuments may emphasise the changing configurations in the settlement of Cumbria, but it is important for another reason too. Such sites lie at the heart of the axe distribution, and in the very areas where these artefacts seem to have been polished. No fewer than three of the sites – the Grey Croft and Castlerigg stone circles, and the henge monument at Mayburgh – are actually associated with

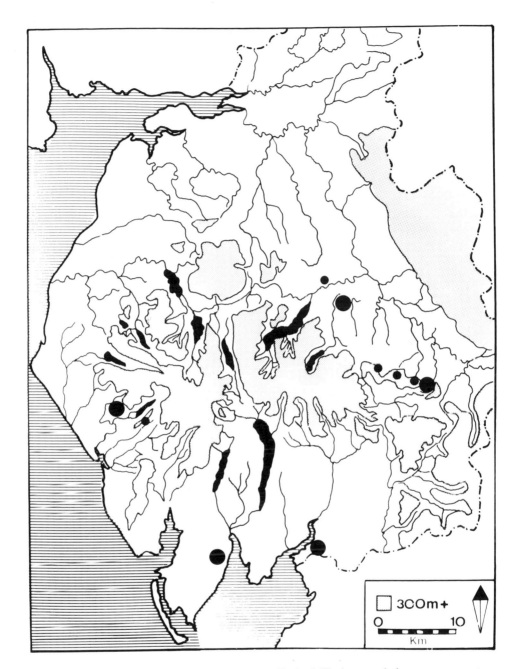

Fig. 7.9 The distribution of long cairns in north-west England. The large symbols represent extant monuments and the smaller symbols possible examples.

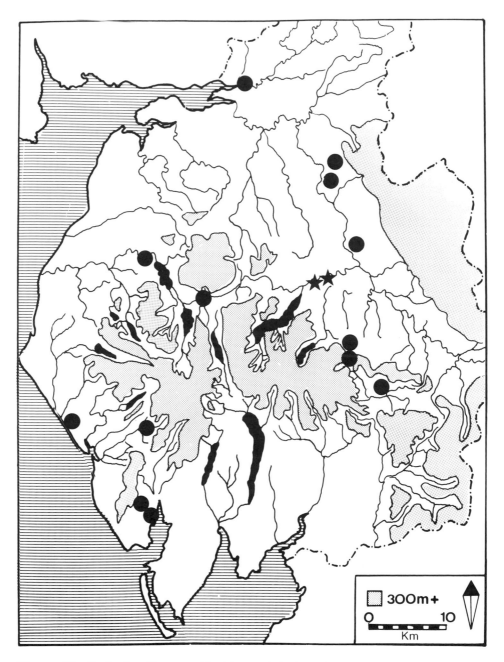

Fig. 7.10 The distribution of henges and 'early' stone circles in north-west England. The henges are shown as stars.

finds of Group VI axes (Burl 1976). In the following chapters we shall consider the possibility that it was through the aggregations that took place at such sites that the axes first changed hands. It may have been from there that they embarked on those journeys that were to take them to the opposite ends of the country. The final part of this book will attempt to explore that process.

III

EXCHANGE SYSTEMS AND THE STUDY OF NEOLITHIC BRITAIN

8

The wider significance of the 'axe trade': the Earlier Neolithic

Introduction

We have now seen how the pattern of settlement in Cumbria developed in parallel with changes in the nature of production methods at Langdale. There are other connections to be made at a national level, and it is the aim of the final section of this book to trace some of these in more detail. The period between about 3500 and 3000 BC saw major changes in the region where the axes were produced, but these processes were echoed across a wider area. It was during the same period that the distribution of Langdale axes altered its structure, from a relatively local concentration near the source, to the pattern of nationwide dispersal which is better known in the literature. As we shall see, that was not the only important change to take place at this time.

During the Later Neolithic period there were to be further developments, but these took a rather different form. Although we have less evidence from the production area itself, study of the finished products reveals a further shift in their distribution, as axes made at other sources increased their representation in parts of southern England. Like the expansion in the production and dissemination of axes, that change can be studied in relation to broader processes in contemporary society. For this reason the period divisions established in our discussion of Neolithic Britain in chapter 2 also provide a structure for this account. The present chapter is concerned with developments occurring up to about 3300 BC, during the Earlier Neolithic period. The Later Neolithic evidence is considered in chapter 9. Both chapters share a common aim. They follow the Cumbrian axes across the country as a whole and seek to interpret their changing contexts, character and associations in terms of the roles that they might have played in contemporary society.

In purely geographical terms one of the major results of research in Cumbria has been to document an important shift in the orientation of settlement. This also applies to the choice of locations for axe manufacture and monuments. In each case there was a significant change of emphasis away from the coastal settlement pattern established during the Mesolithic period towards much greater use of the Eden Valley and other areas close to the foothills of the Pennines. This development may have been under way during much the same period as the reorganisation of axe production at Langdale. It is quite possible that some of these changes took place because people came into the area from north-east England, but this cannot be proved.

These changes may help to account for the unusually high proportion of Cumbrian axes found on the opposite side of the Pennines, and in particular on the Yorkshire

Wolds (Manby 1979), but there are other reasons for stressing the links between these two areas. For a long time it has been clear that broad similarities of material culture extend from Yorkshire through north-west England and south-west Scotland into Ulster. These were originally discussed in terms of agricultural colonisation (Piggott 1954, chapters 4–6; Corcoran 1960; Atkinson 1962), but for our purposes they are more important because they provide evidence for interaction between those areas. Where the original discussion emphasised the importance of ceramics, we can place more weight on the evidence of specialised monuments.

The most important link is also the least well documented. One of the principal features of the Neolithic sequence on the Yorkshire Wolds is the evidence of complex burials. These belong to at least two series, which overlap in time. As in southern England, there are a considerable number of long barrows, associated with collective burials in what have become known as 'mortuary houses' (Manby 1988). The Yorkshire Wolds also see the development of round barrows at a relatively early date (Manby 1988; cf. Kinnes 1979). These monuments can be associated with individual inhumations, accompanied by a distinctive suite of grave goods, particularly arrowheads, but collective burials are also found at these sites. One feature which characterises mounds belonging to both traditions is the use of cremation. This is mainly found with the multiple burials and seems to have involved the firing of the charnel houses which are such a feature of this area. The situation is complicated by the fact that many of these sites were used over a considerable period and show a prolonged sequence of building and modification. In this respect the most informative site is at Whitegrounds (Fig. 8.1), where a circular or slightly oval mound witnessed two distinct periods of use (Brewster 1984). In the first period a number of disarticulated bones had been deposited in some form of mortuary house, with the skulls separated from the rest. This phase was without any grave goods apart from an amber pendant and is dated to about 3800 BC. Subsequent use of the site involved the excavation of a grave to house the articulated body of an adult male, accompanied by a jet belt ornament and a specialised type of polished flint axe of local manufacture. This happened around 3300 BC. Unfortunately, the available information is rarely of such high quality and much of the distinctive material comes from early excavations.

The evidence from Cumbria shares this disadvantage, not least because the same excavator, Canon Greenwell, worked on sites in both areas (Kinnes and Longworth 1985). Although the evidence is by no means satisfactory, several features which Greenwell would have recognised from his work in Yorkshire also occur in a small group of monuments close to the Eden Valley (Masters 1984). There seems little doubt that at least four of these belong to this period. One of the more informative sites was at Raiset Pike, where two round cairns may have been incorporated into a later long cairn. Each of these early monuments contained a burial 'trench', which sounds from the description very like the mortuary structures found on the Yorkshire Wolds (Greenwell 1877, 510–13; Clare 1979). One of these had been set on fire. In common with Earlier Neolithic practice elsewhere, the human remains from these deposits seem to have been disarticulated.

A third round cairn was recorded at Crosby Garrett nearby (Greenwell 1877,

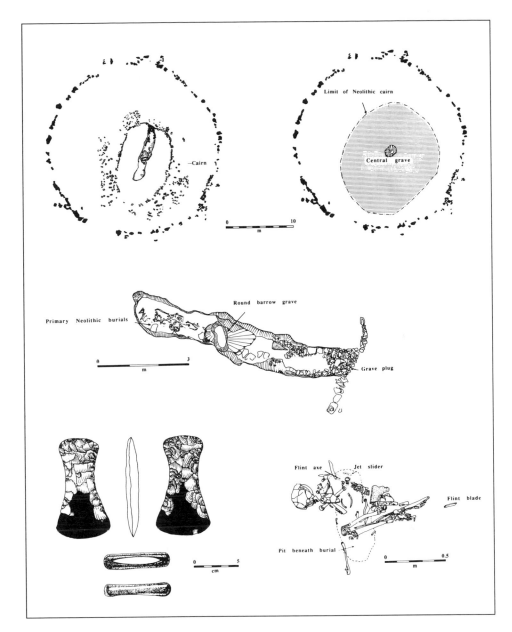

Fig. 8.1 The burial sequence at Whitegrounds (after Brewster 1984). The two successive monuments are shown in the top part of the drawing, the earlier to the right. Details of the earlier burial are shown in the centre of the figure. The later burial, and its associated artefacts, is illustrated at the bottom.

387–9). In this case at least nine individuals were represented by disarticulated remains. Yet another round cairn, this time with a 'cremation trench', was found on Lamb Crag, 30 km south-west of the Eden Valley (Masters 1984, 66–7). Although none of this evidence is of good quality, it may be no accident that all these sites are on the eastern side of the Cumbrian massif. Similar evidence is absent from the coastal plain, but burnt 'mortuary houses' are also found on sites in Ireland, in particular at Doey's Cairn in County Antrim (Evans 1938) and Fourknocks Site II in County Meath (Hartnett 1971).

In Yorkshire itself, barrows of these types are a particular feature of the Wolds. Some of the round mounds had a complex structural history, extending into the Later Neolithic, and air photography has recently shown that in two cases these 'great barrows' are located at the centre of much larger circular enclosures, defined by a causewayed ditch (Fig. 8.2; see Kinnes *et al.* 1983; Manby 1988, 85–6). The same also applies to the sites of at least two of the henge monuments in the Vale of York (Harding and Lee 1987). It is not clear how closely these sites are related to the causewayed enclosures found in southern England and they do not necessarily belong to this phase.

There is one site in Cumbria which closely resembles these enclosures. This is in the Eden Valley, where air photography has identified a large earthwork monument alongside the stone circle known as Long Meg and her Daughters (Pl. 8.1; Soffe and

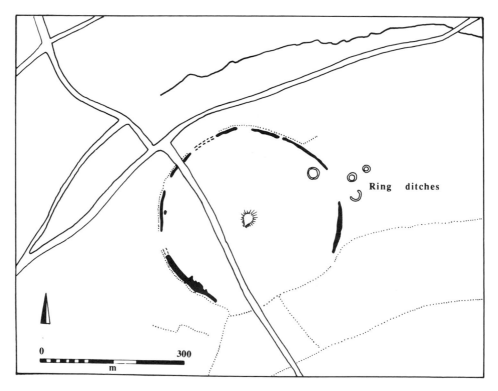

Fig. 8.2 Outline plan of the monument at Duggleby Howe (after Kinnes *et al.* 1983).

Clare 1988). That stone circle is thought to be among the earliest in Britain (Burl 1976, 89–92), but on one side it respects the position of an existing enclosure, and some of the upright stones seem to have fallen into its ditch. The earthwork has a distinctly lobate plan, and the ditch may well have been segmented. It is about the same size as the enclosures already described on the Wolds, and its relationship to the stone circle recalls the juxtaposition of similar enclosures and henge monuments in the Vale of York.

Lastly, a curious earthwork at Trainford Brow in the Eden Valley has sometimes been claimed as a rather exceptional long barrow (Masters 1984, 63–4). This can only be established by excavation, but it is worth making the point that the only comparable structures in northern England are found beyond the Pennines, where they seem to result from secondary extensions built on to more orthodox funerary monuments. The plan and dimensions of this site are not unlike those of two monuments in Yorkshire: East Heslerton and Great Ayton Moor, both of which have been excavated (Vatcher 1965; Hayes 1967). Although some authorities have questioned the identification of this monument, it may be no accident that it should be found in one of the main areas where Langdale axes were finished.

In fact the striking concentration of activity at the edge of the Cumbrian massif has

Plate 8.1 Aerial photograph of Long Meg and her Daughters, showing the stone circle (centre left) and the crop mark of an earlier enclosure surrounding the modern farm. Photograph: Bob Bewley. Crown copyright reserved.

another distinctive feature. Survey on the limestone hills to the south of the Eden Valley has revealed a large number of artefact scatters of prehistoric date (Cherry and Cherry 1987b). Among these is a distinctive group with a mixture of Late Mesolithic and Earlier Neolithic artefact types, including arrowheads and occasional sherds of pottery. One of these sites also produced a Langdale axe. Although the majority of the lithic raw material was of local origin, a significant quantity consisted of fine flint, quite unlike the material used on the Cumbrian coast. It seems likely that this had originated in north-east England.

Both these artefacts and the field monuments in this part of Cumbria have their counterparts on the other side of the Pennines, where large earthworks are much more common (Fig. 8.3). Again the dating evidence leaves much to be desired, but two classes of monument can possibly be assigned to this phase. The first is the distinctive group of enclosures referred to earlier. The other comprises a series of cursus monuments. None of these has been dated by excavation and the argument that some or all of them originated in the later fourth millennium BC depends on extrapolation from excavated sites in southern England (Barrett *et al.* 1991, 36–58). Taken together, the distribution of these two classes of monument presents several features of interest. As might be expected, there is a concentration of these earthworks on the Yorkshire Wolds, where the Rudston cursus complex is much the largest of its kind in northern Britain (Kinnes 1984). Other examples are found near to enclosures with interrupted ditches. The same classes of monument occur, separately or in combination, in two other areas. At Hasting Hill (Tyne and Wear) a causewayed enclosure and a cursus are found together close to the coast (Newman 1976). All the remaining examples, however, are on the lower ground between the Yorkshire Wolds and the eastern margin of the Pennines, where their distribution seems to focus on the major valleys extending into the higher ground. In effect these sites command the main routes across the Pennines into Cumbria. As we shall see, a similar pattern was to develop around the edges of the Lake District during the Later Neolithic.

Even though we know very little about the activities associated with these sites, their distribution is very striking. One group is found at the heart of the Yorkshire Wolds, where Cumbrian axes are discovered in association with Earlier Neolithic pottery (Manby 1988). The main focus of the second group is 75 km to the north-west, and almost the same distance from the main focus of activity in the Eden Valley. There is no reason to suppose that the primary function of those sites was to control the movement of goods, and cursus monuments almost certainly played a more significant role in mortuary rituals. On the other hand, their construction and use would have provided an opportunity for large numbers of people to gather together at a single location, and similar monuments often form the focus for a whole series of earthworks. Such monument complexes also include concentrations of elaborate artefacts, some of them originating in other parts of the country. At present little is known about the monument complexes of northern England, but they most probably drew people from a wider area. It may have been during the ceremonies that took place there that Cumbrian axes were exchanged.

It is unfortunate that little is known about the ways in which these artefacts were treated on the Wolds themselves, but that is probably because so much fieldwork has concentrated on funerary monuments. Axes were only occasionally employed as grave goods at this time, although a few are found in burials and others in hoards (Manby 1979). For the most part it is impossible to assign the latter deposits to any particular part of the Neolithic sequence. On the other hand, a Cumbrian axe was certainly associated with the façade of the Street House long cairn (Vyner 1984, 175). These observations are not sufficient for us to determine the roles that Cumbrian axes played in Yorkshire. However, we have already seen that they are present in large numbers in an area with a more than adequate supply of raw materials of its own. Combined with the observation that they may have been treated differently from the local products, this does suggest that they had been imbued with some significance.

In fact the relationship between flint and stone axes introduces a further complication, for it seems likely that the same forms were being made in a number of areas, from the Yorkshire Wolds to Northern Ireland, but again the chronological evidence is unsatisfactory. The best one can say is that the few flint axes found in Cumbria most probably originated on the other side of the Pennines. What is interesting is that they possess side facets, a characteristic of those axes made of Group VI tuff. That also applies to some of the flint axes found on the Yorkshire Wolds, as well as the porcellanite axes in Ulster. Similar links are suggested by the pronounced butt facets which occur on a small number of Cumbrian axes. They echo similar features on many axes in Yorkshire and Northern Ireland, as well as some from Scotland where this characteristic is not limited to artefacts of Group VI origin (Fig. 8.4). These features are not found in the south. On one level they bear witness to the intensity of interaction between these different areas: links which are also documented by the distribution of non-local artefacts. On another level they may indicate a process of emulation,

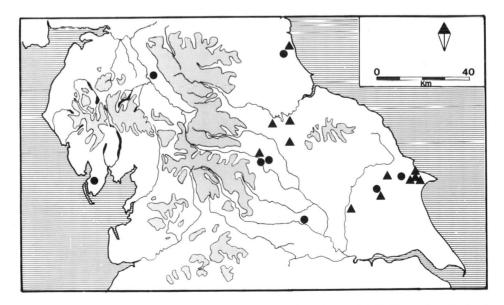

Fig. 8.3 Distribution of cursuses (triangles) and possible early enclosures (circles) in northern England.

although at present it is impossible to say in which direction this operated. Perhaps the greatest prospect of resolving this question comes from work on the Isle of Man, which imported axes from Cumbria and Ulster, as well as producing its own (Coope and Garrad 1988).

Although there is no evidence that goods were moved in bulk, the data suggest that a significant percentage of the products of the Cumbrian sources were exchanged along networks that stretched across the Pennines and into Yorkshire. Axes may have been exchanged through gatherings taking place at specialised monuments, especially the large earthworks of the Vale of York. Some of the same objects are found on the Yorkshire Wolds, an area which had clear cultural links with the eastern fringe of the Lake District. Here a distinctive series of burial rites had developed which stressed the importance of the individual. Although Cumbrian axes rarely feature in the funerary record, there can be little doubt of their importance, and it is even possible that their distinctive forms were imitated in flint.

Faced with such evidence, there is a danger of overemphasising the role played by the movement of axes at this early stage. We have already seen that on a national level the major expansion in the distribution of Langdale products happened during the same period as significant changes in working methods at the stone source. There is no reason to suppose that these changes were in any way *responsible* for the wider changes recognised on the Wolds. The idea that social developments were somehow precipitated by long-distance exchange is refuted by the radiocarbon chronology, and it may be more useful to reverse that equation. Quite simply, the major changes to affect the population of the Yorkshire Wolds were under way *before* the reorganisation of axe production in Cumbria. The round barrow tradition, which was so important in north-east England, was established by 3800 BC, and there were individual burials at Callis Wold by about 3500 BC (Coombs 1976); the use of the quarries on Pike o' Stickle seems to have happened rather later.

There remains the observation that even during the Earlier Neolithic period the movement of Group VI axes seems to have emphasised the routes across the Pennines. Perhaps the simplest way of explaining this is to suggest that political developments in north-east England precipitated changes in the nature and organisation of production, rather than the other way round. That would be consistent with the general sequence shown by axe production sites in Britain. During an early phase production is on a small scale and the products are distributed over a limited area; only later do they travel far across country, and not until that stage are major concentrations of these objects found at any distance from their sources (Cummins 1979; Smith 1979). On this basis the changes in the character of axe production at Langdale could have been a response, albeit an indirect one, to changes in the social value placed on these objects – not in the immediate hinterland, but in an area 150 km away which was already experiencing rapid change. In other words, changes in the social contexts in which axes were circulated and consumed may have provided a stimulus for changes in the conditions under which those artefacts were produced.

In chapter 2 we stressed how difficult it is to see these developments in their proper perspective. No doubt the Yorkshire Wolds were an unusually favoured area, just as they were in other periods, but there is the problem that their long history of antiquarian activity means that we know more about the Neolithic in this region than in other parts of eastern England. To a large extent this is because burial mounds still survived in considerable numbers when the first campaigns of barrow digging started. One result of rescue excavation in areas with a longer history of cultivation has been to identify the badly damaged remains of similar sites in lowland environments, extending along the coast, north into parts of Scotland (Kinnes 1985), and south as far as the Thames (Kinnes 1979; Bradley 1992b). Much less is known about the Earlier Neolithic period in these areas, but several features do seem to provide a link with the developments described so far. Such areas, especially Lincolnshire and East Anglia, contain a high proportion of Group VI axes, and they share much the same range of field monuments, including oval-ditched long barrows or enclosures, cursuses and round barrows (Bradley 1992b). Causewayed enclosures, on the other hand, have a more limited distribution. Excavation has shown that some of the

Fig. 8.4 The occurrence of facetted edges on axeheads in Ulster, Scotland and Cumbria.

distinctive burial practices associated with the Yorkshire core area also occur more widely during the Earlier Neolithic. This applies to several characteristic features: the burning of wooden mortuary houses; the existence of similar constructions underneath circular mounds; the presence of articulated inhumations; and the provision of individual grave goods. Other connections are evidenced by a series of portable artefacts, including fine pottery. Sometimes the links are very strong indeed; for example, Swale's Tumulus in Suffolk, which included a cremation burial and a series of Earlier Neolithic ceramics, also produced a fragment of Group VI axe (Briscoe 1956).

For our purposes the most important feature is that so many of these elements are found in areas where Cumbrian axes appear in Earlier Neolithic contexts. Two regions have proved especially helpful in this respect. In the Fenland an important series of intentional deposits of Cumbrian axes have been discovered in excavations at the Etton causewayed enclosure, where a number may have been deliberately smashed before they were buried (F. Pryor pers. comm.). In the light of what was said earlier, it is particularly interesting that some of these axe fragments were deposited in pits together with cremated human bone. Like the Yorkshire Wolds and Lincolnshire, East Anglia is a region with a notable concentration of Group VI axes and an excellent supply of local raw material (Clough and Green 1972).

Another area of special significance is the Thames Valley, where a number of apparently unused Cumbrian axes have been found in the river (Adkins and Jackson 1978; Chappell 1987, 281–2). We lack precise dating evidence in this case, but it seems most likely that such deposits began to form during this period, as Earlier Neolithic pots were also deposited in the Thames (Holgate 1988). In any event it seems possible that the distribution of Group VI axes contracted during the Later Neolithic period. By that time the products of other stone sources were more important in this region.

Such fluctuations are revealing as they remind us that artefact distributions may not have been stable over time. The orientation of local networks could have changed in the course of social competition. The Thames, for example, is only 60 km from a major source of flint axes. Moreover, the use of the Sussex flint mines is a particular feature of the Earlier Neolithic period and began well before 3800 BC (Gardiner 1990).

Having traced the movement of Cumbrian axes into Yorkshire and beyond, it is time to say more about the very different system to which those sites belonged. Such differences are apparent at many levels, but especially because a rather different series of field monuments were constructed in southern England during the Earlier Neolithic. Here we are confronted with a problem. Rather more is known about the Earlier Neolithic monuments in Wessex than those in Sussex, but the Sussex flint mines have been investigated on a far larger scale than any others of this period (Gardiner 1990). Unfortunately this is not because such sites are peculiar to that area, and at least two large groups of flint mines are known in Wessex, at Easton Down and Martin Clump (Stone 1931a; Ride and James 1989). Excavation of those sites has been on a very small scale, and only one radiocarbon date is available. This means that we are better placed to consider the chronology of the flint mines in Sussex, but must compare this with the sequence of field monuments across a wider area. Fortunately this problem may not be as serious as it seems, for characterisation studies have shown that many of the flint mine products dating from the Earlier Neolithic had their origin in Sussex (Craddock *et al.* 1983). That even applies to the axes found at major monuments in Wessex. In the same way, a number of those axes moved as far up the coast as East Anglia (Fig. 8.5).

The Sussex flint mines (Fig. 8.6) have a number of distinctive features. Not only did they begin operation at a very early date: they were also found in an unusual setting. Gardiner (1990) has studied the changing contexts of axe production in southern England. During the Earlier Neolithic period, she suggests, this took place mainly at the mines, which were usually located some distance away from the main settled areas. There is a recurring structure to the way in which the landscape was used. The domestic sites, which are now represented by scatters of surface finds, are discovered in the same areas as the main concentrations of long barrows, although they can extend onto lower ground than those monuments. There is no evidence of axe production on these sites (Gardiner 1984). The flint mines, on the other hand, were situated some distance away from the main areas of settlement (Fig. 8.7). This cannot be explained by the distribution of raw material, which is much more widely available. It seems as

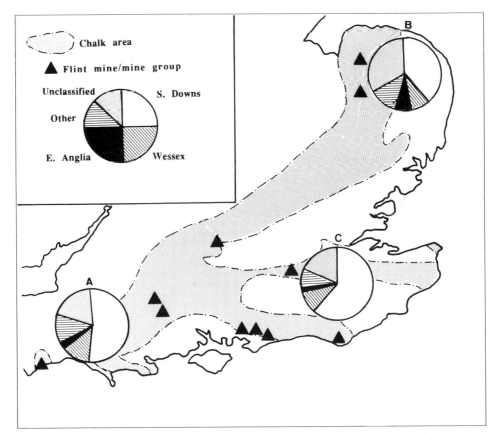

Fig. 8.5 Earlier Neolithic axe distributions in southern England (after Craddock *et al.* 1983).

if the large-scale production of lithic artefacts – mainly axes but also chisels, sickles, knives and projectile points – took place in marginal areas *in between* the main concentrations of domestic activity (Edmonds in press).

This evidence is found over a wide area, and it receives support from an unexpected source. As we saw in chapter 2, for some time it was supposed that the causewayed enclosures of the Earlier Neolithic had acted as central places in a dispersed pattern of settlement; to some extent their distribution had been taken to reflect the extent of domestic activity, as we find in Drewett's reconstruction of Earlier Neolithic territorial organisation in Sussex (Drewett *et al.* 1988, fig. 2.9). With more intensive field survey, combined with the thorough examination of well-provenanced collections of surface finds, it has become apparent that this model was flawed. The long barrows and lithic scatters did occur in the same basic areas, but the causewayed enclosures adopted more marginal positions in the landscape, around the edges of those concentrations of domestic activity. Some of them were built in limited woodland clearings (Thomas 1982), and like the flint mines, they were towards the edges of the settlement pattern as a whole (Gardiner 1984 and 1990).

This observation is especially helpful as there are certain links between these causewayed enclosures and the process of axe manufacture. These exist on several levels. There are areas, such as West Sussex, where flint mines and causewayed enclosures are found in close proximity to one another. Elsewhere axes may have been finished at the enclosures after the initial stages of working had taken place at the stone

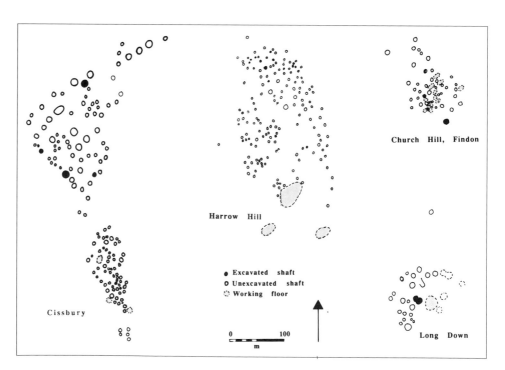

Fig. 8.6 Outline plans of four groups of flint mines in Sussex (after Drewett 1978).

source; this is suggested by the careful deposition of a polishing stone in one such monument on the Fen Edge (F. Pryor pers. comm.). Most important of all is the evidence that flint axes were actually being made inside the causewayed enclosure at Maiden Castle, and that the debitage from their manufacture did not extend into the surrounding area (Edmonds and Bellamy 1991). This recalls the discovery of a small group of flint mines inside the enclosure complex on Hambledon Hill, although these do not seem to have been used for axe production (Mercer 1987).

Such observations have a wider relevance, as they recall Mercer's suggestion that the stone-walled enclosure at Carn Brea controlled one of the major sources of axes in south-west England (1981b, 191–2). But if the stone sources and the enclosures occupied a peripheral position in the Neolithic landscape, how could this have been achieved?

At this juncture we should recall the discussion of causewayed enclosures in chapter 2 (Fig. 8.8). This stressed several points. Although there have been many attempts to work out *the* function of these sites, the evidence from recent excavation stresses their diversity (Edmonds in press). This is not surprising when we consider that in their initial phases they may have provided specialised locations where a number of dispersed groups might come together, a suggestion strongly supported by the variety of partly worked raw materials introduced to Maiden Castle (Edmonds and Bellamy 1991). It also seems that many of these sites were used on an episodic basis, perhaps seasonally. Although the botanical and faunal evidence for the use of these enclosures is equivocal, a low-lying site such as Etton would have been flooded for part of the year (Pryor 1988). Moreover, the distinct episodes of filling, re-excavation and cleaning in their ditches indicate a pattern of intermittent use, in which existing traditions of form and construction were generally maintained (Bamford 1985; Evans 1988).

All these elements serve to emphasise how distinct these enclosures may have been from the main part of the settlement pattern, and from the contexts of day-to-day experience. Perhaps the most important characteristic of these sites was precisely that they were situated in such a marginal location. This may also reflect their wider

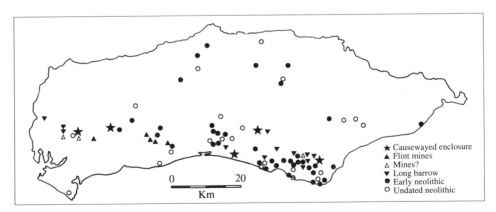

Fig. 8.7 The distribution of Earlier Neolithic enclosures, flint mines and occupation sites in Sussex (after Gardiner 1984).

importance, for if they were *geographically* marginal, they may also have been *socially* liminal (Edmonds in press). This would certainly accord with Holgate's observation that a number of these sites are placed on the boundaries between ceramic style zones (Holgate 1988).

The concept of liminality is fundamental to our understanding of enclosures, particularly if a number of them had played a role in the rites of passage that accompanied the treatment of the dead. Ethnographic studies have demonstrated that such events possess a tripartite structure: an initial stage of *separation* gives way to one of *liminality*, after which order is restored by rites of *reincorporation* (van Gennep 1960; Turner 1969; Bloch 1977). We have already suggested that these enclosures may have been places at which human corpses were exposed or received primary burial, and excavation has revealed a variety of isolated bones, as well as the more formal burials of young people who would normally be underrepresented in long barrows and megalithic tombs (Kinnes 1979, 122–3; Mercer 1980). It also seems possible that bones had been taken away from the latter sites and had circulated as relics. This provides one major point of contrast with the situation in northern England, where the use of cremation would have brought this practice to an end.

Rites of passage are not restricted to the treatment of the dead. A number of thresholds in the life of an individual may be demarcated in a similar fashion. Again it is important that these thresholds should be crossed under formal conditions, perhaps in a specialised environment, for such occasions involve the expression of funda-mental ideas about the social and natural worlds. Activities which may be undertaken in an unconsidered fashion in other contexts may assume a greater degree of explicit significance in these circumstances. Two practices in particular – exchange and consumption – often play an important part in the negotiation of social relationships. Here we should recall that in addition to non-local axes, enclosures contain striking concentrations of food remains, often laid out in formal deposits, together with high frequencies of decorated pottery (Smith 1965; Whittle 1988b).

Such practices are by no means out of place in mortuary rituals, but there are other junctures at which they can play an important role, many of them no doubt embedded in broader cycles of activity. The significance attached to an exchanged item can be transformed as it moves between different spheres, and it is this transformation which is often crucial to the maintenance of relations within and between groups (Barrett 1989; Edmonds in press). For that reason it is often surrounded by proscriptions which delimit the contexts in which such relations may be formed and protected. Activities at these enclosures would have played an extremely powerful role in contemporary society, and for that reason they were a potential source of danger and conflict. They happened in prescribed places, well away from the world of everyday transactions. The episodic nature of enclosure use suggests that constraints may also have been placed on the *times* at which it was appropriate for such events to occur (Edmonds in press). If they provided places where relations between the living and the dead were transacted, they were also places where different 'regimes of value' could overlap, and where exotic artefacts could pass from one social network to another. In this way the meanings and associations of those items could be controlled.

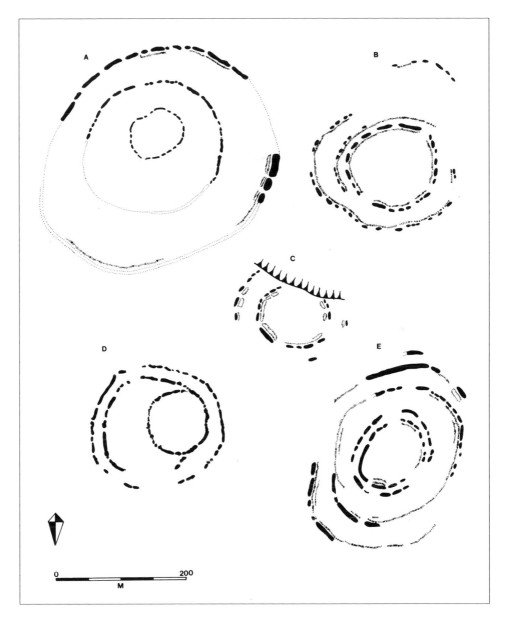

Fig. 8.8 Outline plans of selected causewayed enclosures. A, Windmill Hill; B, The Trundle; C, Coombe Hill; D, Briar Hill; E, Whitehawk.

If the exchange of special artefacts was subject to such proscriptions, it seems less surprising that the same should apply to the circumstances under which these objects were made. We have seen that in Sussex flint mines share some of the locational attributes of those monuments. Again there is no evidence that these mines were used all year round – this would have been inefficient and also dangerous – and it is easy to overestimate the amount of labour invested in winning the raw material. Given the enormous period of time over which the southern English mines were in operation, few of the shafts need have been open together. Again it is important to emphasise that these locations were not selected because they would have provided the only sources of suitable raw material. Rather, the placing of early flint mines away from settlement areas is better understood when we set them in a similar framework to our discussion of causewayed enclosures. They provide evidence of the same process of separating the contexts in which important items were obtained from those in which they circulated. In this sense the procurement of flint axes could have been 'embedded' not only in an economic framework but also in a broader conceptual scheme. Separation from the wider community might have provided the context in which to obtain items that carried a special significance, as markers of social identity within the local community, and thus as potentially important media for exchange (Edmonds in press).

Such links may help to explain why a few of the causewayed enclosures seem to be particularly closely integrated into the production and circulation of flint axes. We see the same link between axe production and the operation of other specialised monuments. Another polishing stone had been deposited in the entrance of an earthwork of this date at Llandegai in North Wales, together with a human cremation (Houlder 1968, 218), and the same pattern is even more obvious at West Kennett long barrow where one of the orthostats at the entrance of the megalithic tomb bears a series of 'axe polishing grooves' (Pl. 8.2; Piggott 1962, 19 and 21). A similar feature is found on one of the corbels of the passage tomb at Newgrange (O'Kelly 1982, 183). In such cases it seems possible that the final stages in the production process were undertaken in the context of ritual activity.

Because the southern English flint mines went out of use during the Earlier Neolithic period, it is rather easier to demonstrate the special importance of their products than it is in the case of Cumbrian axes. Some of the arguments are very similar to those already applied to Group VI artefacts. Flint mine axes of Sussex origin are found in ten of the fourteen hoards that have been characterised (Craddock *et al.* 1983). They also occur in high proportions in Wessex and East Anglia during this period – both of them regions which resemble the Yorkshire Wolds in having perfectly adequate flint supplies of their own. Most striking of all is an observation made recently by Gardiner (1990). She notes that polished axes apparently originating in the Sussex flint mines are commonly found in the Weald, but in contrast to those discovered nearer to the source area, a significant proportion of these artefacts are unbroken. By contrast, unpolished axes, which could have been used over the same period, are rarely found in one piece. This means that some of the flint mine products were used and/or deposited in a more specialised manner *away from the area of origin*.

It is clear that the principal monuments of southern England were related to one

Plate 8.2 Axe-polishing grooves in the entrance of West Kennet long barrow. Photograph: Stuart Piggott.

another in a complex manner. Long barrows were generally found in the same areas as settlement sites but, unlike those in the north, they usually contained an undifferentiated mixture of unburnt human bones. Despite the special circumstances in which some types of flint artefact had been made, they do not seem to have been used as grave goods. At the same time, the more marginally located sites also played a part. Certain of the causewayed enclosures may have provided the setting for the preliminary treatment of corpses. Some of the dead were buried there, whilst the bones of others were taken away to circulate in the home area, where they are sometimes found in long barrows and less often on settlement sites. Specialised flint artefacts may also have been produced and exchanged on the edge of the settled landscape, but again they contribute to the assemblages found on occupation sites. In a few cases they form part of structured deposits in pits (see Healy 1987), but elsewhere they can be found in flint scatters or in isolation. Such variations in the treatment and deposition of artefacts emphasise the fluid character of material culture. The ideas associated with axes may have been drawn upon to varying degrees in different contexts. In many cases, this may have occurred at a largely tacit or unconsidered level. In others, specific ideas could have been drawn into sharper focus.

Nearly all these features were to change by the end of the Earlier Neolithic period. Although such developments took many forms and were not distributed evenly across southern England, they do share one common element. Both settlements and burials provide more evidence of differentiation – the drawing of explicit references to distinctions within society that had previously been masked.

In the light of our discussion of the situation in northern England, some of these elements have a familiar ring. At the same time, there were significant changes in the deposits found beneath long barrows. Fewer sites were associated with deposits of unfleshed bones, and instead we find a series of fully articulated inhumations. The number of burials changes, and fewer individuals are represented at these monuments. Single or double burials can be found, and in common with developments on the Yorkshire Wolds, there is a greater emphasis on adult males. A small number of these deposits were provided with grave goods (Fig. 8.1; Barrett *et al.* 1991, 51–3).

If these changes recall our description of burials in northern England, there is one extremely important difference. In the north there is a general tendency for round barrows with individual burials to supersede the long barrows and for burnt mortuary houses to disappear (Kinnes 1979). In southern England there were more limited changes in the form of the covering monument and long barrows continued to predominate in areas south of the Thames. A number of these earthworks did take slightly different forms; the newer mounds tended to have a rather more oval outline than their predecessors, and the flanking ditches were sometimes extended around one or both ends of the earthwork, as if to cut off all access to the human remains deposited beneath them (Drewett 1986; Barrett *et al.* 1991, 36–43 and 51–3). On at least three sites in Wessex, late long barrows were without any human bones at all (Ashbee, Smith and Evans 1979, 228–300; Barrett *et al.* 1991, 36–8 and fig. 2.10). In other cases they might be built on a rather smaller scale.

In the Thames Valley the situation was much more fluid, and here small long barrows could be rebuilt to an oval, or even circular plan (Bradley and Holgate 1984, 116–20). As we have seen, oval long barrows of similar form are found across large parts of lowland Britain, including the Midlands and East Anglia (Loveday and Petchey 1982). It may be no accident that the Thames Valley is also on the southern edge of the main distribution of Neolithic round barrows (Kinnes 1979, fig. 5.2), although a small number of examples have been found in Wessex. In both areas these were first built during the Earlier Neolithic period, and like the round barrows of northern and eastern England, some of these covered articulated inhumations.

These changes in the burial record have their counterparts in the evidence from causewayed enclosures. As we mentioned in chapter 2, many of the difficulties of interpreting these sites developed because Neolithic scholars had been looking for a single all-embracing interpretation. Now that these enclosures have been excavated on a larger scale, and studies of these sites are supported by radiocarbon dates, it is clear that some of the enclosures took on new roles during the later fourth millennium BC. This applies particularly to the few sites which have been interpreted as settlements (Mercer 1980; Sharples 1991; Dixon 1988, 47–8). Although the evidence is not documented in sufficient detail, it appears that nearly all the enclosures containing Neolithic structures had changed their character at a late stage in their history. When

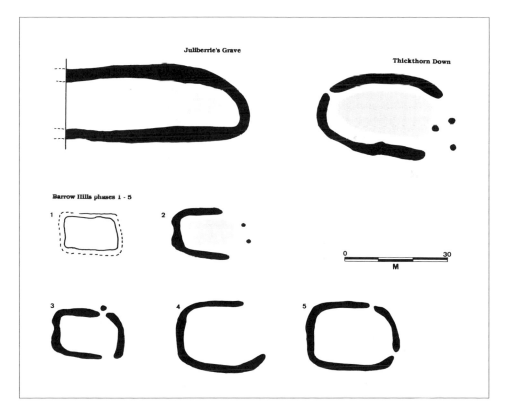

Fig. 8.9 Outline plans of three late long barrows in southern England.

they were originally constructed, they had interrupted ditches, which formed the focus for a whole series of formal deposits, including those groups of human and animal bones referred to earlier. A small number of the sites were to see striking changes. The ditches were replaced by continuous earthworks, and the ramparts were rebuilt until they formed a more substantial barrier (Bradley 1984a, 34–5, and 1984b). Two of the enclosures were supplemented by outworks, and several were provided with timber gates. At Hambledon Hill, as many as three separate enclosures were brought together within a single circuit which would have been one of the largest and most impressive monuments built during this period (Mercer 1980).

It is difficult to relate the evidence from the interiors of these enclosures to the changes that were made to the surrounding earthworks, but at Crickley Hill, where good stratigraphic evidence survives, it seems likely that the excavated houses belong to a late stage in the development of the site (Dixon 1988). The same could be true of Carn Brea where some of the internal structures had been burnt, perhaps during the conflict that led to the deposition of several hundred arrowheads, and possibly the collapse of the defensive wall on the site (Mercer 1981). Similar episodes can be identified at Hambledon Hill, Crickley Hill, Maiden Castle and perhaps Hembury, and in each case they come towards the end of the sequence (Dixon 1988; Mercer 1980; Sharples 1991, 47–8; Todd 1984, 253–9; see also Brown 1989).

Early accounts of causewayed enclosures compared these earthworks to the hill forts built during later prehistory (Curwen 1930), and there are cases in which such sites were excavated under the impression that they were actually built at that time. Those links have been less prominent in recent writing, simply because so many examples have now been found on lower ground; the hilltop enclosures considered by Curwen are no longer typical of the group as a whole. In the light of recent field-work it seems that opinion may have moved too far, and Neolithic enclosures with continuous ditches have been found on the Sussex downs (Bedwin 1981). The evidence from several areas of southern England seems to indicate that a small number of prominent earthworks, which no doubt began life as ceremonial sites, gradually developed into specialised and defended settlements. That is not to say that their original functions were lost, but they may have gained some new ones. If a few of these enclosures really did emerge as a special class of settlement, they provide evidence of social differentiation to set alongside the changes in the burial record.

There are several specific reasons for making this connection, and these are of fundamental significance if we are to arrive at any interpretation of the role played by long-distance exchange.

One of the most important features is the pairing of some of the causewayed enclosures in Wessex and the Thames Valley with late long barrows, or even with round barrows belonging to the same period (Bradley 1992a). This is particularly striking as such enclosures are usually displaced from the main concentrations of burial mounds. Recent work has shown that this applies to many of the enclosures in these two areas, and on a number of sites, including Hambledon Hill, Knap Hill, Abingdon and probably Maiden Castle, excavation suggests that the two were in use together. This is especially important in view of what has been said about the evidence for social differentiation discovered at both kinds of monument. In fact single or double burials of Earlier Neolithic date have now been found in the mounds alongside three enclosed sites: Hambledon Hill, Knap Hill and Abingdon. All were articulated inhumations, and, as we shall see, those from Abingdon were accompanied by grave goods.

Another significant change is evidenced by the radiocarbon dates from causewayed enclosures and flint mines. If some of the enclosures were changing their character from 3300 BC onwards, the mines were going out of use *at very much the same time*. As mentioned earlier, there are problems in comparing the dates from flint mines in Sussex with the chronology of monuments with a much wider distribution, but the pattern is sufficiently consistent to command attention (Gardiner 1990). This change is especially striking as the end of the Sussex flint mines coincided with the expansion in the movement of stone axes from highland areas and a shift in the character of production at Great Langdale (Smith 1979).

Much of the evidence for this extension in the distribution of stone axes comes from the causewayed enclosures, which provide some of the best dated stratigraphic sequences in southern England, but it is particularly interesting that not all of these sites started life at this time. At a number of excavated enclosures, including Windmill Hill (Smith 1965), Whitehawk (Curwen 1936), Briar Hill (Bamford 1985), Etton (Pryor 1988) and Staines (Robertson-Mackay 1987), it is clear that the non-flint axes belong to a developed stage in the sequence. This has been overlooked in considering the part that these enclosures seem to have played in the dispersal of exotic artefacts. The enclosures were *already well established*, before this extension in their long-distance contacts. This development is not related to the initial construction and use of these monuments but to the transformation that happened at a late stage in their history. The appropriate equation to make is with the period in which a few of these sites were rebuilt as defended settlements.

The clearest demonstration of some of these links comes from Abingdon in the Thames Valley (Avery 1982). The causewayed enclosure on this site has been excavated on three separate occasions and its interpretation is controversial, but one reading of the evidence suggests a structural sequence very like that at Hambledon Hill (Bradley 1992a). The site could have started life as a specialised enclosure associated with formal deposits of antler, animal bone, human remains and decorated pottery, but at a late stage in its history the original monument was contained within a much larger earthwork, with a considerable revetted rampart. There was a Cumbrian axe in a high level of the inner enclosure ditch. At the same time, late in the development of this complex, a small oval long barrow was built close to the inner ditch of the enclosure. At one end of the mound were a series of formal deposits matching those in the ditch of the causewayed enclosure. A shallow grave beneath this mound contained two articulated inhumations, both of them accompanied by artefacts (Fig. 8.9).

The selection of grave goods is especially revealing. They consist of a leaf-shaped arrowhead, a fine polished flint knife and a shale or jet belt ornament. They are mentioned here because all three would be more at home in contemporary burials on the Yorkshire Wolds (Bradley 1992a); indeed the belt slider was almost certainly made in north-east England. The only other example found in a recent excavation is from the burial at Whitegrounds mentioned earlier (Brewster 1984). The radiocarbon dates from these two sites are virtually the same.

This small collection of grave goods seems to epitomise the changes that were happening in three separate parts of the archaeological record: the appearance of individual burials owing as much to northern practice as they did to local prototypes; the transformation of a small number of causewayed enclosures into defended settlements; and the replacement of local exchange networks based on flint mine products by the long-distance movement of artefacts originating in upland Britain.

How should these links be interpreted? It seems as though much of the stimulus for change came from outside the immediate region, in that broader interaction sphere dominated by the evidence from the Yorkshire Wolds. If that is the case, the first appearance of an appreciable number of non-local axes in the south becomes an important issue. That is particularly true if this process undermined the symbolic associations of flint mine products to such an extent that their sources on the Sussex downs went out of use. Axes from more distant areas such as Cumbria may have usurped their special status.

We have described the rather rigid controls that appear to have existed in the Earlier Neolithic societies of southern England: mortuary rituals seem to have effaced whatever distinctions might have found expression in life, although it is obvious that very few people were buried on the sites of long barrows; specialised sites such as causewayed enclosures made the major demands on human labour whilst ordinary settlements are extraordinarily evanescent; the production of high-quality artefacts at flint mines was purposefully distanced from the settled area. The changes that seem to have happened from 3300 BC onwards involved a gradual break with all these inhibitions, but, in particular, they seem to reflect the extension of exchange relations over a larger area than in earlier centuries. In forming links with more distant communities, who conducted their lives in such different ways, groups in southern England drew upon a powerful source of new ideas. The process of social differentiation that looms so large during the closing years of the Earlier Neolithic may perhaps be understood as a result of these new relationships. Alliance, emulation and the exchange of portable artefacts may all have played a part in those changes of political geography that resulted in the emergence of a distinctive class of fortified settlement and the first signs of armed conflict in the British Isles.

Such changes were not *caused* by the influx of Cumbrian axes in the south, any more than their appearance in Yorkshire brought changes in that area, but the forces that made these objects so much more important than local products must be some indication of a wider transformation of political alignments, and perhaps of social roles, within the British Isles. That is not to say that the only stimulus came from the Yorkshire core area, or even that Group VI axes travelled south by way of that region; to some extent we are still constrained by imbalances in the distribution of fieldwork. What is clear, however, is that these drastic changes in the scale and orientation of exchange networks prefigure many of the characteristic features of the Later Neolithic. They will be considered in chapter 9.

9

The wider significance of the 'axe trade': the Later Neolithic

Introduction

In chapter 8 we traced a gradual expansion in the movement of Cumbrian axes across the British Isles until that process reached its peak towards the end of the fourth millennium BC. It seemed to run in parallel with developments at Great Langdale, where the character of axe making changed over the same period. This extension in the scale of production and distribution had its social implications, and we were able to suggest how the wider roles of some of these artefacts may have altered as they moved into more distant areas, until their adoption in southern England seemed to be related to a rather broader transformation of contemporary culture.

This chapter adopts a similar approach to the developments that took place during the Later Neolithic period. At one level it traces a contraction in the areas over which the Cumbrian products are found, but at another it returns to one of the main issues identified in our earlier account. Almost the defining characteristic of the Later Neolithic is the way in which long-distance exchange seems to have gained in importance, compared with the more local networks that characterised so much of the previous period. Such long-distance links were undoubtedly important, but they were also rather unstable, and this discussion will concern itself with the competition that seems to have developed between people who were able to control the movement or consumption of different classes of material. This identifies the two main themes running throughout this chapter: the increasingly volatile relationship between different exchange networks, and the ways in which this affected the significance of Cumbrian axes.

The production and distribution of Cumbrian axes

Neither of these topics can be discussed in detail as there are still serious gaps in the archaeological record. The sequence at the stone source shows changes in the ways in which axes were made, but the finished products did not alter their form. For that reason the chronology of Group VI axes is best assessed through closed associations with other artefacts, or through radiocarbon dates. In principle that should pose no problem, but in fact two difficulties do arise from the outset. The chronology of Later Neolithic pottery is not well understood and depends very largely on typological arguments that have yet to be tested by absolute dating (Smith 1974). That problem applies to the evidence of Peterborough Ware rather than Grooved Ware. At the same time, the imbalance in fieldwork towards certain parts of the country, such as Wessex, the Thames Valley, the Fenland and the Yorkshire Wolds, means that associations between axes and other kinds of artefacts are more likely to be identified in some areas than in others. There seems no prospect of resolving either of these difficulties in the immediate future, and this account makes use of what information is currently available.

With that caveat, the distribution of Group VI axes does seem to have contracted. Fewer examples are found in Later Neolithic contexts south of the Thames, and possibly south of the Fenland (Chappell 1987). This is not entirely the result of gaps in the archaeological record, as axes belonging to Group I are associated with Later Neolithic artefacts in the south. By contrast, Cumbrian axes appear in contemporary contexts in East Anglia (Clough and Green 1972) and are recorded in greater numbers in Yorkshire, where they are associated with both Peterborough Ware and Grooved Ware (Manby 1979). They may have been current in other core areas, but the evidence is too slight for the position to be clear. On the other hand, it is notable that the distributions of the main types of axe which could have replaced Group VI – Group I from Cornwall, and Groups VII and VIII from Wales – do not extend north of the Yorkshire Wolds (Clough and Cummins 1988, maps 2, 7 and 8).

If the distribution of Cumbrian axes did contract, it is difficult to relate that change to any developments at the stone source. Despite the scale of recent survey at Great Langdale, the latest date, 2850–3250 BC (BM 676), comes from the 'finishing site' on Thunacar Knott, yet axes made in this region are discovered in association with pottery of much later origin (Manby 1974 and 1979). Several possibilities might be considered in future work, although none can be assessed in the absence of radio-carbon dates. One is that after reaching a peak during the Earlier Neolithic, axe production reverted to the less intensive procedures established during the first phase of working. This cannot be demonstrated, although the date just quoted certainly suggests that the two methods of making these artefacts could have coexisted. A second possibility is that *quarrying* came to an end, at least on Pike o' Stickle. We have already shown how this activity must have extended up the mountainside with time. Site 95, however, was located close to the top of the Group VI outcrop, yet it returned dates in the Earlier Neolithic period. It seems clear that the process could hardly have gone much further on this part of the mountain. Either quarrying was transferred to locations along the outcrop which were not investigated by excavation, or more use was made of material already obtained during earlier phases of exploitation. This is precisely the pattern observed at Dungeon Ghyll, where the second phase of axe production involved the systematic re-use of raw material discarded during an earlier period of stoneworking. It is unfortunate that this secondary phase of activity could not be dated, as it might have provided the best clue to the nature of axe production after quarrying on Pike o' Stickle had ended. That is speculation; suffice it to say that all the radiocarbon dates from Langdale belong to the period when the distribution of Group VI axes was still increasing.

The changing contexts of consumption
In fact the distribution of Group VI axes in southern England altered during a period when raw materials were being used in a new way. A particular feature of this phase is

an emphasis on polished flint. Although the evidence for artefact production is more fully analysed in Sussex and Wessex, it was along the North Sea coast that such artefacts may have played their most obvious role (Manby 1974, chapter 3; Bradley 1992b). They occur in a number of forms, but in each case the distinctive qualities of the raw material were enhanced by polishing. Among them were artefacts made of banded flint or of flint of unusual colours. At the same time we encounter significant changes in the contexts in which they were consumed. We shall start by considering those changes that ran in parallel with the Peterborough Ware tradition. A later section will review the distinctive role played by the Grooved Ware network.

At a general level it is true to say that the Later Neolithic period saw an extension in the range of artefacts and raw materials imbued with particular significance, including jet, amber, bone and antler (Manby 1974, chapter 3). These changes are most evident from the burial record, where we have the advantage of dealing with assemblages rather than individual types. Again the key sequence is from Yorkshire, although similar artefacts are found widely in northern and eastern England. It is here that Kinnes (1979) has identified an important change, from burials containing projectile points to Later Neolithic deposits with personal ornaments (Fig. 9.1). Few of the sites provide a stratigraphic sequence, but there are two important exceptions in this respect: Whitegrounds and Duggleby Howe.

Whitegrounds is a recently excavated site (Brewster 1984) and the sequence of burials there was summarised in chapter 8. It is the latest of those burials that concerns us now. This contained a single male inhumation associated with a jet belt slider, similar to the example found outside the Abingdon causewayed enclosure, but with it was a polished flint axe of the specialised 'Seamer' type. These were associated with a radiocarbon date of about 3300 BC. This is important for two reasons. It shows that types of artefact traditionally assigned to a date in the Later Neolithic were already in circulation by the end of the previous phase. More important, it creates a bridge with a far more elaborate sequence of burials found in an older excavation, at Duggleby Howe.

Duggleby Howe is the key site for our understanding of the sequence of burials on the Yorkshire Wolds (Kinnes *et al.* 1983; Manby 1988). A massive round barrow built up over several phases, it lies at the centre of one of the 'causewayed' enclosures described in the previous chapter. Excavation in 1890 provided evidence for a remarkable sequence of graves, and for this reason the site has been taken to epitomise the precocious development of individual burial in northern England.

The features belonging to the initial phase included a crouched inhumation, associated with decorated pottery in the earlier Towthorpe tradition, but among the burials assigned to the following period of activity were a more remarkable series of artefacts: a high-quality lozenge-shaped arrowhead, a macehead made of antler, a large flint adze and a completely polished flint knife. The following phase saw the deposition of boars' tusks, utilised beaver teeth, a bone pin and a series of transverse arrowheads (Fig. 9.2).

Three of these types are especially important in the wider region (Manby 1974, chapter 3). Polished flint knives are among the finest and most elaborate flint artefacts made in Britain, and almost certainly were never intended for use. The flint adze from the site is a large waisted implement, related to the axe from Whitegrounds, whilst the antler macehead appears to provide the prototype for a series of carefully-made stone maceheads whose main distribution extends along the coast from northern Scotland to the Thames Estuary (Roe 1979). There are further types of artefact which may originate in this area, although they are not represented at these two sites. They include a wider variety of fine projectile points and a series of partly or completely polished knives. The latter are found in a wider range of shapes than the example from Duggleby Howe (Manby 1974, chapter 3).

Although many of these types were used as grave goods, other examples are also found in hoards, occasionally as secondary deposits in existing burial mounds. Again polished flint artefacts play a most important role. Among the finds from the hoards in this region are flint axes with ground edges, a polished flint chisel and the

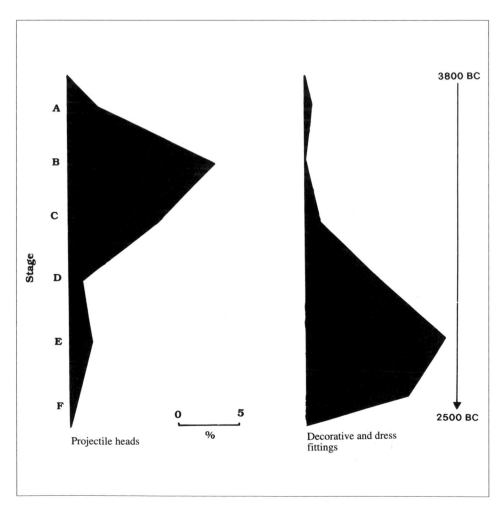

Fig. 9.1 The chronological distribution of projectile points and decorative fittings in Neolithic burials (after Kinnes 1979).

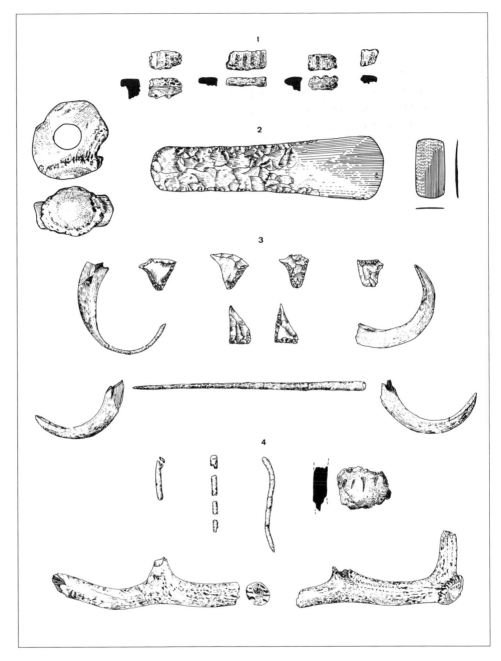

Fig. 9.2 Selected artefacts from Duggleby Howe (after Kinnes 1979 and Manby 1988).

specialised form of flint axe which comes from the eponymous site of Seamer Moor (Smith 1921).

In addition, the distribution of some of the most elaborate lithic artefacts focuses on the Rudston cursus complex. This applies to polished flint knives, stone maceheads, Seamer axes, Duggleby adzes and polished-edge chisels. The same is also true of the finest arrowheads in the area (Pierpoint 1980, 271–7). It seems most improbable that this extraordinary concentration of elaborate artefacts resulted from chance loss, and for this reason it is tempting to consider a number of these finds as intentional deposits. As we have seen, some of the raw material used to make them was particularly distinctive. It probably originated on the North Sea coast.

It is clear that once again the evidence from the Yorkshire Wolds plays such a prominent part in our discussion because of the way in which early excavators concentrated on the burial mounds of that area. In fact examples of the same types of artefact have been identified over a much wider region, although they seem to occur at a lower density. Thus specialised knives and axes may be identified along the North Sea coast, into Scotland in one direction (Kinnes 1985) and at least as far as East Anglia in the other (Bradley 1992b). The distribution of Later Neolithic burials extends over much the same area, although the number of sites is extremely small. The distribution of axe hoards also includes examples in Lincolnshire and East Anglia (Smith 1921), and stone maceheads are found in the Thames (Roe 1979). To some extent we may be witnessing the intensification of contacts already evidenced by the distribution of Cumbrian axes.

Such axes remain a regular feature of the archaeological record in eastern England, and on the Yorkshire Wolds non-flint axes certainly appear in two of the hoards. They are also found on settlement sites with Peterborough Ware (Manby 1975 and 1988). There is one link between these types that is worth exploring here. We have already mentioned the distinctive classes of flint axe and adze, named after the sites at Seamer Moor and Duggleby Howe respectively. The most striking features of these artefacts are their narrow waists and expanded cutting blades. Both are features which they share with Group VI axes in Yorkshire, and Manby (1979) has suggested that the imports were deliberately imitating a prestigious local form. On the other hand, similar features have been identified among the Group VI axes in Cumbria. Such resemblances seem more than a coincidence, but it is not clear which area provided the source of inspiration. Even so, the fact that flint is harder to polish than tuff emphasises the increasing significance of local materials in eastern England.

Raw material sources and the changing pattern of settlement

The growing importance of high-quality flint artefacts is also reflected by changes in the use of raw material sources in the south. These are intimately connected with wider changes in the pattern of settlement.

As in earlier periods, the best evidence is provided by lithic scatters, and domestic structures are rare. These surface finds have a number of novel characteristics. They are much more extensive than the domestic sites of the previous phase, and for this reason they are easier to identify in the field (Bradley 1987). They are far more frequent, and their distribution is wider, extending onto the higher parts of the chalk-land. On excavation, the structural evidence consists of occasional pits, together with stake holes. Little is known about the spatial organisation of these 'sites' and it is not clear how long they were in use. There is little to suggest a sedentary pattern of settlement: the plant remains recovered from the pits indicate a continued reliance on wild resources (Moffet *et al.* 1989), but the animal bones include a high proportion of domesticates, mainly cattle and pig (Grigson 1981).

The lithic industry changed drastically, away from lightweight, easily portable artefacts based on blades or narrow flakes. During the Earlier Neolithic much of this material had been utilised, but later sites contain a much higher proportion of debitage. Multipurpose artefacts gave way to a wider range of formal implement types (Edmonds 1987). The earlier tool kit had features in common with hunter-gatherer equipment and seems to have been designed to be both flexible and portable, but the flint industry of the Later Neolithic suggests a lower level of mobility (Bradley 1987; Edmonds 1987). A number of the new artefact types would have been difficult to transport, and a significant proportion of these collections consists of expedient tools.

Although these developments are chiefly important for the light they shed on the changing character of occupation sites, the development of a more varied tool kit has another implication. If one characteristic of the Earlier Neolithic assemblage was its emphasis on lightweight multipurpose tools, the artefacts of the following period seem to have been much more elaborate and sometimes received very careful treatment. Some of them show areas of polishing or pressure flaking that would have done nothing to improve their mechanical performance. Moreover, many of these items reflect an increased emphasis upon distinctive raw materials. Only axes and projectile points would have lent themselves to this treatment during the earlier phase; now they were joined by a variety of artefact types which could have helped to mark divisions of age, gender and status in contemporary society (see Edmonds and Thomas 1987).

Most important of all, sites on the chalk of southern England provide evidence of a different relationship between domestic activity and the major sources of raw material. We have already seen how the mines had been kept apart from contemporary settlements, as reflected by lithic scatters; the same is true of the main axe quarries. The mining of flint ceased during the Earlier Neolithic, although a few of these locations were probably re-used as domestic sites, exploiting the raw material found on the surface (Gardiner 1990). More important, some of the largest occupation sites are located at major sources of raw material on the clay with flints, where there is considerable evidence of artefact production, including the making of axes, arrow-heads and fine discoidal knives. Although the raw material would have been easy to obtain, this may not be why these sites were chosen. By locating some of the larger settlements at raw material sources it would have been easier to control access to the objects made there. This tendency is best documented in Sussex and Wessex (Gardiner 1990; Barrett *et al.* 1991, 59–70), but it is by no means limited to those areas. The same pattern has been identified by field survey at Beer Head, which seems to have been the main source of chalk flint in south-west England (M. Tingle pers.

comm.). It was also the procedure followed at Grand Pressigny in western France, where the best sources of raw material were chosen as occupation sites (Giot *et al.* 1986).

Although this development contrasts markedly with earlier practice, the evidence needs careful handling. It does not mean that the artefacts produced at these locations necessarily enjoyed a special significance in the immediate area – in fact non-flint axes may be discovered there (Barrett *et al.* 1991, 64). Moreover, in regions with a range of specialised monuments, flint axes were still *imported*, despite the abundance of local products. The patterns documented by field survey provide evidence of changes in the way in which raw material sources were controlled, but they do not imply any lessening in the intensity with which certain artefacts were exchanged. Rather, they indicate a still closer supervision of the production process.

The clearest demonstration of this point perhaps comes from Yorkshire, although much fieldwork still needs to be undertaken in this area. The flint itself was obtained from the beaches around Flamborough Head, and preliminary working certainly took place close to those locations (Manby 1979, 71 and 1988, 73; Henson 1989, 11–17). It is not clear whether these sites were distanced from the broader pattern of settlement, and there are finds of hearths, pottery and even structures to suggest that this did not happen (Moore 1964). In the case of a particularly elaborate artefact type, the polished knife, pre-forms were probably taken a short distance inland to an area denoted by one of the main flint scatters on the edge of the Wolds, and the artefacts were finished there. This activity seems to have been confined to only part of the site, and the debris from making these objects is found within a surface scatter of retouched and utilised material (T. Durden pers. comm.). The pattern is very similar to that recorded in the south.

It is unfortunate that these striking developments cannot be compared directly with changes in the making of non-flint axes, but only Langdale has been investigated with that idea in mind, and here the excavated evidence is apparently of earlier date. On the other hand, similar developments to those just described have been identified in the important sequence at the Breton quarry of Plussulien (Le Roux in Giot *et al.* 1979, 359–66). In its earlier phases this site was well away from the areas with evidence of contemporary occupation, but during a developed stage in the sequence it came to be integrated much more closely in the local pattern of settlement.

The changing status of stone axes

This discussion raises some important issues. There is no clear evidence for the operation of flint mines between the Earlier Neolithic and the development of Grimes Graves in the mid third millennium BC. Nor is there any indication that new axe quarries developed in highland Britain before that time; indeed, some of the smaller production sites in south-west England, those making axes of Groups IVa, XVI and XVII, may have been abandoned (Smith 1979). The main expansion in the distribution of the Group VII axes from North Wales ran in parallel with the development of the Cumbrian stone source, but its products were found over a smaller area, although axes belonging to this group are associated with finds of Later Neolithic date in Wessex (Smith 1979; cf. Clough and Cummins 1988, map 7). Axe production at Tievebulliagh may have started rather later, about 3500 BC, but its products are quite thinly scattered across England and Scotland (Clough and Cummins 1988, map 9). It was the Cumbrian quarries which were the most prolific source of stone axes, and yet the distribution of their products contracted during this period. How can this be explained?

At the end of chapter 8 we suggested that some of the more striking developments in southern England around 3500 BC might be explained if communities had begun to form long-distance alliances, which brought a new range of artefacts into the closed social networks to which they belonged. Non-local axes may have been deployed in these familiar settings, but the ultimate effect of doing so was to subvert existing practice. We also drew attention to the growing links between this area and developments in northern England and suggested that the growth of long-distance relations was one archaeologically detectable feature in a process of accelerated social change. A tangible element in that relationship was the introduction of Cumbrian axes into southern Britain.

Having established that link, people may have found it difficult to exploit to good effect. We have already suggested that there was a relationship between social developments on the Yorkshire Wolds and the expansion of axe production on the opposite side of the Pennines. Although those axes had the signal merit of being relatively exotic, it is difficult to see how communities in eastern England could have exercised any sort of control over the *quantities* that became available, and for that reason any major influx of Group VI artefacts would eventually have threatened the special status of these objects. The only way to cope with the problem would be to restrict the contexts in which it was appropriate to undertake exchange. Such difficulties may be behind two largely new developments which now took place in north-east England. A wider range of complex artefacts was adopted (Manby 1974, chapter 3). No doubt some of these developed in succession as different types became too widely available. At the same time, more emphasis was placed on the complex treatment of *local* raw materials, where the scale of production could be controlled more closely. The evidence from northern England is severely limited, but it seems as if communities in the south may again have followed suit. Here we find drastic changes in the organisation of artefact production, and major sources of surface flint were selected as settlement sites. The production of a number of artefact types might have taken place under closer control. This may not have entailed a loss of status for axes *per se*, but it does seem as if polished flint artefacts of several kinds took on some of the social roles that they had played. Indeed, a wider range of social differences may have been signalled by an increasing array of distinctive items. At present the details elude us, and this is an area which cries out for new research.

A crucial link is provided by the evidence of stone maceheads. These may have developed from antler prototypes found with round barrow burials (Kinnes 1979, fig. 6.2), and they have a very wide distribution along the east coast (Fig. 9.3; Roe 1979). Over the same area we find an unusual series of stone axeheads, which seem to show evidence of secondary modification (Bradley 1990b). These come from a variety

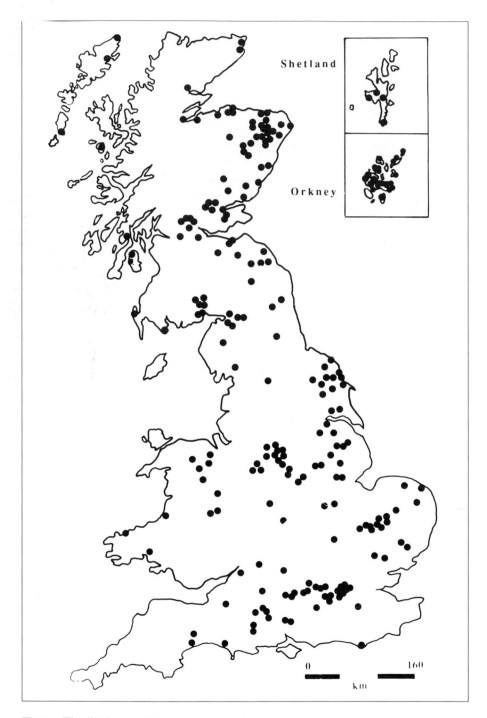

Fig. 9.3 The distribution of stone maceheads (after Roe 1979).

of source areas, but apart from a few which could have been made from glacial erratics, none is found anywhere near its original area of origin (Fig. 9.4). The modifications made to these objects take two basic forms. One small group, including the Cumbrian axeheads, as well as three others made of Continental jadeite, were perforated at the butt, perhaps for use as personal ornaments (Pl. 9.1). The remainder have a perforation at the centre of the blade, making them useless as woodworking tools, but suitable as maceheads. The evidence is of generally poor quality, and it would be easy to exaggerate the number of examples involved. Even so, it does provide an indication that at some stage during the Later Neolithic period the status of non-flint axes was coming into question. It may have been for this reason that some of these well-travelled artefacts were converted into locally appropriate forms.

Developments of the system

The developments described so far were under way before the general adoption of Grooved Ware. When that happened, from about 3000 BC, it entailed a drastic modification of these patterns. This included a renewed interest in the 'axe trade'.

As we mentioned in chapter 2, the Grooved Ware tradition has its origin at the outer edge of the British Isles, in Orkney, and its geographical distance from the other 'core areas' of the Later Neolithic may well have added to its allure. It would take another

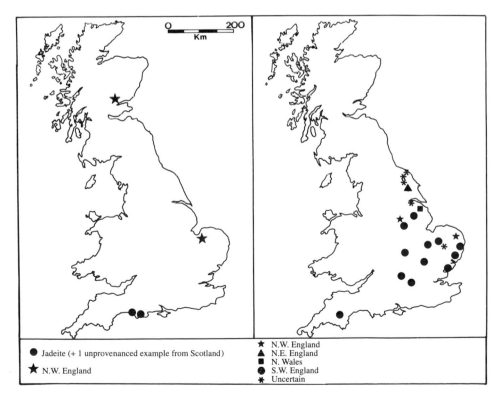

Fig. 9.4 The distribution of perforated stone axeheads. (Left) Axes with perforated butts; (right) axes with perforated blades.

book to account for the rise of this distinctive phenomenon, and we must content ourselves with a briefer summary of a number of ideas suggested in recent work.

The original impetus for social change in Orkney may have come from its involvement in the passage tomb tradition, and, in particular, its close links with the Boyne Valley (Renfrew 1979; Sharples 1985). At all events Orkney includes a group of funerary monuments as complex as any described in this account. As in so many areas, the earliest sites provide little evidence of social differentiation. There are two main series of funerary monuments, whose chronology overlaps to an uncertain extent. The 'stalled cairns' of Orkney may have contained as many as thirty bodies, but the dead were not provided with individual grave goods. Those bodies were introduced whilst they retained their articulation, but underwent considerable disturbance and rearrangement at a later stage (Richards 1988). Stalled cairns come in a variety of forms, but they share the common characteristic that they are widely distributed around the islands. In most cases they are found close to areas of fertile soil (Fraser 1983).

In this respect, they contrast markedly with Orcadian passage tombs, which were probably adopted at a later date than the first stalled cairns. These were more massive structures, fairly evenly spaced across the landscape, and dominating a series of natural regions (Fraser 1983). They made much greater demands on human labour and were built in more prominent positions than other cairns. A few examples are associated with carved decoration of a style found in Ireland. Unlike the stalled cairns, these monuments can be associated with Grooved Ware, a ceramic tradition which took some of its distinctive decoration from the same source. Fraser has argued that these sites became the dominant funerary monuments of the Orkney landscape, and their first appearance may well provide an indication of important social changes. Such arguments are greatly strengthened by Richards' reassessment of the human remains from these sites (Richards 1988). It has always been apparent that they contain a large number of disarticulated bones, and yet there is little order in their deposition, or even in the radiocarbon dates that they provide. He has pointed out that the bones that are best represented in the passage tombs are precisely those that seem to have been abstracted from the stalled cairns, some time after their initial deposition. He argues that the people responsible for building the great passage tombs were appropriating ancestral remains from other monuments and incorporating these in the new constructions. In combination with Fraser's spatial analysis, this provides evidence of a significant political change.

This last point receives support from Sharples' study of these sites (Sharples 1985). He traces the later history of these tombs, suggesting that a number of sites were destroyed or substantially modified, when they were replaced by open-air monuments more suitable for public rituals. This development may be linked with the building of henges. The henges of Later Neolithic Orkney were massive structures, and were also associated with Grooved Ware, but on this occasion their characteristic features were copied outside the Northern Isles. By 2500 BC Grooved Ware was in use over an enormous area, extending down into south-west England, whilst the decorative devices that characterise this style of pottery were shared with other media in Scotland

and beyond (Bradley and Chapman 1986). More important, henge monuments were adopted in many of the core areas of Neolithic Britain.

It is impossible to encapsulate these changes in a short summary, but one feature stands out from all the rest: the way in which the sequence seems to show a growing emphasis on special forms of monument and, perhaps, on relations with the super-natural. These are the characteristics of the Grooved Ware network that seem to set it apart from its predecessors in the Later Neolithic. Indeed, it might be argued that they have more in common with the developments considered in chapter 8. At all events, such features provided the impetus for changes in the production and circulation of axes.

It is important to see these developments in their proper perspective. Although the Orcadian sequence has its own fascination, it was only with the development of henge monuments that it had a much wider impact, and the Grooved Ware network, as it affected other regions of the country, was limited to special-purpose enclosures and the use of portable artefacts. These do not constitute a unified 'cultural' assemblage. They were adopted piecemeal over a considerable period of time. The first henge monuments in eastern Scotland date from about 3000 BC; those in southern England

Plate 9.1 Perforated axehead of Group VI tuff from Cargill, Perthshire. Photograph: Royal Museum of Scotland.

are significantly later in date and may not have been important for several hundred years. Moreover, the Grooved Ware assemblage lacks any real unity, apart from the pottery itself. It has an eclectic range of associations. Some of them, like carved stone balls, are virtually confined to Scotland (Marshall 1977; Edmonds 1992), whilst others seem to have originated before this style of pottery was adopted (Fig. 9.5). The latter include many of the types originally associated with round barrows and single graves in north-east England (Bradley 1984a, 57–61).

Such observations hardly suggest the expansion of a cohesive artefact assemblage. Rather, they seem to indicate the piecemeal adoption of exotic artefacts and ideas from a distant area of the British Isles. It seems likely that this assemblage was used on sites with specialised roles in ritual and ceremonial, and some of the main assemblages of Grooved Ware are found in the large henge monuments of Wessex. Even where this material is discovered on ostensibly domestic sites, it seems to have been deposited with considerable formality (Richards and Thomas 1984; J. Thomas 1991, chapter 4). Although the characteristic decoration found on the pottery recalls the repertoire of passage tomb art, Grooved Ware plays little role in the funerary record. At present it is by no means clear whether the use of this material coexisted with a tradition of individual burial, or whether its adoption in different parts of the country brought existing practices to an end. Until a more exact chronology becomes available, it is impossible to resolve this question, although the Grooved Ware and Peterborough Ware traditions often had different geographical emphases. Perhaps some communities sought exchange links with the Grooved Ware network, whilst others remained aloof.

Whatever the solution to this problem, it is clear that these developments brought changes in the movement of portable artefacts, even if this process was less important than the interchange of ritual knowledge. It seems safe to say that the middle years of the third millennium BC saw greater competition for exotic goods and for links with distant areas.

This is apparent from the changes that affected the distribution of axes. Their ceramic associations are revealing. Flint and stone axes are found with Peterborough Ware in roughly equal numbers, but up to 85% of those associated with Grooved Ware come from highland sources (Bradley 1984a, table 3.5). There is evidence for new developments in the latter area. The Graig Lwyd quarries included a stone plaque bearing the same style of decoration as Grooved Ware (Warren 1922), whilst the production and distribution of Group I Cornish axes expanded drastically at this time (Smith 1979). This is especially striking in view of what has been said about the rather static nature of stone axe production over the period from about 3200 BC. Axes of Cornish origin are very widely distributed and, like those made in Cumbria, they occur in especially large numbers in areas well away from the source (Cummins 1979). Outside their area of origin they are particularly associated with Grooved Ware (Wainwright and Longworth 1971, 261). Although such finds extend into north-east England, Cumbrian axes are usually found with Grooved Ware in that area, together with those originating in North Wales (Manby 1979).

In fact the main distributions of Cornish and Cumbrian axes largely complement

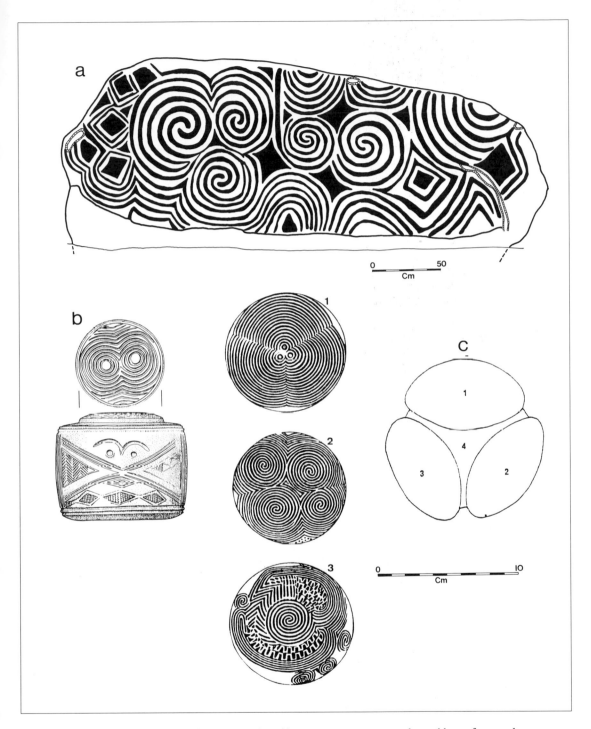

Fig. 9.5 Examples of decoration shared between passage graves and portable artefacts. a, the entrance stone at Newgrange; b, chalk drum from Folkton, Yorkshire; c, stone ball from Towie, Aberdeenshire.

one another. Those made in south-west England seem to fill the void left as the distribution of Group VI artefacts contracted (Clough and Cummins 1988, map 2), whilst they are found less frequently in the north-east where Cumbrian products retained a hold (map 6). Thus one exchange network extended along the south coast as far as the Thames estuary and East Anglia, whilst the other crossed the Pennines and the Solway Firth and reached down the North Sea coast to the Fenland. Although axes from both source areas are found together with Grooved Ware, there are important differences between these two networks. In Burl's analysis the same broad areas are associated with different styles of henge monument (Fig. 9.6; Burl 1976, fig. 13), and that geographical division can also be recognised in Barnatt's analysis of stone circles, the earliest of which most probably began life during this period (1989, chapter 4). Although the evidence is tenuous, it seems possible that the movement of stone axes was caught up in larger political alignments (see Elliott, Ellman and Hodder 1978).

These observations are certainly strengthened by the evidence from the flint mines at Grimes Graves (Fig. 9.7; see Mercer 1981a). Their inception coincides with the wider dissemination of Cornish axes, and the choice of location is extremely striking. The flint mines are found in the marginal zone between these two major exchange systems – in fact axes of Cornish origin have been found at the mines themselves. Recent fieldwork at Grimes Graves is only partly published and for this reason we must confine our comments to a few key points.

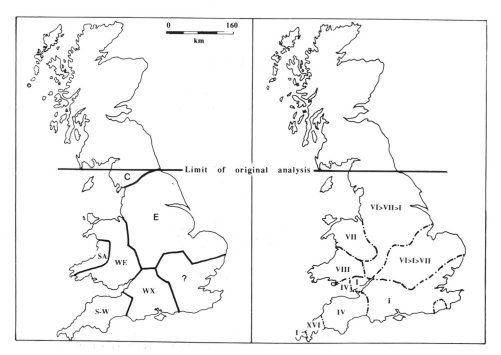

Fig. 9.6 Stone axe distributions in England and Wales (after Cummins 1980) and the regional styles of henges (after Burl 1976).

The site is associated with Grooved Ware, and artefact production may have been directed towards the north, as well as the southern network characterised by Group I axes. There are several reasons for taking this view. In the first place, it is clear that these mines did not serve the immediate area, since the lithic industries found at nearby settlement sites do not seem to have made very much use of mined flint (Healy 1991); clearly, Grimes Graves played a more important part in *non-local* exchange. The movement of its products needs to be studied by scientific characterisation, but purely stylistic criteria do provide some clues. Axes form only part of the output of this site and do not seem to have been made with particular skill (Saville 1981). Even so, they can exhibit a striking feature. A number of these artefacts have poorly polished but expanded cutting edges which appear to copy the distinctive form of examples made in south-west England.

A similar argument is suggested by a more detailed analysis of the artefacts being produced on this site. It has always been assumed that flint mining was undertaken in order to obtain high-quality nodules suitable for making axes, but careful analysis of recently excavated material from Grimes Graves shows that these were not the only products. Saville's study of the finds from a shaft excavated in 1971–2 suggests that its

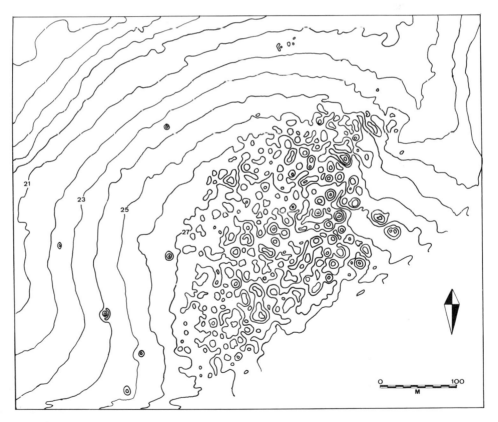

Fig. 9.7 Plan of the surviving flint mines at Grimes Graves (after Mercer 1981a). The contours are at 1 m intervals.

main output consisted of discoidal knives (Saville 1981). This is of especial significance when we remember that artefacts of this type form part of the distinctive
coast, and in particular on the Yorkshire Wolds. Such types seem to have developed
before the adoption of Grooved Ware, but they are also found in Grooved Ware
associations. The inception of mining at Grimes Graves may have supplemented the
output of workshops on the Yorkshire coast, or it may have instigated a period of
competition in which prestigious artefacts were made in a more remote area (cf. Healy
1991). In addition, its position towards the limits of two major axe distributions may
have meant that it was well placed to usurp their distinctive role.

There is a sense in which the siting of Grimes Graves recalls the characteristic
placing of earlier flint mines in the landscape. Again it is set apart from the main settled
area, although only the earlier stages of artefact production are represented. In this
case there are indications that the winning of stone was attended by ritual practices not
unlike those taking place on other sites, and a deliberate deposit of fine pottery at the
bottom of the shaft excavated by Mercer recalls very similar material from henges
(1981a, 23). Still more important is the setting of Grimes Graves in the wider cultural
landscape, for its placing towards the margin of two competing exchange systems also
recalls the siting of some of the major ceremonial monuments of the Earlier Neolithic
– the causewayed enclosures.

We have argued that the products of Grimes Graves were influenced by northern
British prototypes. It is only in the latter area that we can take this discussion much
further. Although some of the southern English henge monuments have been
excavated on a very large scale, nothing is known about the contexts in which
Group I axes were made. Nor is it clear whether flint procurement on the chalk
changed its character with the adoption of new pottery styles. In northern Britain, on
the other hand, the situation is much more satisfactory. Again we have still to identify
the extraction sites used during this phase, but we can say rather more about the
changing circumstances under which their products moved across country.

We began our discussion of the Earlier Neolithic by considering the ways in which
Cumbrian axes first played a part in long-distance exchange. Much of that discussion
concerned the circumstances under which these artefacts first crossed the Pennines.
It is appropriate that our best evidence for the movement of *Later* Neolithic axes
concerns the same geographical area. This brings us back to the all-important
production sites in Cumbria, at the same time as it illustrates the changes that came
about in the ways in which stone axes circulated.

Again there is a significant link between developments on the limestone above the
Eden Valley and those on the Yorkshire Wolds, and in some cases these connections
take a similar form. We have already presented some evidence for Earlier Neolithic
burial monuments in this area, several of which have features in common with better-
known examples in north-east England. That link remained in force during the Later
Neolithic. Not far from three of the sites discussed in chapter 8 was another excavated
by Canon Greenwell: Crosby Garrett 174. This was an oval cairn associated with a
number of burials (Greenwell 1877: 389–91). Two of these, both adult males, were
accompanied by grave goods, including artefact types which they share with Duggleby

Howe – boars' tusks and an antler macehead. The remaining artefacts include a side-looped bone pin which would also be at home in Yorkshire (Kinnes and Longworth 1985, 98). Like Duggleby Howe, the body of the mound contained a series of human cremations. Other funerary monuments in the area may also date from the same period, although the evidence is less clearcut. Perhaps the best contender is a burial from Orton, associated with a polished stone chisel (Greenwell 1877, 395–6).

Such links may seem rather tenuous, but they are more than matched by the evidence of domestic activity, which increased sharply during the Later Neolithic. Where only two groups of surface finds seem to have been associated with Earlier Neolithic pottery, later material from the same area includes eleven collections containing Peterborough Ware and four containing Grooved Ware (Cherry and Cherry 1987b). More important, this group of sites now includes a much larger component of imported flint, almost certainly originating on the Yorkshire coast. A certain number of flint artefacts, principally knives, are of types that are common in that area. With them are fragments of Group VI tuff, evidently from the reworking of axes.

The limited representation of Grooved Ware in these collections may be quite fortuitous, but it could result from a growing emphasis on the river valley, for it is here that a major group of henges is found. These have not been dated by excavation, but there seems no reason to suppose that they lie outside the normal chronology for this kind of monument. The same applies to the large stone circles of Cumbria, which Burl considers to be one of the same date (Fig. 9.8; Burl 1976, chapter 4 and 1988). One of those sites, Long Meg and her Daughters, overlies an earthwork enclosure tentatively assigned to the Earlier Neolithic (Soffe and Clare 1988).

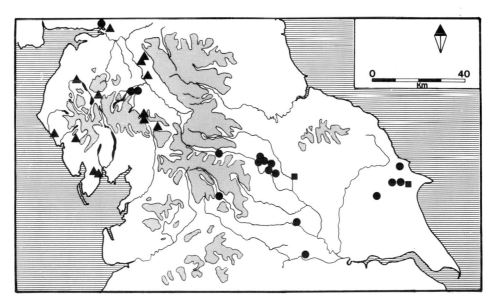

Fig. 9.8 The distribution of Later Neolithic enclosures and other monuments in northern England. Henges are shown by circles, large monoliths by squares and large stone circles by triangles.

In chapter 8 we considered the possibility that the exchange of Cumbrian axes was facilitated by the existence of large monuments. Not only might these have provided focal points at which such transactions could take place: like causewayed enclosures, they lay outside the orbit of everyday life and offered a neutral location where such encounters could be managed. There is one important difference between the developments in these two periods. During the Earlier Neolithic the major groups of monuments – cursuses and possibly enclosures – were found to the east of the Pennines, one in the Vale of York and the other on the Yorkshire Wolds. These were well placed to command the major routes across country. During the Later Neolithic a new series of earthwork monuments – henges – developed in both of those areas; indeed, at Thornborough one of the henges was superimposed on the existing cursus (Thomas 1955; Vatcher 1962). Only limited changes were made to the earlier pattern. The distribution of henges emphasised three crossing routes rather than two, and the main density of sites in the lowlands is found rather nearer to the Pennines. In addition, henges were built in two of the major valleys leading into the high ground.

On the opposite side of the Pennines, however, new developments took place (Fig. 9.8). Where there had been only one large enclosure in this area, a whole series of henges and early stone circles were built, with a distribution that picks out the main valleys leading to the Cumbrian massif (Burl 1976, chapter 4, and 1988; Barnatt 1989, fig. 60). Again the major concentration of these sites was in the Eden Valley, towards the opposite ends of the routes to north-east England – in one case the interval between sites on either side of the Pennines was as little as 40 km. The same distribution of sites continues to the north, with a second group of henges and early stone circles around the Solway Firth (Burl 1988, fig. 7.1; Barnatt 1989, fig. 54). It has long been suggested that these monuments might have played some part in the movement of Group VI artefacts, and poorly recorded finds of stone axes at three of the sites could lend a measure of support (Burl 1976, fig. 12; 1988, 83–4).

At one level the Earlier and Later Neolithic systems have many features in common, but there is also a sense in which they differ radically. Although the basic pattern to the east of the Pennines remained essentially the same, that was not the case in Cumbria where one early ceremonial centre – itself of uncertain date – was replaced by as many as ten. These seem to be concentrated in the lowland area where roughout axes were finished, and they most probably belong to a period in which the movement of specialised artefacts played an even more distinctive role. These sites were strategically located in relation to the easiest routes to the stone source, but they also commanded the major crossing points of the Pennines. We still know very little about the latest stages of axe production at Langdale, but the setting of these major monuments surely provides some clue as to how their products were distributed.

Conclusion

This account has stressed the instability of exchange systems during the Later Neolithic and has raised the possibility that groups in different parts of the country competed more actively for access to, and control over, exotic goods and specialised knowledge. That may provide one explanation for the shifting configurations in the distribution of stone artefacts. At the same time, it may also be why long-established sources suddenly increased their output whilst others were used for the first time. We have seen evidence for developments in the ways in which raw material sources were perceived and controlled. We have identified changes in the contexts in which artefact production took place. We have even suggested a process of emulation by which the distinctive stylistic features developed in one part of the country were copied in other areas, or in other materials. This is in striking contrast to the evidence from the Earlier Neolithic.

Very much the same features must lie behind the demise of the 'axe trade'. The direct archaeological evidence is limited, but it seems as if none of the stone sources continued in operation into the second half of the third millennium BC. The advent of the first metal axes had a drastic effect on the systems of exchange and consumption that had developed over the previous thousand years.

Our work at Great Langdale has not shed any light on the processes that brought stone axe production to an end (Smith 1979). It was not among the sources that produced perforated tools during the Bronze Age, and there are no indications, from artefacts or the pollen record, that the area was of any significance for several hundred years. But the real solution to the problem may not be found at the stone source, or, indeed, at any of the other Neolithic quarries in Britain. The exchange systems of the Later Neolithic are characterised by a growing instability and by an ever more urgent quest for novelty. The introduction of metals and other material items from outside the country altogether may simply have continued that process.

10

Retrospect

Throughout this book we have emphasised the study of relationships between different kinds of data as a prerequisite for broader interpretation. We have drawn on the idea that specific categories of material may play an important role in social reproduction and have argued that the creation, use and manipulation of those categories provide important media through which particular principles are negotiated (Miller 1985). Similar themes underlie the use of texts as analogies for material culture (Moore 1986; Hodder 1989).

That analogy can be useful, but it should not lead us to assume that people can transform the conditions of their existence simply by manipulating the meanings of material items. It is for that reason that we have placed a greater emphasis on the relationship between specific forms of production and the social and historical conditions in which meanings were maintained or altered. As we argued in chapter 1, the idea that objects may be 'read' in different ways according to context has major implications for our approach to prehistoric exchange systems. We shall never understand the purposes served by exchange if we continue to study distribution patterns in isolation. Equal attention has to be paid to the conditions under which they were created, and to the ways in which they were integrated into local traditions.

That we have been able to explore the implications of these arguments is a testament to the detailed and painstaking work conducted in Britain over the last few decades, most of all the analyses undertaken by the Implement Petrology Committee. Even so, the processes of contrasting these different strands of information, and of weaving them together to create a narrative, raises almost as many questions as it answers. At one level we would claim that this research provides some insights into changes in the nature and significance of the 'axe trade' in Neolithic Britain. At another, it leaves us in a better position to identify those questions that still remain unanswered. Only now can we begin to specify how they should be addressed.

Source criticism

First, we need to consider the questions raised by our work at Great Langdale itself. It is clear that finely grained volcanic tuffs were already being exploited for tools and blades by the later Mesolithic period. Similar pre-Neolithic exploitation is known from Anglesey, where flakes of Groups VIII and XXI stone have been found in unequivocal Mesolithic contexts (Ireland and Lynch 1973), whilst ground stone axes of the same date are known in Ireland and Wales (Woodman 1978; David 1989). For this reason the presence of worked tuff cannot be used as dating evidence. Still more important, we must abandon the assumption that stone axes provide direct evidence of the presence of *farmers*, cutting a swathe through a forested landscape. The evidence from north-west England suggests that this early phase of exploitation may have centred on the use of pebbles and erratics which occur widely in rivers and tills. Although we cannot exclude some use of the Cumbrian massif, it seems unlikely that exploitation of the source began before the early fourth millennium BC. As we have seen, its discovery could have been achieved by following pebbles of the appropriate material up the streams to the primary outcrops, a practice beautifully evoked in Primo Levi's account of ore prospection (Levi 1985, 83).

This brings us to one of the main questions that arise from our work. The sequence at Great Langdale provides a clear indication that the conditions under which rough-out production took place changed over time, even though axes seem to have been polished in lowland Cumbria throughout the Neolithic period (Manby 1965). These changes ran in the opposite direction to the development of lithic assemblages in Britain. From about 3300 BC less care was invested in the procurement and production of most kinds of flint artefact, but at Langdale this was when there was an increase in the control and precision exercised in making stone axes. It is not clear whether a similar trend can be identified at other major sources, but this disjuncture shows that the same constraints did not affect the production of all stone tools.

The results of our fieldwork document an increasing level of control and precision in stone axe production, accompanied by the development of more regular routines and a greater demarcation of space. Are we justified in inferring the emergence of a class of specialist producers (cf. Torrence 1986)? And how do we account for the fact that the second of our two principal ways of working appears to have developed alongside a more *ad hoc* approach to procurement and production? We are not alone in facing this problem. Even where we can achieve a measure of chronological control, difficulties of interpretation remain. At the Mauna Kea adze quarries Cleghorn (1982) relates variations in stoneworking 'skill' to the activities of specialists and apprentices. It is tempting to apply such a model here, but the terms that Cleghorn uses carry specific sociological implications, and these must be substantiated in contexts away from the stone sources.

Such contexts are largely lacking in the hinterland of the Great Langdale complex. This makes it difficult to avoid falling back on more general arguments that changes in the character and context of axe use in other parts of the country would have precipitated developments within Cumbria itself. This is also the implication of radiocarbon dates from northern England (see p. 164). The sequence at the stone source suggests a change in the conditions under which axe making was undertaken, and in our view this reflects an increased emphasis on production for exchange. But we can interpret the coexistence of two forms of production in several ways. Both could have been practised by the same groups, employing *ad hoc* techniques to make axes for local use, and more structured routines in the creation of axes for exchange. This seems most unlikely, as essentially the same forms would have been realised through polishing. Moreover, such a model conflicts with the view that the practical knowledge involved in material production is to some extent tacit and unconsidered

(Young and Bonnichsen 1985; Edmonds 1990). It is difficult to accept that the makers of axes would have moved back and forth between two radically different approaches to production.

Alternatively, the same pattern might reflect an increasing degree of differentiation, in which specific groups exercised greater control over production for exchange with other communities, particularly those across the Pennines. This need not mean that the axes themselves became important wealth items within the local area. The distribution of monuments in Cumbria suggests that the important threshold across which their significance was transformed was *around the limits* of the region. This alternative model has its attraction, particularly given the broader sequences documented in chapters 8 and 9, but those wider sequences do not offer a sufficient basis for understanding changes in axe production within Cumbria itself. As Sørensen has pointed out, there is a danger of imposing a rigid general model in which the local sequence is 'explained' by developments in exchange networks at a larger geographical scale (Sørensen 1989, 199). That would detract from the idea that objects changed their significance as they circulated in different 'regimes of value'.

There seems little prospect of taking this discussion further without a campaign of fieldwork in the Cumbrian lowlands, for it is here that the major gaps in our knowledge occur. At present the main source of information on the early pattern of settlement is provided by pollen analysis (Walker 1965; Pennington 1975), and outside a few well-researched areas occupation sites have been discovered almost entirely by chance, with the result that we cannot be sure whether they represent a valid sample. This problem arises because so little land is under the plough; in pasture the only way of expanding our information is through systematic test-pitting. The situation is less serious on the west Cumbrian coast, and on the limestone uplands between the Lake District and the Pennines, where some field survey has taken place (Cherry and Cherry 1987a, 1987b), but in both areas we still need the detailed observations that excavation can provide. Moreover, work in the limestone uplands can give us only part of the picture, for it is on the lower ground of the Eden Valley that some of the main monuments are found. Their hinterland remains little known.

If there are difficulties in reconstructing the settlement system within Cumbria, there are equally serious problems in interpreting the monuments found towards its limits. In our account these have been 'dated' by extrapolation from excavated examples in other areas, but this is an unsatisfactory expedient. Thus the henge monuments have been discussed on the basis of radiocarbon dates from different regions, in particular southern England. The large stone circles present another problem. Although Burl has advanced a persuasive case for a rather early date, the chronological evidence is extremely ambiguous (Burl 1988; Barnatt 1989). This difficulty can only be resolved at a local level, and until this happens it is not possible to form precise equations between the development of monuments and the sequence of axe production. At the same time, their role in the circulation of these axes would be better understood if we possessed the detailed contextual evidence that we find on excavated sites elsewhere in Britain.

Because of these limitations there is a sense in which we have been obliged to move too rapidly from the production of axes within Cumbria to their distribution across the country as a whole. Once again we are limited by imbalances in the distribution of fieldwork. Our account has stressed the extraordinary importance of developments on the opposite side of the Pennines, and in particular the significance of the Vale of York and the Yorkshire Wolds. It is most unfortunate that such crucial areas still remain underexplored, with the result that so much of our account depends on a retrospective analysis of the results of old excavations. Happily, this is a problem which is now being addressed by work on the Wolds (T. Manby pers. comm.), but the more exact chronology that should emerge from this will come too late to add detail to our discussion.

By contrast, our information on developments in Wessex and the Thames Valley is very detailed indeed. This is somewhat paradoxical since it is one major premise of our study that social changes in these areas were associated with contacts with north-east England – contacts that are best documented through the circulation of Group VI axes and the distribution of round barrow burial. Again the precise equation between these regional sequences is problematical. The distribution of Group VI axes suggests an emphasis on the North Sea coastline, but the most secure links are between the radio-carbon dates from the stone source at Great Langdale and those tracing the later use of causewayed enclosures in the south. Enough is known, however, to demonstrate that axes exported from Cumbria were used in different ways in different regional systems, and that the main changes in local sequences happened when those systems were brought into contact. This is not to suggest a relationship of cause and effect, in which external connections provided the trigger for social change. Rather, the estab lishment of more extensive networks provided access to a series of material and symbolic resources which could be drawn upon in the resolution of local conflicts of interest.

Further difficulties arise as we trace the sequence into the Later Neolithic period, for again the evidence is severely imbalanced. Two major issues still need to be clarified. First, it is essential that the study of exchange systems based on complex flint artefacts be placed on an equal footing with our reconstruction of the character of axe production at Langdale. This work should focus on the evidence of lithic production along the North Sea coast, and, in particular, on the remarkable series of elaborate artefacts made in the vicinity of Flamborough Head. At present we know all too little about their chronology and distribution and are even further from understanding the contexts in which they were made. Fortunately, such research is now under way (T. Durden pers. comm.).

The second empirical problem concerns chronology. In chapter 9 we suggested that flint and stone axes may have circulated in different ways and that they were chiefly associated with Peterborough Ware and Grooved Ware respectively. It was impossible to take this argument far because the chronological development of Peterborough Ware was so poorly understood. If we are to consider assemblage variability in any but the most superficial terms, the dating of this tradition will need to be refined. Even so, two major trends could be identified during this period, and both are evidenced by so many different observations that they deserve to be taken seriously.

First, there was evidence for the exercise of new controls over the production and circulation of specific categories of object. During the Earlier Neolithic, it seems as if most of the flint mines were situated on the margins of the settled landscape. There is little or no evidence of contemporary occupation at these sites. Like causewayed enclosures, important stone sources may have been located on the edges of the settlement pattern, and specialised transactions such as exchange separated from everyday activities. During the Later Neolithic, however, it seems as if some of the major flint sources were selected as occupation sites. It remains to be shown by spatial analysis, coupled with excavation, whether artefact production was concentrated in particular parts of these complexes, but, if so, this might indicate a further measure of control over access to specific objects. At its simplest this interpretation suggests that the circulation of valuables could have been overseen from the outset.

The second distinctive feature of the Later Neolithic was the widening range of lithic artefacts being made, and the more volatile character of their chronology and distribution. Towards the close of the Earlier Neolithic period we identified a widening in the fields over which exotic artefacts travelled. The earlier third millennium BC saw more interaction between *different* regional networks. There is evidence for a process of emulation by which the distinctive products of one source area were imitated in a different material. We even saw a case in which stone axes were converted into maceheads towards the limits of their distribution. There are also indications that the products of one source area may have supplanted those of another. The changing relationship between flint and stone axes may provide an example of this process. A further instance is offered by the striking interplay between the distributions of axes made in Cornwall, Cumbria and North Wales.

Again the changing associations of these objects show clearly that the meanings attached to them were subject to different interpretations from one area to another. As a wider range of stone artefacts were made, their deposition seems to have been attended by a subtle protocol, so that stone axes are rare in burials but are commonly found in structured deposits close to monuments, or in watery locations. Indeed, variations in their treatment and deposition within particular regions suggest that the concepts associated with axes may have been drawn upon in different ways. During the Earlier Neolithic some of them appear to have been deliberately smashed in the context of rites of passage, perhaps contributing to the transformation of the social individual on death. In other cases, axes were incorporated into formal pit deposits or thrown into rivers such as the Thames.

There is no reason to suppose that all these practices served the same purpose. Formal deposition in pits may have served to 'presence' the properties of individuals in relation to particular activities or places (Barrett *et al.* 1991). By contrast, axes deposited in rivers may have acted as 'gifts to the gods', establishing symbolic exchange relationships that would have important consequences for the distribution of power among the living (Gregory 1980; Bradley 1990a). On the other hand, some of the flint artefacts characteristic of the Yorkshire Wolds were more often used as grave goods. Some of these types can also be found in Grooved Ware deposits in Wessex. These almost certainly postdate the first use of such items in burials in the north, and they provide a further example of the way in which the ideas associated with particular categories of material might have changed across space and time.

The observations made in this study go some way towards providing a genealogy of stone tool production and exchange – a broad sequence documenting developments in the character and context of certain lithic assemblages in the British Neolithic. As we argued in chapters 8 and 9, we come closer to understanding this sequence when it is considered in relation to the evidence of changes in other spheres of social life. We saw how the Neolithic period witnessed important developments in the nature of funerary traditions: in particular a shift away from corporate burial, and an increased emphasis on specific individuals in death. This was apparent at an earlier stage in northern England, but in time it became established across much of the country. These changes seem to indicate a series of transformations in the significance of the ancestors. Once they had served to sustain communal relations, perhaps reproducing divisions based on age and gender; now they were more overtly implicated in competition for dominance.

Our sequence also documents important changes in the character of ceremonial monuments. Whilst causewayed enclosures may originally have provided contexts in which relations between fragmented social groups could be played out, the later horizons at a number of sites suggest fundamental changes in the part that they had played (Edmonds in press). Like the henges that dominate our record for the Later Neolithic, these sites may have taken on more restricted roles, as places where specific practices could be undertaken, and where their interpretation could be controlled. Some of the rituals undertaken at henge monuments were accompanied by episodes of feasting, and it seems likely that exchanges also took place within their limits. Moreover, their association with Grooved Ware, and with important communication routes, reflects the increased emphasis that was placed on objects and ideas derived from distant sources.

These sequences reveal important changes in the character of social relations around 3300 BC. At the same time, they suggest that the manner in which these relations were negotiated may also have been transformed (Kinnes 1985, 43). For a number of authors this period saw the emergence of regional elites, whose position depended on monopolising access to a variety of 'prestige goods' (Thorpe and Richards 1984). We should not reject these arguments, but, given the evidence for local production and the varied ways in which these objects were treated, we should be cautious in subsuming our data within such a general model. These changes may reflect a rather more complex situation, in which distinctions *within and between* groups were mediated through the production, exchange and consumption of portable items (Edmonds and Thomas 1987). From the end of the Earlier Neolithic period, exchange networks became more competitive, and the distribution of axes perhaps reflects changes in the *character* of demand.

We have said enough to show that the movement of stone axes cannot be studied in terms of modern economic principles. Although many issues remain unresolved, it is clear that what we call the 'axe trade' was linked to broader questions of communication and control. In the more competitive climate that seems to have emerged towards 3000 BC the currency of particular status items would seem to be intimately connected to the contexts in which they circulated – their 'regimes of value'. Flint and stone offer very different potentials in this respect. Flint axes could be produced in many areas, making it difficult to maintain effective control over their production, distribution and interpretation. This may help us to understand the increasing elaboration of a number of other flint artefact types, and the use of unusual and easily recognisable raw material. The distinctive form and material of these artefacts may have been important in fixing their association with certain ideas, and perhaps with certain kinds of social relationship.

Other raw materials have restricted natural distributions. The obvious point which arises from this comparison is that the more distant stone sources could have achieved such prominence *precisely because* they were more distant. In other words, the archaeological visibility of these sources cannot be explained by saying that they were the only places at which raw material could be found. Nor is it possible to argue that these sites reflect the selection of particular raw materials because of their inherent physical, mechanical or functional properties (see Bradley *et al.* 1992). Rather, the scale of the deposits on sites like those at Langdale indicates that the effectiveness of Group VI axes in social transactions was maintained over a considerable period. As we argued in chapters 8 and 9, it seems reasonable to suggest that the sequence of change in the nature and organisation of production reflects changes in the nature of the wealth economy beyond the boundaries of Cumbria. The ideas with which these objects were associated may have changed according to context, and it is possible that the specific roles they played also changed through time. Yet the extraordinarily marginal position of the stone source helped to maintain the integrity of the networks within which Lake District axes circulated.

As the title suggests, this chapter offers a retrospect rather than a series of definitive conclusions. There is much that we do not know about the production and circulation of axes, and there may be more that we shall never know. We cannot tell the numbers in which artefacts were made at Langdale, and we cannot recognise many of the items for which they were exchanged. We have suggested the development of competitive strains in Neolithic society, but again the fine details elude us. Although we have summarised some of the main points to arise from this particular project, we have also been concerned with those issues that need more investigation. In doing so, no doubt we have drawn attention to the weak links in the argument, where this is usually left to reviewers. But it would be misleading to give the impression that this avenue of research has been closed. There is much that remains to be done, and we have offered a few suggestions as to where new work might usefully be concentrated. In archaeology, all interpretations are provisional. If we have advanced proposals where we might have insisted on conclusions, 'books are not made to be believed, but to be subjected to enquiry' (Eco 1983).

APPENDIX

Details of the material employed in analysis

Table A.1. *Quantitative assessment of the surface scatters at Great Langdale*

Site/group	No. of sites	Total area (approx.)	Relative flake quantities	Altitude
Troughton Beck	8	1350 m²	9	400–500 m
Stake Beck (N)	7	40 m²	2	500–540 m
Stake Beck (S)	3	106 m²	3	600–640 m
North Scree	25	3080 m²	7	240–420 m
Central Buttress	11	800 m²	8	470–540 m
Central Scree	25	8320 m²	9	255–400 m
Top Buttress	38	1840 m²	11	570–620 m
South Scree	12?	11780 m²	11	250–600 m
Middle Gully	11	450 m²	7	600–640 m
East Gully	8	630 m²	6	600–650 m
Loft Crag	4	270 m²	7	560–660 m
Dungeon Ghyll	8	172 m²	5	620–630 m
Harrison Stickle (W)	11	700 m²	8	580–640 m
Harrison Stickle (E)	13	1140 m²	6	570–610 m
Thorn Crag	4	47 m²	4	460–510 m
Stickle Tarn	5	80 m²	2	480 520 m
Harrison Combe	7	55 m²	1	640–660 m
Great End				
Great End	2	42 m²	1	800–840 m
Scafell Pike				
Brown Tongue	3	6 m²	1	410–430 m
Scafell Pike A	38	387 m²	5	780–820 m
Scafell Pike B	23	69 m²	2	810–830 m
Scafell Pike C	7	30 m²	1	830–840 m
Scafell Pike D	69	604 m²	5	830–890 m
Scafell Pike E	46	186 m²	4	860–900 m
Scafell Pike F	31	1265 m²	5	895–905 m
Scafell Pike G	29	46 m²	5	950–955 m
Scafell Pike H	30	126 m²	4	870–890 m
Scafell Pike I	0	508 m²	5	815–870 m
Seathwaite Fell/Glaramara				
Great Slack	6	13 m²	1	530–550 m
Sprinkling Crags	9	345 m²	4	510–560 m
Red Beck	5	56 m²	2	500–520 m
Hind Side	12	67 m²	1	600–655 m
Glaramara (S)	2	0.7 m²	1	765–775 m
Glaramara (N)	15	158 m²	5	730–750 m

Notes to table A.1

Relative flake quantities: coding
1 0–10
2 10–20
3 20–40
4 40–80
5 80–160
6 160–320
7 320–640
8 640–1250
9 1250–2500
10 2500–5000
11 >5000

This table incorporates data recorded during the period of the survey undertaken by the Cumbria and Lancashire Archaeological Unit and the National Trust (Claris and Quartermaine 1989).

Table A.2. *Technological characteristics of the surface samples at Great Langdale*

Site	Sample	Testing/shaping No %		Mass reduction No %		Thinning No %		Unclass. No %		Hinge fractures No %		Prepared platforms No %		Chips/spalls
Troughton Beck														
1	A	27	13.5	42	21	106	53	25	12.5	97	48.5	79	39.5	★
1	B	58	29	77	38.5	45	22.5	20	10	113	56.5	61	30.5	
2	A	44	22	59	29.5	82	41	15	7.5	87	43.5	69	34.5	★
3	A	31	15.5	40	20	124	62	5	2.5	104	52	87	43.5	★
3	B	57	28.5	72	36	58	29	13	6.5	106	53	59	29.5	
3	C	62	31	112	56	20	10	6	3	117	58.5	54	27	
7	A	34	17	47	23.5	121	55.5	18	9	94	47	108	54	★
7	B	49	24.5	73	36.5	64	32	14	7	121	60.5	84	42	
Stake Beck														
9	A	11	5.5	21	10.5	151	75.5	17	13.5	142	71	66	33	
16	A	14	7	27	13.5	139	69.5	20	10	135	67.5	71	35.5	
16	B	7	3.5	32	16	148	74	13	6.5	124	62	79	39.5	
North Scree														
18	A	48	24	52	26	87	43.5	13	6.5	109	54.5	76	38	★
19	A	38	19	63	31.5	72	36	17	8.5	94	47	81	40.5	★
24	A	27	13.5	38	19	120	60	15	7.5	91	45.5	107	53.5	★
26	A	41	20.5	61	30.5	77	38.5	21	10.5	102	51	88	44	
28	A	48	24	55	27.5	81	40.5	16	8	99	49.5	78	39	
33	A	27	13.5	31	15.5	132	66	10	5	86	43	81	40.5	
Central Scree														
52	A	21	10.5	28	14	128	64	23	11.5	93	46.5	92	46	★
52	B	44	22	68	34	73	36.5	15	7.5	117	57.5	63	31.5	
59	A	29	14.5	37	17.5	112	56	22	11	94	47	94	47	
59	B	48	24	57	28.5	75	37.5	20	10	115	57.5	79	39.5	
60	A	27	13.5	31	15.5	129	64.5	13	6.5	97	48.5	77	38.5	★
62	A	34	17	39	18	102	51	25	12.5	82	41	69	34.5	
62	B	47	23.5	61	30.5	76	38	16	8	76	38	98	49	
63	A	17	13.5	29	14.5	124	62	30	15	88	44	69	34.5	
Central Buttress														
49	A	48	24	86	43	58	29	8	4	62	31	96	48	★(low)
49	B	42	21	73	36.5	67	33.5	18	9	73	36.5	77	38.5	
50	A	27	13.5	42	21	124	62	28	14	94	47	61	30.5	
51	A	34	17	39	19.5	100	50	27	13.5	102	51	66	33	★(low)
52	A	31	15.5	49	24.5	103	51.5	17	8.5	125	62.5	59	29.5	★(low)
52	B	44	22	71	35.5	72	36	13	6.5	137	68.5	52	26	
53	A	49	24.5	97	48.5	40	20	14	7	118	59	58	29	★(low)
55	A	26	13	34	17	111	55.5	29	14.5	104	52	62	31	

Table A.2. (*cont.*)

Site	Sample	Testing/shaping No %	Mass reduction No %	Thinning No %	Unclass. No %	Hinge fractures No %	Prepared platforms No %	Chips/spalls
Top Buttress								
82	A	48 24	95 47.5	43 21.5	14 7	84 42	71 35.5	
83	A	51 25.5	88 44	49 24.5	12 6	98 49	64 32	
84	A	45 22.5	104 52	37 16.5	14 7	102 51	79 39.5	
85	A	31 15.5	63 31.5	86 43	20 10	77 38.5	84 42	*
85	B	42 21	68 34	72 36	18 9	81 40.5	78 39	*(low)
87	A	37 18.5	51 25.5	88 49	24 12	74 37	69 34.5	
91	A	30 15	42 21	112 56	16 8	75 37.5	90 45	*
91	B	39 19.5	72 36	74 37	25 12.5	80 40	78 39	
91	C	47 23.5	77 38.5	60 30	16 8	83 41.5	86 44	
92	A	29 14.5	43 21.5	104 52	24 12	58 29	123 61.5	*
92	B	34 17	52 26	99 49.5	15 7.5	61 30.5	104 52	*(low)
92	C	46 23	61 30.5	83 41.5	10 5	67 33.5	127 63.5	
94	A	29 14.5	37 18.5	119 59.5	15 7.5	49 24.5	141 70.5	*
94	B	33 16.5	49 24.5	100 50	18 9	51 25.5	143 71.5	*
94	C	41 20.5	64 32	81 40.5	14 7	53 26.5	125 62.5	
98	A	23 11.5	28 14	134 67	15 7.5	47 23.5	15 75	*
98	B	28 14	26 13	130 65	16 8	51 25.5	137 68.5	*
98	C	47 23.5	48 24	81 40.5	24 12	53 26.5	141 70.5	
100	A	41 20.5	52 26	99 49.5	18 9	61 30.5	122 61	*
100	B	44 22	48 24	94 47	14 7	59 29.5	120 60	
102	A	52 26	60 30	79 39.5	9 4.5	64 32	127 63.5	*
102	B	31 15.5	41 20.5	117 58.5	11 5.5	57 28.5	133 66.5	*
103	A	20 10	33 19	120 60	28 14	63 31.5	138 69	*
103	B	42 21	53 26.5	90 45	15 7.5	66 33	149 74.5	
104	A	39 19.5	49 24.5	98 49	14 7	69 34.5	132 66	*
106	A	29 14.5	34 17	126 63	11 5.5	60 30	129 64.5	*
106	B	38 19	42 21	99 49.5	21 10.5	71 30.5	139 69.5	
Margins of South Scree								
111	A	29 14.5	34 17	114 57	23 11.5	102 51	71 35.5	*
113	A	62 31	73 36.5	60 30	5 2.5	128 64	61 30.5	
114	A	19 9.5	22 11	118 59	41 20.5	94 47	77 38.5	*
115	A	44 22	59 29.5	70 35	27 13.5	119 59.5	70 35	*
115	B	48 24	68 34	73 36.5	11 5.5	133 66.5	58 29	
117	A	38 19	46 23	81 40.5	35 17.5	121 60.5	64 32	
117	B	69 34.5	74 37	44 22	13 6.5	129 64.5	58 29	
Middle Gully								
127	A	47 23.5	68 34	71 35.5	14 7	66 33	109 54.5	
128	A	43 21.5	62 31	79 39.5	16 8	71 35.5	112 56	
129	A	30 15	44 22	100 50	26 13	68 34	131 65.5	*
130	A	49 24.5	58 29	81 40.5	12 6	77 38.5	117 58.5	
130	B	54 27	75 37.5	51 25.5	20 10	83 41.5	111 55.5	
131	A	23 11.5	37 18.5	121 60.5	19 9.5	68 34	123 61.5	*
134	A	21 10.5	31 15.5	113 56.5	35 17.5	60 30	130 65	*

Table A.2. (*cont.*)

Site	Sample	Testing/ shaping No %		Mass reduction No %		Thinning No %		Unclass. No %		Hinge fractures No %		Prepared platforms No %		Chips/ spalls
East Gully														
135	A	19	9.5	24	12	120	60	37	18.5	73	36.5	124	62	★
135	B	58	29	67	33.5	61	30.5	24	12	80	40	110	55	
138	A	31	15.5	51	25.5	90	45	28	14	64	32	127	63.5	
139	A	29	14.5	38	19	111	55.5	22	11	70	35	136	68	★
139	B	45	22.5	75	37.5	64	32	16	8	86	43	118	59	
Loft Crag														
146	A	54	27	68	34	67	33.5	11	5.5	116	58	74	37	★
146	B	60	30	64	32	61	30.5	15	7.5	108	54	65	32.5	
147	A	43	21.5	54	27	51	25.5	25	12.5	123	61.5	70	35	
147	B	62	31	58	29	59	29.5	21	10.5	134	67	62	31	
Below Thorn Crag														
187	A	11	5.5	19	9.5	143	71.5	27	13.5	114	57	81	40.5	★
188	A	9	4.5	13	6.5	160	80	18	9	128	64	72	36	
Dungeon Ghyll														
150	A	46	23	67	33.5	63	31.5	24	12	142	71	56	28	
151	A	37	18.5	85	42.5	58	29	20	10	126	63	62	31	
Harrison Stickle East														
154	A	26	13	65	32.5	90	45	19	9.5	87	43.5	84	42	★
154	B	48	24	75	37.5	64	32	13	6.5	99	49.5	72	36	
155	A	31	15.5	51	25.5	100	50	18	9	92	46	92	46	★
155	B	58	29	81	40.5	49	24.5	11	5.5	104	52	89	45.5	
156	A	53	26.5	70	35	70	35	7	3.5	111	55.5	78	39	★
156	B	51	25.5	79	49.5	54	27	17	8.5	90	45	68	34	
161	A	24	12	37	18.5	118	59	21	10.5	124	62	64	32	★
161	B	48	24	77	38.5	59	29.5	17	8.5	119	59.5	70	35	
162	A	44	22	53	26.5	81	40.5	22	11	98	49	78	39	★
162	B	51	25.5	69	34.5	61	30.5	19	9.5	104	52	75	37.5	
163	A	48	24	59	29.5	70	35	23	11.5	96	48	81	40.5	
164	A	37	18.5	61	30.5	79	39.5	23	11.5	90	45	71	35.5	
165	A	49	24.5	70	35	60	30	21	10.5	88	44	77	38.5	
Harrison Stickle West														
176	A	59	29.5	68	34	58	29	15	7.5	86	43	82	41	★
180	A	44	22	70	35	72	36	14	7	102	51	70	35	
181	A	32	16	52	26	98	49	18	9	110	55	72	36	
181	B	50	25	74	37	62	31	14	7	132	66	68	34	
185	A	38	19	79	39.5	70	35	13	6.5	120	60	74	37	
Below Harrison Stickle														
170/171		16	8	31	15.5	122	61	31	15.5	94	47	81	40.5	★
174	A	20	10	29	14.5	130	65	21	10.5	88	44	94	47	★

Table A.2. (*cont.*)

Site	Sample	Testing/ shaping No %		Mass reduction No %		Thinning No %		Unclass. No %		Hinge fractures No %		Prepared platforms No %		Chips/ spalls
Scafell Pike A and B														
406	A (100)	6	6	18	18	62	62	14	14	68	68	39	39	★
420	A (100)	14	14	9	9	61	61	16	16	57	57	42	42	★
427	A (200)	20	10	42	16	114	57	24	12	119	59.5	61	30.5	
459	A (100)	12	12	14	14	59	59	15	15	61	61	31	31	
Scafell Pike C														
469	A (100)	2	2	12	12	70	70	16	16	50	50	38	38	
Scafell Pike D														
522	A (100)	11	11	18	18	64	64	7	7	71	71	28	28	
523	A (200)	12	6	29	14.5	140	70	19	9.5	124	62	49	24.5	
529	A (200)	18	9	31	15.5	138	69	12	6	140	70	54	27	★
532	A (200)	41	20.5	43	21.5	102	51	14	7	119	59.5	68	34	
533	A (100)	13	13	29	29	50	50	8	8	77	77	34	34	
540	A (200)	24	12	58	29	98	49	20	10	132	66	37	18.5	
540	B (200)	13	6.5	29	14.5	126	63	32	16	109	54.5	77	38.5	★
Scafell Pike E														
553	A (100)	18	18	19	19	50	50	13	13	67	67	32	32	
577	A (100)	29	29	26	26	35	35	10	10	49	49	42	42	
583	A (100)	13	13	12	12	60	60	15	15	71	71	29	29	
Scafell Pike F														
597	A (100)	6	6	13	13	74	74	7	7	58	58	44	44	★
598	A (200)	24	12	44	22	112	56	20	10	109	54.5	72	36	★
604	A (100)	29	29	17	17	48	48	6	6	64	64	40	40	★
616	A (200)	22	11	49	24.5	119	59.5	10	5	131	65.5	84	42	★
617	A (200)	29	14.5	44	22	108	54	19	8	122	61	66	33	★
619	A (100)	18	18	31	31	41	41	10	10	68	68	29	29	★
620	A (200)	61	30.5	48	24	75	37.5	16	8	140	70	52	26	★
Scafell Pike G														
624	A (200)	37	18.5	66	33	84	42	13	6.5	129	64.5	68	34	
626	A (200)	16	8	28	14	130	65	26	13	109	54.5	72	36	★
627	A (200)	41	20.5	55	27.5	87	43.5	17	8.5	132	66	52	26	
628	A (200)	24	12	37	18.5	119	59.5	20	10	99	49.5	81	40.5	
630	A (200)	39	19.5	61	30.5	81	40.5	19	9.5	116	58	59	29.5	
634	A (200)	57	28.5	70	35	70	35	7	3.5	124	62	64	32	★(low)
635	A (200)	18	9	27	13.5	141	70.5	14	7	101	50.5	70	35	★
636	A (200)	31	15.5	48	24	103	51.5	18	9	111	55.5	58	29	
637	A (200)	24	12	58	29	104	52	14	7	91	45.5	82	41	
638	A (200)	20	10	59	29.5	110	55	11	5.5	106	53	76	38	
641	A (200)	34	17	51	25.5	109	54.5	6	3	121	60.5	68	34	★
642	A (200)	52	26	59	29.5	80	40	9	4.5	117	58.5	79	39.5	
643	A (200)	50	25	67	33.5	74	37	9	4.5	130	65	60	30	
649	A (200)	24	12	34	17	120	60	22	11	104	52	90	45	
651	A (200)	46	23	49	24.5	96	48	9	4.5	120	60	81	40.5	

Table A.2. (*cont.*)

Site	Sample	Testing/ shaping No %		Mass reduction No %		Thinning No %		Unclass. No %		Hinge fractures No %		Prepared platforms No %		Chips/ spalls
Scafell Pike H														
664	A (100)	20	20	31	31	40	40	9	9	62	62	38	38	
670	A (100)	16	16	30	30	48	48	6	6	68	68	32	32	*
670	B (100)	10	10	18	18	68	68	4	4	53	53	49	49	*
682	A (100)	18	18	29	29	47	47	6	6	70	70	37	37	
Scafell Pike I														
709	A (100)	28	28	34	34	34	34	4	4	50	50	30	30	
709	B (200)	40	20	58	29	94	47	8	4	108	54	98	49	
710	A (200)	46	23	61	30.5	79	39.5	14	7	122	61	71	35.5	
711	A (200)	34	17	59	29.5	92	46	15	7.5	98	49	80	40	
715	A (200)	37	18.5	38	19	113	56.5	12	6	90	45	100	50	*
Glaramara South Peak														
755	A (50)	17	34	20	40	10	20	3	6	38	76	9	18	
Glaramara														
757	A (200)	49	24.5	76	38	70	35	5	2.5	130	65	71	35.5	*
761	A (100)	28	28	47	47	20	20	5	5	69	69	41	41	
767	A (200)	46	23	58	29	88	44	8	4	137	68.5	61	30.5	
771	A (200)	21	10.5	43	21.5	121	60.5	15	7.5	104	52	73	36.5	

1. Sample size at each site = 200 flakes (unless otherwise indicated).

2. The presence of significant quantities of small trimming chips is indicated by an asterisk (*).

3. Unless otherwise indicated, multiple samples (A, B, C) are from the top, middle and lower portions of individual screes.

NB Many of the 'sites' on Scafell Pike were too small for sampling. A significant number of these consist of clusters of small flakes and chips, and thus appear to represent the final 'finishing' of implements. However, few scatters reflect the production of anything more than single tools. In all instances where they were recognised, spatial distinctions between different stages of working were on a restricted scale, usually being confined to within a few metres.

Table A.3. *Absolute frequency of flake categories on the excavated sites at Great Langdale*

	A	B	C	D	E	F	Uncl.	Retouched	Total
Stake Beck	22	171	3320	2675	364	540	371	63	7656
Harrison Stickle 1–3	38	217	3714	4649	2309	1741	403	19	13,071
Harrison Stickle 4	12	59	1629	2851	1860	941	103	11	7455
Top Buttress site 98									
Spit AB	30	453	636	764	1624	930	62	—	4499
Spit CD	15	532	702	845	1087	631	105	3	3917
Spit EF	61	484	561	587	520	416	39	—	2688
Spit GH	46	610	717	828	1641	794	52	2	4688
Spit IJ	18	453	752	821	1224	737	71	—	4076
Spit KL	12	375	494	518	537	541	22	—	2499
Spit MN	30	338	556	570	741	463	68	5	2766
Spit O	4	271	632	689	964	643	29	—	3232
Top Buttress site 95									
Spit AB	17	231	476	561	1220	941	37	—	3483
Spit CD	36	337	465	594	634	541	26	1	2633
Spit EF	26	385	408	724	857	623	63	—	3086
Spit GH	44	442	327	689	1431	878	44	2	3855
Spit IJ	31	351	515	786	1119	810	78	—	3690
Spit KL	28	414	461	652	1371	961	29	—	3916
Spit MN	49	362	303	537	319	361	89	1	2020
Spit OP	34	216	352	471	184	292	31	—	1580
Spit Q	13	189	286	314	471	564	49	—	1886
Dungeon Ghyll									
148 Primary	261	2600	1104	421	317	840	132	9	5675
148 Secondary	187	2804	3741	4011	6318	7531	67	2	24,659
148 Tertiary	124	686	403	247	53	160	23	—	1696
Loft Crag (DS 87)									
refit 1	—	6	32	28	13	34	—	—	113
refit 2	—	2	11	38	22	26	—	—	99

Table A.4. *Absolute values for technological attributes on the debitage from excavations at Great Langdale*

Termination types: Regular (feather) vs. Irregular (hinge or step)

Context	A Reg.	A Irreg.	B Reg.	B Irreg.	C Reg.	C Irreg.	D Reg.	D Irreg.
D.G. Primary	121	540	648	1942	479	625	232	189
D.G. Secondary	132	85	2216	588	2968	746	3552	459
D.G. Tertiary	65	59	241	445	126	277	162	185
H. Stickle 1–3	14	24	80	137	2060	1654	3241	1408
H. Stickle 4	6	11	25	34	987	642	1919	932
Stake Beck	7	17	39	132	1024	2296	1123	1552
98 AB	17	13	384	69	552	104	631	133
98 CD	6	9	397	135	587	115	753	110
98 EF	18	43	337	147	483	78	503	84
98 GH	21	25	468	142	593	124	717	111
98 IJ	11	7	338	115	638	114	771	50
98 KL	9	3	283	92	451	43	435	83
98 MN	21	14	227	111	437	119	467	103
98 O	3	1	218	53	508	124	606	83
95 AB	11	6	325	106	381	95	452	119
95 CD	21	15	266	71	414	51	521	73
95 EF	14	12	303	82	361	47	617	107
95 GH	28	16	359	83	294	33	617	72
95 IJ	21	10	237	114	372	143	682	104
95 KL	11	17	325	89	398	63	587	65
95 MN	28	21	245	117	219	84	446	91
95 OP	19	15	166	50	274	78	389	82
95 Q	8	5	114	75	195	91	248	66

Table A.5. *Evidence for platform preparation on flakes (presence/absence) from excavations at Great Langdale*

Context	A		B		C		D	
	Pr.	Ab.	Pr.	Ab.	Pr.	Ab.	Pr.	Ab.
D.G. Primary	I	660	426	2174	354	750	164	257
D.G. Secondary	7	210	1959	845	2944	797	3652	359
D.G. Tertiary	—	124	256	430	187	216	162	85
HS 1–3	—	38	31	186	1656	2056	3021	1628
HS 4	—	17	18	41	965	664	2002	849
Stake Beck	—	24	29	142	449	2871	845	1830
98 AB	4	26	371	82	481	155	609	155
98 CD	2	13	347	185	526	176	686	159
98 EF	8	53	293	191	398	163	483	104
98 GH	6	40	389	221	538	179	763	65
98 IJ	3	15	287	166	594	158	704	117
98 KL	—	12	163	212	374	120	388	130
98 MN	5	30	271	67	426	130	389	181
98 O	—	4	184	87	516	116	547	142
95 AB	3	14	342	89	403	73	483	78
95 CD	5	31	262	125	394	71	482	112
95 EF	7	19	291	94	331	77	553	171
95 GH	8	36	374	68	261	66	586	103
95 IJ	5	26	215	136	385	130	693	93
95 KL	2	26	362	52	282	179	521	131
95 MN	6	43	204	158	194	109	424	113
95 OP	11	23	132	84	224	128	355	116
95 Q	—	13	117	72	217	69	263	51

Table A.6. *Orientation of the dorsal scars on the debitage from excavations at Great Langdale: orientated (O.) vs. not orientated (N.O.) on platform crest*

Context	A O.	A N.O.	B O.	B N.O.	C O.	C N.O.	D O.	D N.O.
D.G. Primary	—	661	596	2004	315	789	296	125
D.G. Secondary	—	217	1885	919	2986	755	3587	424
D.G. Tertiary	—	124	321	365	165	238	168	79
HS 1–3	—	38	40	177	1168	2546	2686	1963
HS 4	—	17	9	50	965	664	1921	930
Stake Beck	—	24	42	129	979	2341	1252	1423
98 AB	—	30	281	172	458	178	655	109
98 CD	—	15	264	168	542	160	775	70
98 EF	—	61	267	217	421	140	496	91
98 GH	—	46	421	189	565	152	748	80
98 IJ	—	18	288	165	588	164	754	67
98 KL	—	12	219	156	389	105	472	46
98 MN	—	35	227	111	345	211	495	75
98 O	—	4	164	107	457	175	588	101
95 AB	—	17	352	79	298	178	458	103
95 CD	—	36	214	123	278	187	476	118
95 EF	—	26	259	126	296	112	686	38
95 GH		44	386	56	259	68	607	82
95 IJ	—	31	226	125	347	168	699	87
95 KL	—	28	245	169	356	105	581	71
95 MN	—	49	189	173	198	105	425	112
95 OP	—	34	104	112	278	74	416	55
95 Q	—	13	97	92	179	107	285	29

BIBLIOGRAPHY

Adkins, R. and Jackson, R. 1978. *Neolithic Axes from the River Thames*. London: British Museum (Occasional Paper 1).

Ammerman, A. and Andrefsky, W. 1982. Reduction sequences and the exchange of obsidian in Neolithic Calabria. In J. Ericson and T. Earle (eds.) *Contexts for Prehistoric Exchange*, 149–72. New York: Academic Press.

Ammerman, A., Matessi, C. and Cavalli-Sforza, L. 1978. Some new approaches to the study of the obsidian trade in the Mediterranean and adjacent areas. In I. Hodder (ed.) *The Spatial Organisation of Culture*, 179–96. London: Duckworth.

Annable, R. 1987. *The Later Prehistory of Northern England*. Oxford: British Archaeological Reports (BAR 160).

Appadurai, A. 1986. Introduction: commodities and the politics of value. In A. Appadurai (ed.) *The Social Life of Things*, 3–63. Cambridge: Cambridge University Press.

Arnold, J., Green, M., Lewis, B. and Bradley, R. 1988. The Mesolithic of Cranborne Chase. *Proceedings of the Dorset Natural History and Archaeological Society* 110, 117–25.

Ashbee, P., Smith, I. and Evans, J. 1979. Excavation of three long barrows near Avebury, Wiltshire. *Proceedings of the Prehistoric Society* 45, 207–300.

Atkinson, R. J. C. 1956. *Stonehenge*. Harmondsworth: Penguin.

1962. Fishermen and farmers. In S. Piggott (ed.) *The Prehistoric Peoples of Scotland*, 1–38. London: Routledge and Kegan Paul.

Avery, M. 1982. The Neolithic causewayed enclosure, Abingdon. In H. Case and A. Whittle (eds.) *Settlement Patterns in the Oxford Region: Excavations at the Abingdon Causewayed Enclosure and Other Sites*, 10–50. London: Council for British Archaeology (Research Report 44).

Bamford, H. 1985. *Briar Hill. Excavations 1974–1978*. Northampton: Northampton Development Corporation (Archaeological Monograph 3).

Barnatt, J. 1989. *Stone Circles of Britain*. Oxford: British Archaeological Reports (BAR 215).

Barrett, J. 1987. Contextual archaeology. *Antiquity* 61, 468–73.

1988. Fields of discourse – reconstituting a social archaeology. *Critique of Anthropology* 7.3, 5–16.

1989. Food, gender and metal: questions of social reproduction. In M. L. Sørensen and R. Thomas (eds.) *The Bronze Age/Iron Age Transition in Europe*. Oxford: British Archaeological Reports (BAR International Series 483).

Barrett, J., Bradley, R. and Green, M. 1991. *Landscape, Monuments and Society: The Prehistory of Cranborne Chase*. Cambridge: Cambridge University Press.

Beale, T. 1973. Early trade in highland Iran: a view from the source area. *World Archaeology* 5, 133–48.

Bedwin, O. 1981. Excavations at the Neolithic enclosure on Bury Hill, Houghton, West Sussex. *Proceedings of the Prehistoric Society* 47, 69–86.

Bettinger, R. 1982. Aboriginal exchange and territoriality in Owens Valley, California. In J. Ericson and T. Earle (eds.) *Contexts for Prehistoric Exchange*, 103–28. New York: Academic Press.

Binford, L. 1987. Data, relativism and archaeological science. *Man* 22, 391–404.

Bloch, M. 1977. The past and the present in the present. *Man* 12, 278–92.

Bonsall, C., Sutherland, D., Tipping, R. and Cherry, J. 1989. The Eskmeals Project: late Mesolithic settlement and economy in north-west England. In C. Bonsall (ed.) *The Mesolithic in Europe*, 175–205. Edinburgh: John Donald.

Bourdieu, P. 1977. *Outline of a Theory of Practice*. Cambridge: Cambridge University Press.
    1990. *The Logic of Practice*. Oxford: Polity Press.

Bradley, R. 1978. *The Prehistoric Settlement of Britain*. London: Routledge and Kegan Paul.
    1982. Position and possession: assemblage variation in the British Neolithic. *Oxford Journal of Archaeology* 1, 27–38.
    1984a. *The Social Foundations of Prehistoric Britain*. Harlow: Longman.
    1984b. Studying monuments. In R. Bradley and J. Gardiner (eds.) *Neolithic Studies*, 61–6. Oxford: British Archaeological Reports (BAR 133).
    1987. Flint technology and the character of Neolithic settlement. In A. Brown and M. Edmonds (eds.) *Lithic Analysis and Later British Prehistory*, 181–5. Oxford: British Archaeological Reports (BAR 162).
    1989. Deaths and entrances: a contextual analysis of megalithic art. *Current Anthropology* 30, 68–75.
    1990a. *The Passage of Arms – An Archaeological Analysis of Prehistoric Hoards and Votive Deposits*. Cambridge: Cambridge University Press.
    1990b. Perforated stone axe-heads in the British Neolithic: their distribution and significance. *Oxford Journal of Archaeology* 9, 299–304.
    1992a. The excavation of an oval barrow beside the Abingdon causewayed enclosure, Oxfordshire. *Proceedings of the Prehistoric Society* 58.
    1992b. Where is East Anglia? Aspects of regional prehistory. *East Anglian Archaeology* 50, 5–13.

Bradley, R. and Chapman, R. 1986. The nature and development of long-distance relations in Later Neolithic Britain and Ireland. In C. Renfrew and J. Cherry (eds.) *Peer Polity Interaction and Sociopolitical Change*, 127–36. Cambridge: Cambridge University Press.

Bradley, R. and Ford, S. 1986. The siting of Neolithic stone quarries – experimental archaeology at Great Langdale, Cumbria. *Oxford Journal of Archaeology* 5, 123–8.

Bradley, R. and Holgate, R. 1984. The Neolithic sequence in the Upper Thames Valley. In R. Bradley and J. Gardiner (eds.) *Neolithic Studies*, 107–34. Oxford: British Archaeological Reports (BAR 133).

Bradley, R., Meredith, P., Smith, J. and Edmonds, M. 1992. Rock physics and the stone axe trade in Neolithic Britain. *Archaeometry*, 34, 323–33.

Bradley, R. and Suthren, R. 1990. Petrographic analysis of hammerstones from the Neolithic quarries at Great Langdale. *Proceedings of the Prehistoric Society* 56, 117–22.

Brewster, T. 1984. *The Excavation of Whitegrounds Barrow, Burythorpe*. Malton: East Riding Archaeological Research Committee.

Briggs, S. 1976. Notes on the distribution of some raw materials in later prehistoric Britain. In C. Burgess and R. Miket (eds.) *Settlement and Economy in the Third and Second Millennia BC*, 267–82. Oxford: British Archaeological Reports (BAR 33).
    1989. Axe-making traditions in Cumbrian stone. *Archaeological Journal* 146, 1–43.

Briscoe, G. 1956. Swale's Tumulus: a combined Neolithic A and Bronze Age barrow at Worlington, Suffolk. *Proceedings of the Cambridge Antiquarian Society* 50, 101–12.

Brown, A. 1989. The social life of flint at Neolithic Hembury. *Lithics* 10, 46–9.

Brumfiel, E. and Earle, T. (eds.) 1987. *Specialisation, Exchange and Complex Societies*. Cambridge: Cambridge University Press.

Bunch, B. and Fell, C. 1949. A stone axe factory at Pike of Stickle, Great Langdale, Westmorland. *Proceedings of the Prehistoric Society* 15, 1–20.

Burl, A. 1976. *The Stone Circles of the British Isles*. New Haven: Yale University Press.
    1988. 'Without sharp north': Alexander Thom and the great stone circles of Cumbria. In C. Ruggles (ed.) *Records in Stone*, 175–205. Cambridge: Cambridge University Press.
Burleigh, R., Hewson, A., Meeks, N., Sieveking, G. and Longworth, I. 1979. British Museum natural radiocarbon measurements, 10. *Radiocarbon* 21, 41–7.
Burton, J. 1980. Making sense of waste flakes: new methods for investigating the technology and economics behind chipped stone assemblages. *Journal of Archaeological Science* 7, 131–48.
    1984a. Quarrying in a tribal society. *World Archaeology* 16, 234–47.
    1984b. Axe Makers of the Wahgi. PhD thesis, Australian National University.
Bush, M. 1988. Early Mesolithic disturbance: a force in the landscape. *Journal of Archaeological Science* 15, 453–62.
Bush, P. and Sieveking, G. 1986. Geochemistry and the provenance of flint axes. In G. Sieveking and M. Hart (eds.) *The Scientific Study of Flint and Chert*, 122–40. Cambridge: Cambridge University Press.
Calvino, I. 1969. The Count of Monte Cristo. In I. Calvino, *t zero*, 137–52. New York: Harcourt Brace Jovanovich.
Care, V. 1982. The collection and distribution of lithic materials during the Mesolithic and Neolithic periods in southern England. *Oxford Journal of Archaeology* 1, 269–85.
Case, H. 1969. Neolithic explanations. *Antiquity* 43, 176–87.
Chappell, S. 1986. Alternative sources in regional exchange systems: a gravity model approach. *Proceedings of the Prehistoric Society* 52, 129–41.
    1987. *Stone Axe Morphology and Distribution in Neolithic Britain*. Oxford: British Archaeological Reports (BAR 177).
Cherry, J. and Cherry, P. 1983. Prehistoric habitation sites in west Cumbria: part 1. *Transactions of the Cumberland and Westmorland Archaeological Society* 83, 1–14.
    1984. Prehistoric habitation sites in west Cumbria: part 2. *Transactions of the Cumberland and Westmorland Archaeological Society* 84, 1–17.
    1985. Prehistoric habitation sites in west Cumbria: part 3. *Transactions of the Cumberland and Westmorland Archaeological Society* 85, 1–10.
    1986. Prehistoric habitation sites in west Cumbria: part 4. *Transactions of the Cumberland and Westmorland Archaeological Society* 86, 1–17.
    1987a. Prehistoric habitation sites in west Cumbria: part 5. *Transactions of the Cumberland and Westmorland Archaeological Society* 87, 1–10.
    1987b. *Prehistoric Habitation Sites on the Limestone Uplands of Eastern Cumbria*. Kendal: Cumberland and Westmorland Archaeological Society (Research Volume 2).
Childe, V. G. 1958. *The Prehistory of European Society*. Harmondsworth: Penguin.
Clare, T. 1979. Raiset Pike long cairn and the Machell manuscripts. *Transactions of the Cumberland and Westmorland Archaeological Society* 79, 144–6.
Claris, P. and Quartermaine, J. 1989. The Neolithic quarries and axe factory sites of Great Langdale and Scafell Pike: a new field survey. *Proceedings of the Prehistoric Society* 55, 1–25.
Clark, J. D. G. 1965. Traffic in stone axe and adze blades. *Economic History Review* (2nd series) 18, 1–28.
Cleal, R. 1984. The Later Neolithic in eastern England. In R. Bradley and J. Gardiner (eds.) *Neolithic Studies*, 135–58. Oxford: British Archaeological Reports (BAR 133).
Cleghorn, P. 1982. *The Mauna Kea Adze Quarry: Technological Analysis and Experimental Tests*. Ann Arbor: University Microfilms.
Clough, T. 1973. Excavations on a Langdale axe chipping site in 1969 and 1970. *Transactions of the Cumberland and Westmorland Archaeological Society* 73, 25–46.
    1988. Introduction. In T. Clough and W. Cummins (eds.) *Stone Axe Studies*, 2, 1–11. London: Council for British Archaeology (Research Report 67).

Clough, T. and Cummins, W. (eds.) 1979. *Stone Axe Studies*. London: Council for British Archaeology (Research Report 23).

1988. *Stone Axe Studies, 2*. London: Council for British Archaeology (Research Report 67).

Clough, T. and Green, B. 1972. The petrological identification of stone implements from East Anglia. *Proceedings of the Prehistoric Society* 38, 108–55.

Coles, J., Heal, V. and Orme, B. 1978. The use and character of wood in prehistoric Britain and Ireland. *Proceedings of the Prehistoric Society* 44, 1–45.

Collins, A. E. P. 1978. Excavations at Ballygalley Hill, County Antrim. *Ulster Journal of Archaeology* 41, 15–32.

Collins, A. L. 1893. Fire setting: the art of mining by fire. *Transactions of the Federal Institute of Mining Engineers (1893)*, 82–92.

Collins, M. 1975. Lithic technology as a means of processual inference. In E. Swanson (ed.) *Lithic Technology: Making and Using Stone Tools*, 15–34. The Hague: Mouton.

Coombs, D. 1976. Callis Wold round barrow, Humberside. *Antiquity* 50, 130–1.

Coope, G. R. 1979. The influence of geology on the manufacture of Neolithic and Bronze Age stone implements in the British Isles. In T. Clough and W. Cummins (eds.) *Stone Axe Studies*, 98–101. London: Council for British Archaeology (Research Report 23).

Coope, G. R. and Garrad, L. S. 1988. The petrological identification of stone implements from the Isle of Man. In T. Clough and W. Cummins (eds.) *Stone Axe Studies, 2*, 67–70. London: Council for British Archaeology (Research Report 67).

Corcoran, J. 1960. The Carlingford Culture. *Proceedings of the Prehistoric Society* 26, 98–148.

Craddock, P., Cowell, M., Leese, M. and Hughes, M. 1983. The trace element composition of polished flint axes as indicator of sources. *Archaeometry* 25, 135–63.

Cummins, W. 1979. Neolithic stone axes: distribution and trade in England and Wales. In T. Clough and W. Cummins (eds.) *Stone Axe Studies*, 5–12. London: Council for British Archaeology (Research Report 23).

1980. Stone axes as a guide to Neolithic communications and boundaries in England and Wales. *Proceedings of the Prehistoric Society* 46, 45–60.

Cummins, W. and Moore, C. N. 1973. Petrological identification of stone implements from Lincolnshire, Nottinghamshire and Rutland. *Proceedings of the Prehistoric Society* 39, 219–55.

Cunnington, M., 1929. *Woodhenge*. Devizes: George Simpson.

Curwen, E. and Curwen, E. C. 1926. Harrow Hill (Sussex) flint mine excavation, 1924–1925. *Sussex Archaeological Collections* 67, 103–38.

Curwen, E., Curwen, E. C., Frost, M. and Goodman, C. 1924. Blackpatch flint mine excavation, 1922. *Sussex Archaeological Collections* 65, 69–111.

Curwen, E. C. 1930. Neolithic camps. *Antiquity* 4, 22–54.

1934. Excavations at Whitehawk Camp, Brighton, 1932–1933. *Antiquaries Journal* 56, 11–23.

1936. Excavations at Whitehawk Camp, Brighton. *Sussex Archaeological Collections* 77, 60–92.

Dalton, G. 1977. Aboriginal economies in stateless societies. In T. Earle and J. Ericson (eds.) *Exchange Systems in Prehistory*, 191–212. New York: Academic Press.

Damon, F. 1984. What moves the Kula: opening and closing gifts on Woodlark Island. In J. Leach and E. Leach (eds.) *The Kula: New Perspectives on Massim Exchange*, 309–42. Cambridge: Cambridge University Press.

Darbishire, R. 1873. Notes on discoveries at Ehenside Tarn, Cumberland. *Archaeologia* 44, 273–92.

Darvill, T. 1987. *Prehistoric Britain*. London: Batsford.

1989. The circulation of Neolithic stone and flint axes: a case study from Wales and the mid-west of England. *Proceedings of the Prehistoric Society* 55, 27–43.

David, A. 1989. Some aspects of the human presence in west Wales during the Mesolithic. In C. Bonsall (ed.) *The Mesolithic in Europe*, 241–53. Edinburgh: John Donald.

Davidson, J. and Henshall, A. 1989. *The Chambered Cairns of Orkney*. Edinburgh: Edinburgh University Press.

Davis, D. 1985. Hereditary emblems: material culture in the context of social change. *Journal of Anthropological Archaeology* 4, 149–76.

Davis, R. V. 1985. Implement petrology: the state of the art. In A. P. Phillips (ed.) *The Archaeologist and the Laboratory*, 33–5. London: Council for British Archaeology (Research Report 58).

Dixon, J., Cann, J. and Renfrew, C. 1986. Obsidian and the origins of trade. *Scientific American* 218, 38–46.

Dixon, P. 1988. The Neolithic settlements on Crickley Hill. In C. Burgess, P. Topping, C. Mordant and M. Maddison (eds.) *Enclosures and Defences in the Neolithic of Western Europe*, 75–87. Oxford: British Archaeological Reports (BAR International Series 403).

Douglas, M. 1966. *Purity and Danger*. London: Routledge and Kegan Paul.

Drewett, P. 1978. Neolithic Sussex. In P. Drewett (ed.) *Archaeology in Sussex to AD 1500*, 23–9. London: Council for British Archaeology.

    1986. The excavation of a Neolithic oval barrow at North Marden, West Sussex, 1982. *Proceedings of the Prehistoric Society* 52, 31–55.

Drewett, P., Rudling, D. and Gardiner, M. 1988. *The South East to AD 1000*. Harlow: Longman.

Earle, T. 1977. A reappraisal of redistribution: complex Hawaiian chiefdoms. In T. Earle and J. Ericson (eds.) *Exchange Systems in Prehistory*, 213–39. New York: Academic Press.

    1982. Prehistoric economies and the archaeology of exchange. In J. Ericson and T. Earle (eds.) *Contexts for Prehistoric Exchange*, 1–12. New York: Academic Press.

    1989. The evolution of chiefdoms. *Current Anthropology* 30, 84–8.

Earle, T. and D'Altroy, T. 1982. Storage facilities and state finance in the Upper Mantaro Valley, Peru. In J. Ericson and T. Earle (eds.) *Contexts for Prehistoric Exchange*, 265–90. New York: Academic Press.

Earle, T. and Ericson, J. (eds.) 1977. *Exchange Systems in Prehistory*. New York: Academic Press.

Eco, U. 1983. *The Name of the Rose*. London: Secker and Warburg.

Edmonds, M. 1987. Rocks and risk: problems with lithic procurement strategies. In A. Brown and M. Edmonds (eds.) *Lithic Analysis and Later British Prehistory*, 155–79. Oxford: British Archaeological Reports (BAR 162).

    1989. The Gift of Stones: The Production and Exchange of Stone Axes in the Neolithic of Britain. PhD thesis, Reading University.

    1990. Description, understanding and the *chaîne opératoire*. *Archaeological Review from Cambridge* 9, 55–70.

    1992. Their use is wholly unknown. In N. Sharples and A. Sheridan (eds.) *Vessels for the Ancestors*, 179–93. Edinburgh: Edinburgh University Press.

    In press. Interpreting causewayed enclosures in the present and the past. In M. Shanks and C. Tilley (eds.) *Interpretative Archaeology*. London: Routledge.

Edmonds, M. and Bellamy, P. 1991. The lithic assemblage from Maiden Castle. In N. Sharples (ed.) *Maiden Castle: Excavations and Field Survey, 1985–1986*, 214–29. London: English Heritage.

Edmonds, M. and Sheridan, A. in press. Survey and excavation at Creag na Caillich, Perthshire. *Proceedings of the Society of Antiquaries of Scotland*, 121.

Edmonds, M. and Thomas, J. 1987. The Archers: an everyday story of country folk. In A. Brown and M. Edmonds (eds.) *Lithic Analysis and Later British Prehistory*, 187–99. Oxford: British Archaeological Reports (BAR 162).

Edwards, K. 1982. Man, space and the woodland edge – speculations on the detection and interpretation of human impact in pollen profiles. In M. Bell and S. Limbrey (eds.) *Aspects of Woodland Ecology*, 5–22. Oxford: British Archaeological Reports (BAR International Series 146).

Ekholm, K. 1977. External exchange and the transformation of Central African social systems. In J. Friedman and M. Rowlands (eds.) *The Evolution of Social Systems*, 115–36. London: Duckworth.

Elliott, K., Ellman, D. and Hodder, I. 1978. The simulation of Neolithic axe dispersal in Britain. In I. Hodder (ed.) *Simulation Studies in Archaeology*, 79–87. Cambridge: Cambridge University Press.

Eogan, G. 1986. *Knowth and the Passage-Tombs of Ireland*. London: Thames and Hudson.

Ericson, J. 1977. Egalitarian exchange systems in California: a preliminary view. In T. Earle and J. Ericson (eds.) *Exchange Systems in Prehistory*, 109–26. New York: Academic Press.

1982. Production for obsidian exchange in California. In J. Ericson and T. Earle (eds.) *Contexts for Prehistoric Exchange*, 129–48. New York: Academic Press.

Ericson, J. and Earle, T. (eds.) 1982. *Contexts for Prehistoric Exchange*. New York: Academic Press.

Ericson, J. and Purdy, B. (eds.) 1984. *Prehistoric Quarries and Lithic Production*. Cambridge: Cambridge University Press.

Evans, C. 1988. Acts of enclosure: a consideration of concentrically-organised causewayed enclosures. In J. Barrett and I. Kinnes (eds.) *The Archaeology of Context in the Neolithic and Bronze Age: Recent Trends*, 85–96. Sheffield: Sheffield University Department of Archaeology and Prehistory.

Evans, E. E. 1938. Doey's Cairn, County Antrim. *Ulster Journal of Archaeology* 1, 59–78.

Evans, J. G., Rouse, A. and Sharples, N. 1988. The landscape setting of causewayed camps: some recent work on the Maiden Castle enclosure. In J. Barrett and I. Kinnes (eds.) *The Archaeology of Context in the Neolithic and Bronze Age: Recent Trends*, 73–84. Sheffield: Sheffield University Department of Archaeology and Prehistory.

Evens, E., Smith, I., Piggott, S. and Wallis, F. 1962. Fourth report of the sub-committee of the South-Western Federation of Museums and Art Galleries on the petrological identification of stone axes. *Proceedings of the Prehistoric Society* 28, 209–66.

Evens, E., Smith, I. and Wallis, F. 1972. The petrographic identification of stone implements from south-western England: Fifth report of the sub-committee of the South-Western Federation of Museums and Art Galleries. *Proceedings of the Prehistoric Society* 38, 235–75.

Feinman, G. and Neinzel, J. 1984. Too many types: an overview of prestate societies in the Americas. In M. Schiffer (ed.) *Advances in Archaeological Methods and Theory* 7, 39–102. New York: Academic Press.

Felder, P. J. 1979. Prehistoric flint mining at Rijckholt-St Gertruid (Netherlands) and Grimes Graves (England). *Staringia* 6, 57–62.

Fell, C. 1950. The Great Langdale stone axe factory. *Transactions of the Cumberland and Westmorland Archaeological Society* 50, 1–13.

1954. Further notes on the Great Langdale axe factory. *Proceedings of the Prehistoric Society* 20, 238–9.

1964. The Cumbrian type of polished stone axe and its distribution in Britain. *Proceedings of the Prehistoric Society* 30, 39–55.

Fell, C. and Davis, V. 1988. The petrological identification of stone implements from Cumbria. In T. Clough and W. Cummins (eds.) *Stone Axe Studies*, 2, 71–7. London: Council for British Archaeology (Research Report 67).

Finbow, F. and Bolognese, M. 1980. An initial examination of prehistoric obsidian exchange in Hidalgo County, New Mexico. *The Kiva* 45, 227–51.

1982. Regional modelling of obsidian procurement in the American south-west. In J. Ericson and T. Earle (eds.) *Contexts for Prehistoric Exchange*, 53–81. New York: Academic Press.

Flannery, K. 1972. Evolutionary trends in social exchange and interaction. In E. Wilmsen (ed.) *Social Exchange and Interaction*, 129–35. Ann Arbor: University of Michigan Press (University of Michigan, Museum of Anthropology Paper 46).

Fleming, S. 1979. *Thermoluminescence Techniques in Archaeology*. Oxford: Clarendon Press.

Frankenstein, S. and Rowlands, M. 1978. The internal structure and regional context of early Iron Age society in south-west Germany. *Bulletin of the University of London Institute of Archaeology* 15, 73–112.

Fraser, D. 1983. *Land and Society in Neolithic Orkney*. Oxford: British Archaeological Reports (BAR 117).

Friedman, J. and Rowlands, M. 1977. Notes towards an epigenetic model of the evolution of 'civilisation'. In J. Friedman and M. Rowlands (eds.) *The Evolution of Social Systems*, 201–76. London: Duckworth.

Gardiner, J. 1984. Lithic distributions and Neolithic settlement patterns in central southern England. In R. Bradley and J. Gardiner (eds.) *Neolithic Studies*, 15–40. Oxford: British Archaeological Reports (BAR 133).

   1990. Flint procurement and Neolithic axe production on the South Downs: a reassessment. *Oxford Journal of Archaeology* 9, 119–40.

Giot, D., Mallet, N. and Mallet, D. 1986. Les silex de la région du Grand-Pressigny (Indre-et-Loire). Recherche géologique et analyse pétrographique. *Revue Archéologique du Centre de la France* 25, 21–36.

Giot, P.-R., L'Helgouac'h, J. and Monnier, J.-L. 1979. *Préhistoire de la Brétagne*. Rennes: Ouest-France.

Godelier, M. 1977. *Perspectives in Marxist Anthropology*. Cambridge: Cambridge University Press.

Green, H. S. 1980. *The Flint Arrowheads of the British Isles*. Oxford: British Archaeological Reports (BAR 75).

Greenwell, W. 1877. *British Barrows*. Oxford: Clarendon Press.

Gregory, C. 1980. Gifts to men and gifts to god: gift exchange and capital accumulation in contemporary Papua. *Man* 15, 628–52.

   1982. *Gifts and Commodities*. London: Academic Press.

Grigson, C. 1981. [Neolithic] fauna. In I. Simmons and M. Tooley (eds.) *The Environment in British Prehistory*, 191–9. London: Duckworth.

Grimes, W. F. 1979. The history of implement petrology in Britain. In T. Clough and W. Cummins (eds.) *Stone Axe Studies*, 1–4. London: Council for British Archaeology (Research Report 23).

Hallam, B., Warren, S. and Renfrew, C. 1976. Obsidian in the western Mediterranean: characterisation by neutron activation analysis and optical emission spectroscopy. *Proceedings of the Prehistoric Society* 42, 85–110.

Harding, A. and Lee, G. 1987. *Henges and Related Monuments in Britain*. Oxford: British Archaeological Reports (BAR 190).

Harding, J. 1991. Using the unique as the typical: monuments and the ritual landscape. In P. Garwood, D. Jennings, R. Skeates and J. Toms (eds.) *Scared and Profane*, 141–51. Oxford: Oxford University Committee for Archaeology.

Hartnett, P. 1971. The excavation of two tumuli at Fourknocks (Sites II and III), Co. Meath. *Proceedings of the Royal Irish Academy* 71 (C), 35–89.

Hartwell, B. 1991. Ballynahatty – a prehistoric ceremonial centre. *Archaeology Ireland* 5.4, 12–15.

Hayden, B. and Cannon, A. 1983. Where the garbage goes: refuse disposal in the Maya Highlands. *Journal of Anthropological Archaeology* 2, 117–63.

Hayes, R. 1967. *The Chambered Cairn and Adjacent Monuments on Great Ayton Moor, North-East Yorkshire*. Scarborough: Scarborough and District Archaeological Society (Research Report 7).

Healey, E. and Robertson-Mackay, R. 1983. The lithic industries from Staines causewayed enclosure and their relationship to other Earlier Neolithic industries in southern Britain. *Lithics* 4, 1–27.

Healy, F. 1984. Farming and field monuments: the Neolithic in Norfolk. In C. Barringer (ed.) *Aspects of East Anglian Prehistory*, 77–140. Norwich: Geo Books.

1987. Prediction or prejudice? The relationship between field survey and excavation. In A. Brown and M. Edmonds (eds.) *Lithic Analysis and Later British Prehistory*, 9–17. Oxford: British Archaeological Reports (BAR 162)

1991. The hunting of the floorstone. In A. J. Schofield (ed.) *Interpreting Artefact Scatters*, 29–37. Oxford: Oxbow Books (Oxbow Monograph 4).

Helms, M. 1988. *Ulysses' Sail*. Princeton: Princeton University Press.

Henson, D. 1989. Away from the core? A northerners' view of flint exploitation. In I. Brooks and P. Phillips (eds.) *Breaking the Stony Silence*, 5–31. Oxford: British Archaeological Reports (BAR 213).

Higham, N. 1986. *The Northern Counties to AD 1000*. Harlow: Longman.

1987. Landscape and land use in northern England: a survey of agricultural potential. *Landscape History* 9, 35–44.

Hodder, I. 1974. Regression analysis of some trade and marketing patterns. *World Archaeology* 6, 172–89.

1978. Some effects of distance on patterns of human interaction. In I. Hodder (ed.) *The Spatial Organisation of Culture*, 155–78. London: Duckworth.

1982a. *The Present Past*. London: Batsford.

1982b. Towards a contextual approach to prehistoric exchange. In J. Ericson and T. Earle (eds.) *Contexts for Prehistoric Exchange*, 199–211. New York: Academic Press.

1989. This is not an article about material culture as text. *Journal of Anthropological Archaeology* 8, 250–69.

1991. *Reading the Past*, second edition. Cambridge: Cambridge University Press.

Hodder, I. and Lane, P. 1982. A contextual examination of Neolithic axe distribution in Britain. In J. Ericson and T. Earle (eds.) *Contexts for Prehistoric Exchange*, 213–35. New York: Academic Press.

Hodder, I. and Orton, C. 1976. *Spatial Analysis in Archaeology*. Cambridge: Cambridge University Press.

Holgate, R. 1988. *Neolithic Settlement of the Thames Basin*. Oxford: British Archaeological Reports (BAR 194).

Houlder, C. 1961. The excavation of a Neolithic stone implement factory on Mynydd Rhiw in Caernarvonshire. *Proceedings of the Prehistoric Society* 27, 108–43.

1968. The henge monuments at Llandegai. *Antiquity* 52, 216–21.

1976. Stone axes and henge monuments. In G. Boon and J. Lewis (eds.) *Welsh Antiquity*, 55–62. Cardiff: National Museum of Wales.

1979. The Langdale and Scafell Pike axe factory sites: a field survey. In T. Clough and W. Cummins (eds.) *Stone Axe Studies*, 87–9. London: Council for British Archaeology (Research Report 23).

Ingold, T. 1986. *Evolution and Social Life*. Cambridge: Cambridge University Press.

Ireland, J. and Lynch, F. 1973. More Mesolithic flints from Trwyn Du, Aberffraw. *Transactions of the Anglesey Antiquarian Society and Field Club* (1973), 170–5.

Jacobi, R., Tallis, J. and Mellars, P. 1976. The southern Pennine Mesolithic and the archaeological record. *Journal of Archaeological Science* 3, 307–20.

Jope, E. M. 1952. Porcellanite axes from factories in north-east Ireland. Part 1: archaeological survey. *Ulster Journal of Archaeology* 15, 31–55.

Junghans, S., Sangmeister, E. and Schröder, M. 1960. *Metallanalysen kupferzeitlicher und frühbronzezeitlicher Bodenfunde aus Europa – Studien zu den Anfängen der Metallurgie 1*. Berlin: Römisch-Germanisches Zentralmuseum.

Keen, L. and Radley, J. 1971. Report on the petrological identification of stone axes from Yorkshire. *Proceedings of the Prehistoric Society* 37, 16–37.

Keiller, A., Piggott, S. and Wallis, F. 1941. First report of the sub-committee of the south-western group of museums and art galleries on the petrological identification of stone axes. *Proceedings of the Prehistoric Society* 7, 50–72.

Kinnes, I. 1979. *Round Barrows and Ring-Ditches in the British Neolithic*. London: British Museum (Occasional Paper 7).

  1984. Prehistoric sites in the Great Wold Valley. *Archaeological Journal* 141, 36–7.

  1985. Circumstance not context: the Neolithic of Scotland as seen from outside. *Proceedings of the Society of Antiquaries of Scotland* 115, 15–57.

  1988. The Cattleship Potemkin: the first Neolithic in Britain. In J. Barrett and I. Kinnes (eds.) *The Archaeology of Context in the Neolithic and Bronze Age: Recent Trends*, 2–8. Sheffield: Sheffield University Department of Archaeology and Prehistory.

Kinnes, I. and Longworth, I. 1985. *Catalogue of the Excavated Prehistoric and Romano-British Material in the Greenwell Collection*. London: British Museum.

Kinnes, I., Schadla-Hall, T., Chadwick, P. and Dean, P. 1983. Duggleby Howe reconsidered. *Archaeological Journal* 140, 83–108.

Knowles, W. J. 1906. Stone axe factories near Cushendall. *Journal of the Royal Society of Antiquaries of Ireland* 16, 383–94.

Kristiansen, K. 1984. Ideology and material culture: an archaeological perspective. In M. Spriggs (ed.) *Marxist Perspectives in Archaeology*, 72–100. Cambridge: Cambridge University Press.

Larick, R. 1985. Spears, style and time among Maa-speaking pastoralists. *Journal of Anthropological Archaeology* 4, 206–20.

  1986. Age grading and ethnicity in Loikop (Samburu) spears. *Journal of Anthropological Archaeology* 4, 269–83.

Leach, E. 1973. Concluding address. In C. Renfrew (ed.) *The Explanation of Culture Change*, 761–71. London: Duckworth.

Leach, J. and Leach, E. (eds.) 1983. *The Kula: New Perspectives on Massim Exchange*. Cambridge: Cambridge University Press.

Lederman, R. 1986. *What Gifts Engender*. Cambridge: Cambridge University Press.

Lemonnier, P. 1986. The study of material culture today: towards an anthropology of technical systems. *Journal of Anthropological Archaeology* 5, 147–86.

Levi, P. 1985. *The Periodic Table*. London: Michael Joseph.

Lévi-Strauss, C. 1969. *The Elementary Structures of Kinship*. Boston: Beacon Press.

LiPuma, E. 1987. *The Gift of Kinship*. Cambridge: Cambridge University Press.

Longworth, I., Ellison, A. and Rigby, V. 1988. *Excavations at Grimes Graves, Norfolk, 1972–1976. Fascicule 2: The Neolithic, Bronze Age and Later Pottery*. London: British Museum.

Loveday, R. and Petchey, M. 1982. Oblong ditches: a discussion and some new evidence. *Aerial Archaeology* 8, 17–24.

McBryde, I. 1979. Petrology and prehistory: lithic evidence for exploitation of stone resources and exchange systems in south-eastern Australia. In T. Clough and W. Cummins (eds.) *Stone Axe Studies*, 113–26. London: Council for British Archaeology (Research Report 23).

  1984. Kulin greenstone quarries: the social contexts of production and distribution for the Mount William site. *World Archaeology* 16, 267–85.

McBryde, I. and Harrison, D. 1981. Valued good or valuable stone? Consideration of the distribution of greenstone artefacts in south-eastern Australia. In F. Leach and J. Davidson (eds.) *Archaeological Studies of Pacific Stone Resources*, 183–208. Oxford: British Archaeological Reports (BAR International Series 104)

MacCormack, C. 1981. Exchange and hierarchy. In A. Sheridan and G. Bailey (eds.) *Economic Archaeology*, 159–66. Oxford: British Archaeological Reports (BAR International Series 96).

Mallory, J. 1990. Trial excavations at Tievebulliagh, Co. Antrim. *Ulster Journal of Archaeology* 53, 15–28.

Manby, T. 1965. The distribution of rough-out 'Cumbrian' and related axes of Lake District origin in northern England. *Transactions of the Cumberland and Westmorland Archaeological Society* 65, 1–37.

　　1974. *Grooved Ware Sites in Yorkshire and the North of England*. Oxford: British Archaeological Reports (BAR 9).

　　1975. Neolithic occupation sites on the Yorkshire Wolds. *Yorkshire Archaeological Journal* 47, 23–59.

　　1979. Typology, material and distribution of flint and stone axes in Yorkshire. In T. Clough and W. Cummins (eds.) *Stone Axe Studies*, 65–81. London: Council for British Archaeology (Research Report 23).

　　1988. The Neolithic in eastern Yorkshire. In T. Manby (ed.) *Archaeology in Eastern Yorkshire*, 35–88. Sheffield: Sheffield University Department of Archaeology and Prehistory.

Marshall, D. 1977. Carved stone balls. *Proceedings of the Society of Antiquaries of Scotland* 108, 40–72.

Masters, L. 1984. The Neolithic long cairns of Cumbria and Northumberland. In R. Miket and C. Burgess (eds.) *Between and Beyond the Walls*, 52–73. Edinburgh: John Donald.

Mauss, M. 1954 [1925]. *The Gift*. London: Cohen and West.

Megaw, J. V. S. and Simpson, D. D. A. 1979. *Introduction to British Prehistory*. Leicester: Leicester University Press.

Meillassoux, C. 1968. Ostentation, destruction, reproduction. *Economie et Société* 2, 760–72.

　　1981. *Maidens, Meal and Money. Capitalism and the Domestic Economy*. Cambridge: Cambridge University Press.

Mellars, P. 1976. Fire ecology, animal populations and man: a study of some ecological relationships in prehistory. *Proceedings of the Prehistoric Society* 42, 15–48.

Mercer, R. 1980. *Hambledon Hill – A Neolithic Landscape*. Edinburgh: Edinburgh University Press.

　　1981a. *Grimes Graves, Norfolk. Excavations 1971–72*. London: HMSO.

　　1981b. Excavations at Carn Brea, Illogan, Cornwall – a Neolithic fortified complex of the third millennium bc. *Cornish Archaeology* 20, 1–204.

　　1986. The Neolithic in Cornwall. *Cornish Archaeology* 25, 35–80.

　　1987. A flint quarry in the Hambledon Hill Neolithic enclosure complex. In G. Sieveking and M. Newcomer (eds.) *The Human Uses of Flint and Chert*, 159–63. Cambridge: Cambridge University Press.

Miller, D. 1985. *Artefacts as Categories*. Cambridge: Cambridge University Press.

Moffet, L., Robinson, M. and Straker, V. 1989. Cereals, fruits and nuts: charred plant remains from Neolithic sites in England and Wales and the Neolithic economy. In A. Milles, D. Williams and N. Gardner (eds.) *The Beginnings of Agriculture*, 243–61. Oxford: British Archaeological Reports (BAR International Series 496).

Moholy-Nagy, H. 1976. Spatial distribution of flint and obsidian artefacts at Tikal, Guatemala. In T. Hester and N. Hammond (eds.) *Maya Lithic Studies*, 91–108. San Antonio: Center for Archaeological Research.

Moore, H. 1986. *Space, Text and Gender*. Cambridge: Cambridge University Press.

Moore, J. 1964. Excavations on Beacon Hill, Flamborough Head. *Yorkshire Archaeological Journal* 41, 191–202.

Morgan, F. de M. 1959. The excavation of a long barrow at Nutbane, Hants. *Proceedings of the Prehistoric Society* 25, 15–51.

Mortimore, R. 1979. The engineering domains and classification of chalk in relation to Neolithic flint mining, with special reference to Grimes Graves (England) and Rijckholt (Holland). *Staringia* 6, 30–5.

Muller, J. 1987. Salt, chert and shell: Mississippian exchange and economy. In E. Brumfiel and T. Earle (eds.) *Specialisation, Exchange and Complex Societies*, 10–21. Cambridge: Cambridge University Press.

Newman, T. 1976. A crop-mark site at Hasting Hill, Tyne and Wear. *Archaeologia Aeliana* 5th series 4, 183–4.

O'Kelly, M. J. 1982. *Newgrange. Archaeology, Art and Legend*. London: Thames and Hudson.

Olausson, D. 1983. *Flint and Groundstone Axes in the Scanian Neolithic*. Lund: Scripta Minora 2.

Pelegrin, J. 1990. Prehistoric lithic technology: some aspects of research. *Archaeological Review from Cambridge* 9, 116–25.

Pelegrin, J., Karlin, C. and Bodu, P. 1988. Chaînes opératoires: un outil pour le préhistorien. In J. Tixier (ed.) *Technologie paléolithique*, 55–62, Paris: CNRS.

Pennington, W. 1970. Vegetational history in the north-west of England – a regional study. In D. Walker and R. G. West (eds.) *Studies in the Vegetational History of the British Isles*, 41–80. Cambridge: Cambridge University Press.

1975. The effect of Neolithic man on the environments of north-west England: the use of absolute pollen diagrams. In J. G. Evans, S. Limbrey and H. Cleere (eds.) *The Effect of Man on the Landscape: The Highland Zone*, 74–86. London: Council for British Archaeology (Research Report 11).

Pierpoint, S. 1980. *Social Patterns in Yorkshire Prehistory*. Oxford: British Archaeological Reports (BAR 74).

Piggott, S. 1954. *The Neolithic Cultures of the British Isles*. Cambridge: Cambridge University Press.

1963. *The West Kennet Long Barrow. Excavations 1955–56*. London: HMSO.

Pires-Ferreira, J. 1976. Obsidian exchange in formative Mesoamerica. In K. Flannery (ed.) *The Early Mesoamerican Village*, 292–305. New York: Academic Press.

Plint, R. G. 1962. Stone axe factory sites in the Cumbrian fells. *Transactions of the Cumberland and Westmorland Archaeological Society* 62, 1–26.

1978. More stone axe factory sites in the Cumbrian fells. *Transactions of the Cumberland and Westmorland Archaeological Society* 78, 1–4.

Plog, F. 1977. Modelling economic exchange. In T. Earle and J. Ericson (eds.) *Exchange Systems in Prehistory*, 127–40. New York: Academic Press.

Powell, T., Oldfield, F. and Corcoran, J. 1971. Excavations in Zone VII peat at Storrs Moss, Lancashire, England. *Proceedings of the Prehistoric Society* 37, 112–37.

Pryor, F. 1988. Etton, near Maxey, Cambridgeshire: a causewayed enclosure on the Fen Edge. In C. Burgess, P. Topping, C. Mordant and M. Maddison (eds.) *Enclosures and Defences in the Neolithic of Western Europe*, 107–26. Oxford: British Archaeological Reports (BAR International Series 403).

Purdy, B. 1984. Quarry studies: technological and chronological significance. In J. Ericson and B. Purdy (eds.) *Prehistoric Quarries and Lithic Production*, 119–28. Cambridge: Cambridge University Press.

Rackham, O. 1976. *Trees and Woodland in the British Landscape*. London: Dent.

Rathje, W. 1975. Last tango at Mayapan: a tentative trajectory of production-distribution systems. In J. Sabloff and C. Lamberg-Karlovsky (eds.) *Ancient Civilisation and Trade*, 409–48. Albuquerque: University of New Mexico Press.

Renfrew, C. 1969. Trade and culture process in European prehistory. *Current Anthropology* 10, 151–69.

1973. Monuments, mobilisation and social organisation in Neolithic Wessex. In C. Renfrew (ed.) *The Explanation of Culture Change*, 539–58. London, Duckworth.

1975. Trade as action at a distance: questions of integration and communication. In J. Sabloff and C. Lamberg-Karlovsky (eds.) *Ancient Civilisation and Trade*, 3–60. Albuquerque: University of New Mexico Press.

1977. Alternative models for exchange and spatial distribution. In T. Earle and J. Ericson (eds.) *Exchange Systems in Prehistory*, 71–90. New York: Academic Press.

1979. *Investigations in Orkney*. London: Society of Antiquaries (Research Report 38).

Renfrew, C., Cann, J. and Dixon, J. 1968. Further analysis of Near Eastern obsidian. *Proceedings of the Prehistoric Society* 34, 319–31.

Renfrew, C. and Cherry, J. (eds.) 1986. *Peer Polity Interaction and Sociopolitical Change*. Cambridge: Cambridge University Press.

Renfrew, C. and Dixon, J. 1976. Obsidian in western Asia: a review. In G. Sieveking, I. Longworth and K. Wilson (eds.) *Problems in Economic and Social Archaeology*, 137–50. London: Duckworth.

Renfrew, C. and Shennan, S. (eds.) 1982. *Ranking, Resource and Exchange*. Cambridge: Cambridge University Press.

Richards, C. 1988. Altered images: a re-examination of Neolithic mortuary practices in Orkney. In J. Barrett and I. Kinnes (eds.) *The Archaeology of Context in the Neolithic and Bronze Age: Recent Trends*, 42–56. Sheffield: Sheffield University Department of Archaeology and Prehistory.

Richards, C. and Thomas, J. 1984. Ritual activity and structured deposition in Later Neolithic Wessex. In R. Bradley and J. Gardiner (eds.) *Neolithic Studies*, 189–218. Oxford: British Archaeological Reports (BAR 133).

Richards, J. 1990. *The Stonehenge Environs Project*. London: English Heritage.

Ride, D. and James, D. 1989. An account of an excavation of a flint mine at Martin's Clump, Over Wallop, Hampshire. *Proceedings of the Hampshire Field Club* 45, 213–15.

Robertson-Mackay, R. 1987. The Neolithic causewayed enclosure at Staines, Surrey: excavations 1961–63. *Proceedings of the Prehistoric Society* 53, 23–128.

Roe, F. 1979. Typology of stone implements with shafthole. In T. Clough and W. Cummins (eds.) *Stone Axe Studies*, 23–48. London: Council for British Archaeology (Research Report 23).

Roux, V. 1990. The psychosocial analysis of technical activities. *Archaeological Review from Cambridge* 9, 143–53.

Rowlands, M. 1982. Processual archaeology as historical social science. In C. Renfrew, M. Rowlands and B. Segraves (eds.) *Theory and Explanation in Archeology: the Southampton Conference*. New York: Academic Press.

1987. Core and periphery: a review of a concept. In M. Rowlands, M. Larsen and K. Kristiansen (eds.) *Centre and Periphery in the Ancient World*, 1–11. Cambridge: Cambridge University Press.

Rowlands, M., Larsen, M. and Kristiansen, K. (eds.) 1987. *Centre and Periphery in the Ancient World*. Cambridge: Cambridge University Press.

Royal Commission on the Ancient and Historical Monuments of Wales 1956. *Caernarvonshire, vol. 1*. London: HMSO.

Sahlins, M. 1972. *Stone Age Economics*. London: Tavistock.

1976. *Culture and Practical Reason*. Chicago: Chicago University Press.

Saville, A. 1981. *Grimes Graves, Norfolk. Excavations 1971–72. Vol. 2: The Flint Assemblage*. London: HMSO.

Schiffer, M. 1987. *Formation Processes of the Archaeological Record*. Albuquerque: University of New Mexico Press.

Shanks, M. and Tilley, C. 1982. Ideology, symbolic power and ritual communication: a reinterpretation of Neolithic mortuary practices. In I. Hodder (ed.) *Symbolic and Structural Archaeology*, 129–54. Cambridge: Cambridge University Press.

1989. Archaeology into the 1990s. *Norwegian Archaeological Review* 22.1, 1–17.

Sharples, N. 1985. Individual and community: the changing role of megaliths in the Orcadian Neolithic. *Proceedings of the Prehistoric Society* 51, 59–74.

1991. *Maiden Castle*. London: Batsford.

Shee Twohig, E. 1981. *The Megalithic Art of Western Europe*. Oxford: Clarendon Press.

Sheets, P. 1975. Behavioural analysis and the structure of a prehistoric industry. *Current Anthropology* 16, 369–91.

1978. From craftsman to cog: quantitative views of Mesoamerican lithic technology. In R. Sidrys (ed.) *Papers on the Economy and Architecture of the Ancient Maya*, 40–71. Los Angeles: University of California, Los Angeles (Monograph 8).

Shennan, S. 1986. Interaction and change in third millennium BC Western and Central Europe. In C. Renfrew and J. Cherry (eds.) *Peer Polity Interaction and Sociopolitical Change*, 137–48. Cambridge: Cambridge University Press.

Sheridan, A. 1986. Porcellanite artefacts: a new survey. *Ulster Journal of Archaeology* 49, 19–32.

Sidrys, R. 1976. Classic Maya obsidian trade. *American Antiquity* 41, 449–64.

1977. Mass-distance measures for the Maya obsidian trade. In T. Earle and J. Ericson (eds.) *Exchange Systems in Prehistory*, 91–108. New York: Academic Press.

Simmons, I. and Innes, J. 1987. Mid-Holocene adaptations and later Mesolithic forest disturbance in northern England. *Journal of Archaeological Science* 14, 385–403.

Singer, C. and Ericson, J. 1977. Quarry analysis at Bodie hills, Mono County, California: a case study. In T. Earle and J. Ericson (eds.) *Exchange Systems in Prehistory*, 171–90. New York: Academic Press.

Smith, I. 1965. *Windmill Hill and Avebury*. Oxford: Clarendon Press.

1966. Windmill Hill and its implications. *Palaeohistoria* 12, 469–83.

1971. Causewayed enclosures. In D. Simpson (ed.) *Settlement and Economy in Neolithic and Early Bronze Age Britain and Europe*, 89–112. Leicester: Leicester University Press.

1974. The Neolithic. In C. Renfrew (ed.) *British Prehistory – A New Outline*, 100–36. London: Duckworth.

1979. The chronology of British stone implements. In T. Clough and W. Cummins (eds.) *Stone Axe Studies*, 13–22. London: Council for British Archaeology (Research Report 23).

Smith, R. 1921. Hoards of Neolithic celts. *Archaeologia* 71, 113–24.

Soffe, G. and Clare, T. 1988. New evidence of ritual monuments at Long Meg and her Daughters, Cumbria. *Antiquity* 62, 552–7.

Sørensen, M. L. 1989. Ignoring innovation, denying change. In R. Torrence and S. van der Leeuw (eds.) *What's New?*, 180–203. London: Unwin Hyman.

Spence, M. 1982. The social context of production and exchange. In J. Ericson and T. Earle (eds.) *Contexts for Prehistoric Exchange*, 173–97. New York: Academic Press.

Stone, J. F. S. 1931a. Easton Down, Winterslow, S. Wilts, flint mine excavation, 1930. *Wiltshire Archaeological Magazine* 45, 350–65.

1931b. A settlement site of the Beaker period on Easton Down, Winterslow, S. Wilts. *Wiltshire Archaeological Magazine* 45, 366–72.

Stone, J. F. S. and Wallis, F. S. 1951. Third report of the south-western group of museums and art galleries on the petrological identification of stone axes. *Proceedings of the Prehistoric Society* 17, 99–158.

Stonehouse, P. 1988. Mesolithic sites on the Pennine watershed. *Greater Manchester Archaeological Journal* 3, 5–17.

Strathern, A. 1971. *The Rope of Moka*. Cambridge: Cambridge University Press.

Strathern, M. 1984. Subject or object? Women and the circulation of valuables in Highland New Guinea. In R. Hirscon (ed.) *Woman and Property, Woman as Property*, 158–75. London: Croom Helm.

1988. *The Gender of the Gift*. Berkeley and Los Angeles: University of California Press.

Thomas, J. 1988. Neolithic explanations revisited: the Mesolithic-Neolithic transition in Britain and South Scandinavia. *Proceedings of the Prehistoric Society* 54, 59–66.

1991. *Rethinking the Neolithic*. Cambridge: Cambridge University Press.

Thomas, J. and Whittle, A. 1986. Anatomy of a tomb: West Kennet revisited. *Oxford Journal of Archaeology* 5, 129–56.

Thomas, K. 1982. Neolithic enclosures and woodland habitats on the South Downs, Sussex, England. In M. Bell and S. Limbrey (eds.) *Aspects of Woodland Ecology*, 147–70. Oxford: British Archaeological Reports (BAR International Series 146).

Thomas, N. 1955. The Thornborough Circles, near Ripon, North Riding. *Yorkshire Archaeological Journal* 38, 425–45.

1991. *Entangled Objects. Exchange, Material Culture and Colonialism in the Pacific*. Cambridge, Massachusetts: Harvard University Press.

Thorpe, I. 1984. Ritual, power and ideology: a reconstruction of Earlier Neolithic rituals in Wessex. In R. Bradley and J. Gardiner (eds.) *Neolithic Studies*, 41–60. Oxford: British Archaeological Reports (BAR 133).

Thorpe, I. and Richards, C. 1984. The decline of ritual authority and the introduction of Beakers into Britain. In R. Bradley and J. Gardiner (eds.) *Neolithic Studies*, 67–84. Oxford: British Archaeological Reports (BAR 133).

Tilley, C. 1984. Ideology and the legitimation of power in the Middle Neolithic of southern Sweden. In D. Miller and C. Tilley (eds.) *Ideology, Power and Prehistory*, 111–46. Cambridge: Cambridge University Press.

Todd, M. 1984. Excavation at Hembury (Devon) 1980–83: a summary report. *Antiquaries Journal* 64, 251–68.

Torrence, R. 1986. *Production and Exchange of Stone Tools*. Cambridge: Cambridge University Press.

Traube, E. 1986. *Cosmology and social life*. Chicago: Chicago University Press.

Turner, V. 1969. *The Ritual Process*. Chicago: Aldine.

van Gennep, A. 1960 [1909]. *The Rites of Passage*. London: Routledge and Kegan Paul.

Vatcher, F. 1962. Thornborough Cursus, Yorkshire. *Yorkshire Archaeological Journal* 40, 169–82.

1965. East Heslerton long barrow, Yorkshire. *Antiquity* 39, 49–52.

Vemming, P. and Madsen, B. 1983. Flint manufacture in the Neolithic: an experimental investigation of a flint axe manufacture site at Hastrup Vaenget, East Zealand. *Journal of Danish Archaeology* 2, 43–59.

Vyner, B. 1984. The excavation of a Neolithic cairn at Street House, Loftus, Cleveland. *Proceedings of the Prehistoric Society* 50, 151–95.

Wade, A. G. 1924. Ancient flint mines at Stoke Down, Sussex. *Proceedings of the Prehistoric Society of East Anglia* 4, 82–91.

Wainwright, G. 1989. *The Henge Monuments*. London: Thames and Hudson.

Wainwright, G. and Longworth, I. 1971. *Durrington Walls: Excavations 1966–1968*. London: Society of Antiquaries (Research Report 29).

Walker, D. 1965. The post-glacial period in the Langdale Fells, English Lake District. *New Phytologist* 64, 488–510.

Warren, S. H. 1922. The Neolithic stone axes of Graig Lwyd, Penmaenmawr. *Archaeologia Cambrensis* 77, 1–35.

Waterhouse, J. 1985. *The Stone Circles of Cumbria*. Southampton: Camelot Press.

Weiner, A. 1983. A world of made is not a world of born. In J. Leach and E. Leach (eds.) *The Kula: New Perspectives on Massim Exchange*, 147–70. Cambridge: Cambridge University Press.

1985. Inalienable wealth. *American Ethnologist* 12.2, 210–27.

Whelan, C. B. 1934. Further excavations at Ballynagard, Rathlin Island, Co. Antrim. *Proceedings of the Belfast Natural History and Philosophical Society* (1933–4), 107–11.

Whittle, A. 1977. *The Earlier Neolithic of Southern England and its Continental Background*. Oxford: British Archaeological Reports (BAR International Series 35).

1978. Resources and population in the British Neolithic. *Antiquity* 52, 34–42.

1988a. Contexts, activities, events – aspects of Neolithic and Copper Age enclosures in Western and Central Europe. In C. Burgess, P. Topping, C. Mordant and M. Maddison (eds.) *Enclosures and Defences in the Neolithic of Western Europe*, 1–20. Oxford: British Archaeological Reports (BAR International Series 403).

1988b. *Problems in Neolithic Archaeology*. Cambridge: Cambridge University Press.

1990. Prolegomena to the study of the Mesolithic-Neolithic transition in Britain and Ireland. In D. Cahen and M. Otte (eds.) *Rubané et cardial*, 209–27. Liège.

Whyte, I. 1985. Shielings and the upland pastoral economy of the Lake District in medieval and early modern times. In J. Baldwin and I. Whyte (eds.) *The Scandinavians in Cumbria*, 103–17. Edinburgh: Scottish Society for Northern Studies.

Williams, B. 1990. The archaeology of Rathlin Island. *Archaeology Ireland* 4, 47–51.

Wilmsen, E. (ed.) 1972. *Social Exchange and Interaction*. Ann Arbor: University of Michigan, Museum of Anthropology (Anthropological Paper 46).

Wood, W. and Johnson, D. 1980. A survey of disturbance processes in archaeological site formation. In M. Schiffer (ed.) *Advances in Archaeological Method and Theory* vol. 1, 131–98. New York: Academic Press.

Woodman, P. 1978. *The Mesolithic in Ireland*. Oxford: British Archaeological Reports (BAR 58).

Woodward, P. 1988. Pictures of the Neolithic: discoveries from the Flagstones House excavations, Dorchester, Dorset. *Antiquity* 62, 266–74.

Wright, G. 1969. *Obsidian Analysis and Prehistoric Near Eastern Trade*. Ann Arbor: University of Michigan, Museum of Anthropology (Anthropological Paper 37).

Wright, H. and Zeder, M. 1977. The simulation of a linear exchange system under equilibrium conditions. In T. Earle and J. Ericson (eds.) *Exchange Systems in Prehistory*, 133–54. New York: Academic Press.

Wymer, J. 1977. *Gazetteer of Mesolithic Sites in England and Wales*. London: Council for British Archaeology (Research Report 20).

Young, D. and Bonnichsen, R. 1985. *Understanding Stone Tools: A Cognitive Approach*. Orono: University of Maine, Center for the Study of Early Man.

INDEX

Compiled by James Smith